CW01653919

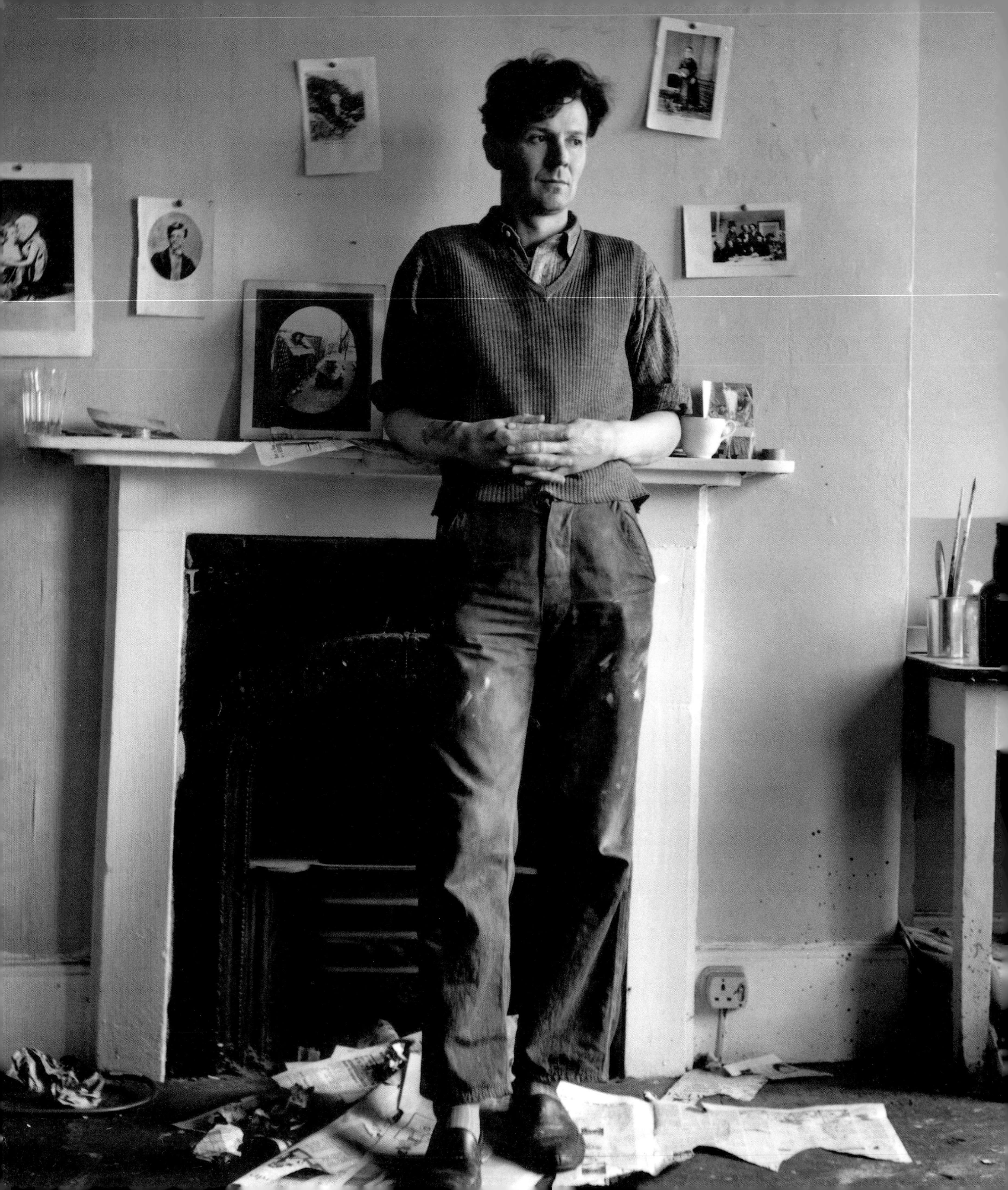

Michael Andrews

William Feaver and Paul Moorhouse

Tate Publishing

Exhibition supported by

B&Q

Published by order of the Tate Trustees by
Tate Publishing, a division of
Tate Enterprises Ltd
Millbank
London SW1P 4RG

© Tate Trustees 2001

This catalogue is published to accompany
the exhibition at Tate Britain
19 July – 7 October 2001

A catalogue record for this book
is available
from the British Library

ISBN 1 85437 368 4

Designed and typeset by Kate Stephens

Printed by Conti Tipocolor, Italy

Dimensions of works are in centimetres,
height before width

Front cover:
Lights II: The Ship Engulfed (detail, no.38)
Arts Council Collection, Hayward Gallery, London

Frontispiece:
Michael Andrews
Photo: John Deakin
© The James Moores Collection

Contents

Sponsor's foreword

Until recently Tate and B&Q might have seemed unusual bedfellows but we have proved what a successful combination we can be. This year, we launched the Tate range of paints together, and we are delighted that our association now extends to the mounting of this important exhibition, *Michael Andrews*.

We believe this exhibition will help to confirm and enhance Andrews's deserved prominence in the story of modern art in Britain. It has been a pleasure to help make it happen.

George Adams
Managing Director, B&Q Commercial

Foreword

Michael Andrews (1928–1995) was one of Britain's finest late twentieth-century painters, yet much of his work has remained little known to a wide public. As the first ever retrospective of his whole career, this exhibition aims to be both milestone and revelation. Indeed, thanks to the generosity and enthusiasm of those who have collected and own his work, we have been able to assemble here a remarkably high proportion of his total output as an artist. His career from the Slade in the early fifties to the final series of Thames paintings in the nineties thereby unfolds through the show, providing a distinctive, perhaps definitive, sequel to the mid-career survey exhibition of his work organised so successfully by the Arts Council in 1980.

Tate Britain's exhibition has been selected by William Feaver, writer and critic, and Paul Moorhouse, Tate Curator. They have also written this accompanying catalogue which, amongst much else, draws imaginatively on the extensive Andrews archive that has been generously presented to Tate by June Andrews, the artist's widow. We are also extremely grateful to her for encouraging and assisting the project in countless ways. Ben Tufnell, Assistant Curator at Tate Britain, has been central to its implementation too and I would like to thank him for his diligence and calm efficiency throughout. Nick Serota, never far from the making of a Tate show, has stayed particularly close to the creation and genesis of the exhibition: selection, installation and catalogue have all benefited greatly from his guidance.

William Feaver and Paul Moorhouse would also like to thank the following for their help: Melanie Andrews, Richard Calvocoressi, Jeffery Camp, Michelle Gillard, Adrian Glew, Rosemary Harris, Sophie Lawrence, Fran Matheson, Richard Morphet, Mary Richards, Andrea Rose, Andy Shiel, Peter Snow, Kate Stephens, Colin St John Wilson, Tim Taylor and the staff of the Timothy Taylor Gallery, especially Terry Danziger Miles, Robin Vousden of the Anthony d'Offay Gallery, Sheena Wagstaff and Glen Williams.

Finally, we acknowledge with thanks the support of the exhibition's sponsors, B & Q.

Stephen Deuchar
Director, Tate Britain

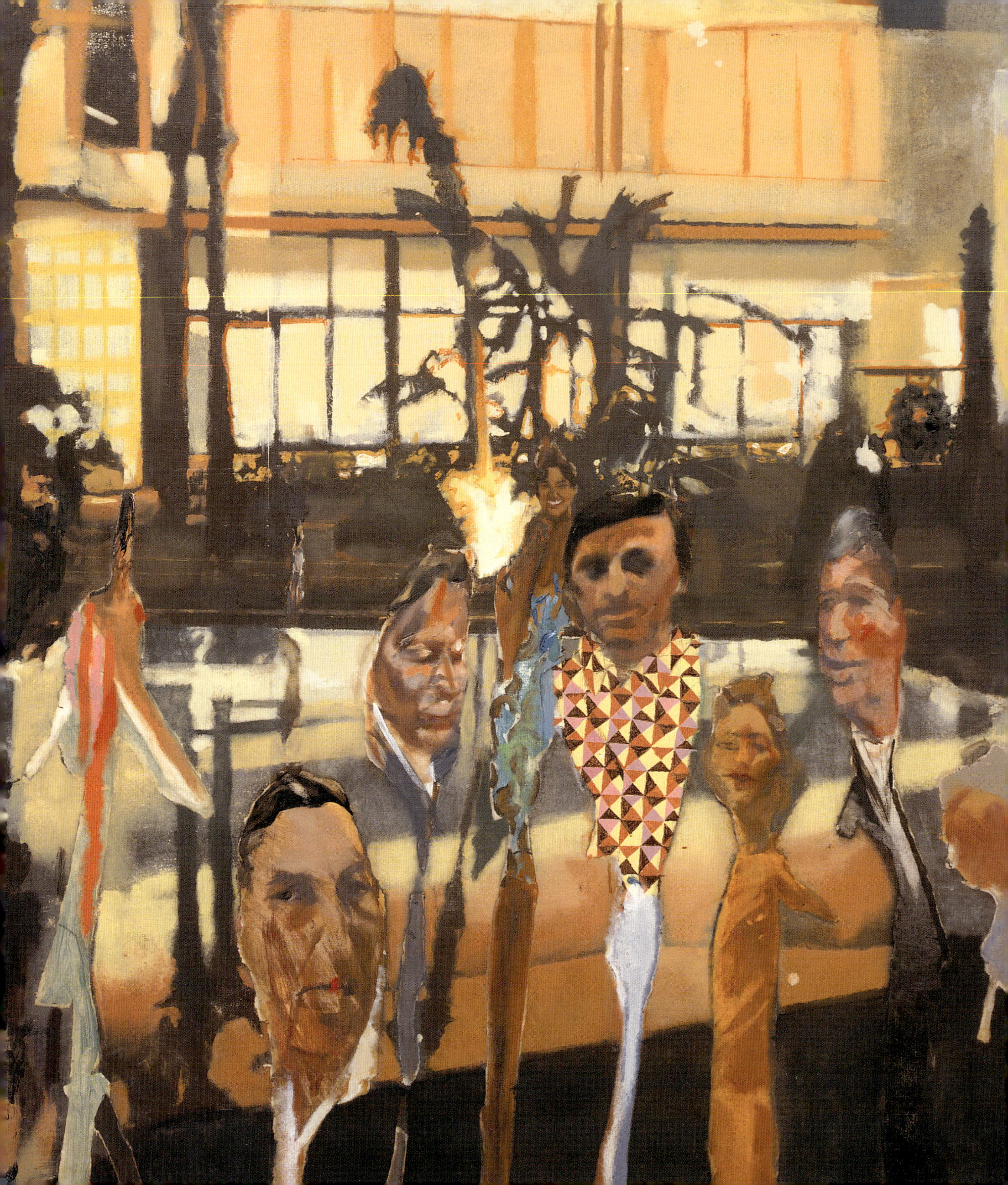

'Strange Consolation': The Art of Michael Andrews

Paul Moorhouse

This exhibition presents the first opportunity to survey the entire career of Michael Andrews, who died in 1995. Andrews was a notoriously slow worker. Consequently his oeuvre is relatively small and during his lifetime he had few solo exhibitions. Yet despite this modest output and limited exposure he is rightly regarded as one of Britain's leading post-war painters.

Indeed, since the 1980s it has become customary to identify Andrews as one of the so-called 'School of London', a controversial term which has nevertheless gained international currency. Together with Frank Auerbach, Francis Bacon, Lucian Freud and Leon Kossoff, Andrews has become linked with a very particular figurative tendency in British art. This tendency is usually described in terms of the personal and professional connections which existed between these artists from the early 1950s, and by reference to their shared preoccupation with representing the human figure. Unswayed by a succession of avant-garde artistic developments inimical not only to figuration but in some cases to the tradition of painting, their total identification with the act and process of painting is also cited as a key characteristic of the artists grouped beneath the 'School of London' banner.

By omitting the many differences between these artists' work, such descriptions propose a degree of commonality; and, in general terms, this account frames the context and broad thrust of Andrews's work. From the outset, his painting demonstrated an unswerving concern with the representation of people – alone, in situations involving a small number of protagonists, as family groups, or in social gatherings. In particular, his portraits and paintings of figures convey an acute sensitivity to the human presence and they evoke the subtle relationships – physical and psychological – which arise when individuals interact.

But, when applied to Andrews – and, indeed, to all these artists – the effort to articulate a group identity conceals a complex and unique artistic vision which resists classification. In the course of a career lasting forty-five years, Andrews's art proceeded according to very personal, deeply held values and perceptions, sustained by the development of technical means which answered particular needs. The result is a body of work which is manifestly the evidence of a singular view of the world in which certain preoccupations are prominent. Central among these is what Andrews described as 'the nature of being'. Eschewing illustration – a simple reliance on reproducing the appearance of things – Andrews's art, at a fundamental level, functions as a means of enquiry: as a way of forming a deeper, personal appreciation or understanding of certain real issues; and, through his engagement with them, these issues are transposed into the subjects of his art. For Andrews, probing the mysteries of human nature in order to form a fuller sense of our purpose and position in the world was an enduring concern.

In this respect, his art has an unmistakable existential character. Given the intellectual atmosphere in which his career and ideas took shape this is perhaps not surprising. As an art

FIG. I
Detail from *Good and Bad at Games* 1964–8 (no.21)

student in the early 1950s, Andrews was exposed to the philosophical sensibility emanating from the Continent whose defining spirits were Jean-Paul Sartre, Albert Camus and, of particular relevance to Andrews, Sören Kierkegaard. The questions posed by these writers about man's nature and purpose, and the answers they sought in an examination of human action, were of fundamental importance for Andrews. He later observed of this formative time as a student at the Slade: '[it was] not social protest realism that concerned us. That was too narrow. It was existentialist, it was a search for the nature of being.' [1]

In common with such artists as Auerbach, Bacon, Freud and Kossoff, whose careers also unfolded against the intellectual and social backdrop provided by London's art schools and – in some cases – the bars in Soho, for Andrews the representation of the human figure has a significance which transcends straightforward depiction of the subject's appearance. As with these other artists, representation is synonymous with interpretation. It is the way the motif is refracted through the artist's sensibility, investing the subject with a weight of meaning and expressive information, that commands attention. This said, the particular means of addressing his subject, and the precise nature of his concerns, set Andrews's work somewhat apart from these other artists.

From the outset, Andrews's depiction of people rarely engages in the kind of extreme distortion associated especially with, for example, Bacon and Auerbach. Prior to *Good and Bad at Games* 1964–8 (no.21, p.88) (in which, unusually for Andrews, the figures are physically altered) his paintings frequently have a rich, painterly, sometimes even awkward quality; but seldom is there a sense that his subject's appearance has been radically transformed. Rather, his work of the 1950s and early 1960s achieves its interpretative and expressive ends through a characteristic fusion of naturalistic depiction and imagination. This is the phase of Andrews's work to which his phrase 'mysterious conventionality'[2] is most appropriately applied. Apparently ordinary situations appear strange through imaginative invention or by bringing together real elements from disparate sources. The way that Andrews refracts reality through an imaginative lens is completely distinctive – the evidence of an apparent desire to experience certain real situations by inventing virtual images of them.

This paradox – the will to engage with and to understand aspects of the real world through a parallel imaginative engagement – stands at the heart of Andrews's art. It is its defining characteristic and its driving force. It is responsible not least for the important technical development in Andrews's work from the 1960s onwards, of using photographs and other images culled from a variety of sources. This collage-related method was employed not only for appropriating motifs for a composition, but as a means of deepening his imaginative engagement with a particular subject while making a painting.

Underpinning this paradox is, however, a coherent, consistent and explicit artistic motive. For Andrews, the existential quest for 'the nature of being' was not entirely a metaphysical affair. Rather, as the following examination of the development of his work reveals, his firmly held conviction was that some sense of the world and our place in it can be formed from reflecting on human nature. For that reason, people, the rich diversity and causes of behaviour, and identity are his abiding subjects; even when people are not physically present in his work – as in his paintings of balloons, fish and certain landscapes – such images are redolent with human significance. For Andrews, the activity of painting was a way of asking questions about the nature of being and contained the potential for sharing whatever insights were gained. Towards the end of his career, in a telling reflection on the purpose of his art he observed: 'In painting, through a process of definition, I realise how I am disposed – it is reassuring to know. As none of us are so different we can share the realization ... hence strange consolation.'

Early work

Andrews studied at the Slade School of Art from 1949 to 1953 and, after a shaky start, his development there was rapid. He arrived feeling that, unlike most of his fellow students, he had had virtually no previous art education and regarded himself as 'very ignorant.' In fact, in 1947, in his last year at school, he had taken Saturday morning oil-painting lessons for a term at Norwich School of Art; and he had continued to draw and paint during a subsequent period of national service, nineteen months of which was spent in Egypt. However, neither Andrews nor his tutor at the Slade, William Townsend, attached much importance to this previous experience. When Andrews showed Townsend some examples of his work, the older man pronounced them 'tricky'. Andrews was shocked. His surprise was compounded when Townsend went on to express a clear preference for some other, less finished sketches. Though Andrews regarded these as 'perfunctory', Townsend's comments redeemed them on the grounds that they were more direct. In retrospect, Andrews saw that Townsend's criticism, though apparently adverse, had been a useful corrective.

Andrews's training at the Slade emphasised the importance of life drawing. William Coldstream had been appointed Professor the same year that Andrews commenced as a student. Yet, despite the importance placed by Coldstream on observation and exacting measurement – in his own work – no such rigid system was passed on to the students. Instead, as Andrews later recalled: 'Bill gave me my first enlightenment. He persuaded me of the paramount value of looking, of appraisal and, in transcription, of direct statement of which he said "just write it down". It was so simple and unforgettable.' Although Andrews's work subsequently gravitated away from observation from life, Coldstream's advice remained with Andrews. And, surprising though it might at first seem, the ethos of the direct statement laid the foundations of Andrews's mature work, in which there is a vital imaginative dimension.

The key to this is the way that Andrews understood the notion of directness to mean addressing the motif or subject without preconceptions. In the life room this entailed allowing a visual response to form naturally by letting it evolve directly from the experience of the model. This realisation is an integral element of Andrews's subsequent practice when working from an imaginative source. Here, too, the response to the subject was permitted to evolve intuitively and, in taking shape in this way, revealed the artist's attitude to that subject. Andrews encapsulated this approach in his observation: 'The activity is for me the most

FIG.2
Self-Portrait 1943,
pencil on paper,
24.2 x 33
Private Collection

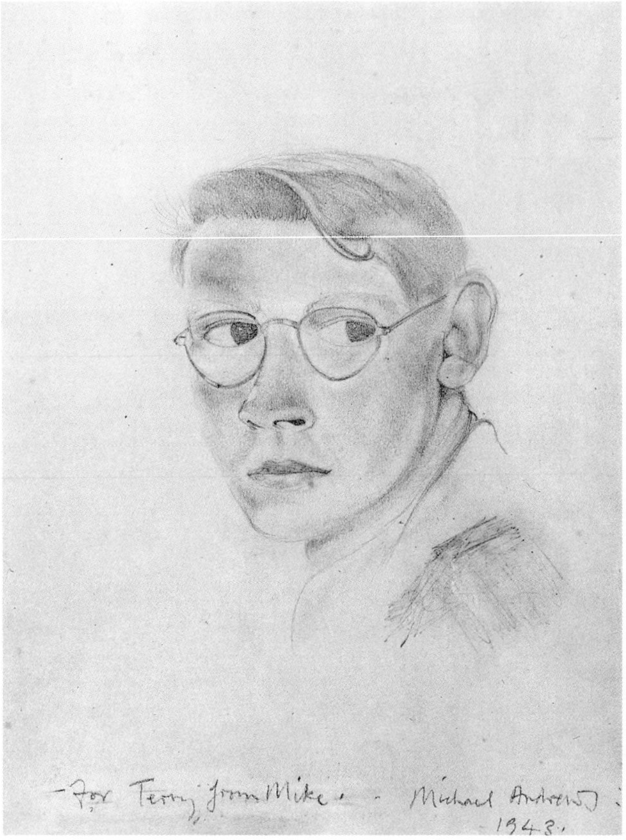

FIG.3
Wheelers, Old Compton Street, London, 1962. Left to right: Tim Behrens, Lucian Freud, Frank Auerbach, Andrews. Photo: John Deakin

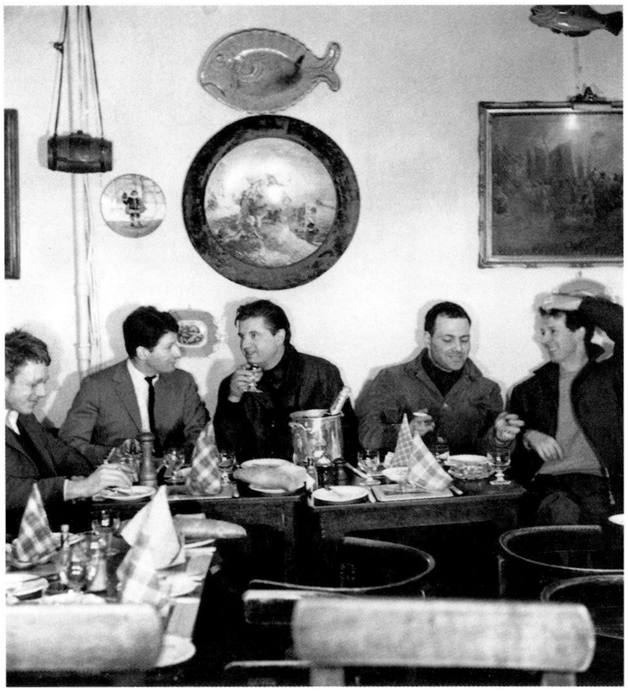

FIG.4
Still from *Together* 1955: Andrews and Eduardo Paolozzi

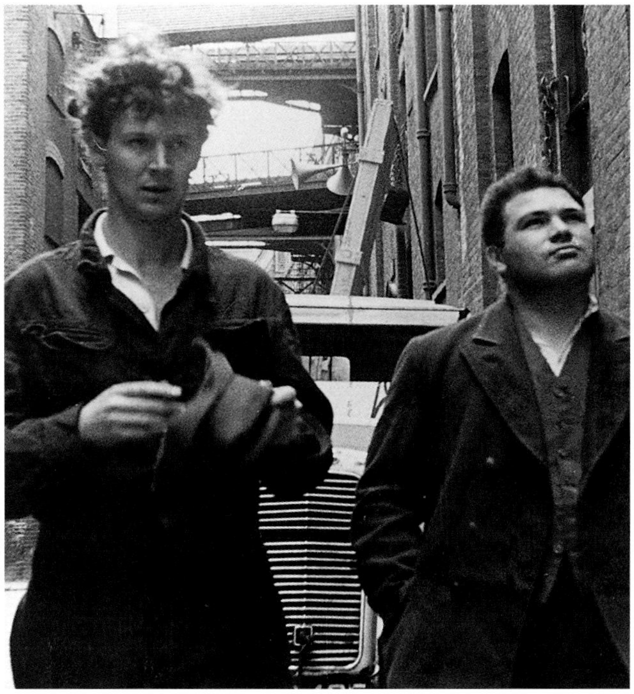

marvellous, elaborate, complete way of making up my mind.'

This way of working forms the basis of two paintings completed by Andrews in his second and third year at the Slade. Despite being youthful productions, both are confidently unconventional, their subject matter strikingly idiosyncratic. The first, *August for the People* 1951 (no.1, p.64), depicts a middle-aged man walking on a beach. He is dressed rather formally in a dark suit while, around him, younger people dressed in swimwear relax or daydream absent-mindedly. In an inversion of the behaviour usually associated with youth and maturity, the older man looks distinctly uncomfortable, self-conscious and embarrassed. The second of the two works, *A Man Who Suddenly Fell Over* 1952 (no.4, p.66), is a similarly odd image, also fitting no recognisable category or genre. Another man – perhaps the same one – is shown crashing to earth. Bald-headed and dressed in a three-piece suit, he is depicted in mid-fall – his momentary loss of equilibrium and sudden descent caught for our prolonged gaze. Andrews has chosen to focus on that exact moment when surprise, alarm, embarrassment and a rather futile attempt at recovering composure all converge in the subject's mind. His resulting facial expression is a study in consternation.

What is the significance of these strange images? Their origins lay in student assignments. It was Coldstream's practice to set the students a literary subject to be developed in visual terms, and both works have literary connections. *August for the People*, which was Andrews's prize-winning summer composition, relates to the poem by W.H. Auden whose opening line reads: 'August for the people and their favourite islands'. For the second painting – which was included in the Slade Diploma Examination – Andrews chose a poem by Peter Stanford, a friend he had first met in 1947 at the start of national service. Entitled 'A Man Who Cried Out', Stanford's poem describes the misfortune of a man: 'hat in hand and black umbrella / he runs and falls headlong'. Literature would continue to be a source of inspiration for Andrews but, as both these works suggest, only as a starting point for subsequent imaginative development. In both cases, the paintings leave their ostensible literary origins behind and explore concerns of a more personal nature.

August for the People marks the beginning of Andrews's interest in human behaviour as subject. Visually the work is understated and at first sight apparently without any obvious point. Rather, it describes a situation to which the viewer must respond, engaging imaginatively in order to glimpse an undertow of meaning. The painting's significance becomes apparent when we reflect on the man's awkwardness and begin to speculate about his accompanying feelings. The relationship between behaviour and implied, underlying emotion is the central theme of *A Man Who Suddenly Fell Over*. On the surface, there is an evident interest, in particular, in the man's behaviour – positioned as he is, between composure and absurdity. But, as Andrews commented later, 'it's about the complete upsetting of someone's apparently secure equilibrium and about their almost immediate attempts at recovery and their attempt to conceal that they have been perhaps badly hurt or upset which would only be allowed to show if they were by themselves'.[3] In other words, the meaning of the image resides not simply in its ostensible visual facts, but also in how we interpret the feelings associated with the human situation which Andrews has created.

Andrews came to see *A Man Who Suddenly Fell Over* as the first painting he had done which interested him. Certainly it is significant for the way it signals some key characteristics of his subsequent work. Prominent among these are: an interest in implied narrative (in the way that the picture invites an interpretative reading); the vital role of imagination in creating a credible 'real' situation; and, not least, a fascination with human behaviour and its causes.

Portraits

With such paintings as *A Man Who Suddenly Fell Over* it is apparent that a key element in the creation of Andrews's paintings of people, and also in their appreciation, is empathy: the capacity for intellectual and emotional identification with another human being. One of the great strengths of the portraits of acquaintances and friends that Andrews made in the 1950s and 1960s is their power not only to describe their subject's appearance, but also to suggest character and to invite a response as to how the subject seems as a living, feeling person.

The seeds of this ability can be detected in a small, yet subtly effective picture, *Little Boy Running*, that Andrews painted in 1953. If the more ambitious *August for the People* and *A Man Who Suddenly Fell Over* can be seen as addressing the way it feels to be an older person in a certain situation, *Little Boy Running* takes a look backwards, recovering all the uncertainty and vulnerability of youth. Painted in the year that Andrews left the Slade, when he was facing the uncertain prospect of a career as an artist in the outside world, it is hard not to see an echo of Andrews's own feelings in the little boy's flight.

Certainly, for the remainder of the decade Andrews's situation remained unfixed, his direction unclear. Having won a scholarship in painting at the British School in Rome – an opportunity he accepted with some misgivings – Andrews set off for Italy, only to return six months later having failed to settle. During his time in Rome, Andrews did, however, commence a portrait of Lorenza Mazzetti, another ex-student from the Slade. In this painting we find, applied to the depiction of an actual person, convincing evidence of the aesthetic which Andrews described in the following way: 'All true appreciations of people are bound to be blurred (I think this goes for images too). Finding a bit here, a bit there, – its all approximate. Everything is "more or less" in my opinion.'

The painting certainly bears out Andrews's ideas about approximation and the compilation of disparate sources. It was painted partly from memory of the subject, partly from a photograph, and partly from the experience of meeting Lorenza Mazzetti's identical sister in Rome. From these different elements Andrews has created an image which is not so much unfinished (though it appears so), as precise about those impressions which are clear and those which are necessarily vague. Lorenza's face is described with clarity and conviction, yet other parts of the composition appear blurred, tentative and uncertain. As such, it evokes with veracity the experience of encountering a friend: facial recognition is the strongest, most definite sensation, while other details – of costume and background – register less clearly. The image is thus not simply a record of the subject's appearance: it corresponds to the impression made by the subject in a certain situation. The pictorial image is about the way the subject *seems*. The nature of the artist's response – his interpretation – becomes an integral part of the subject.

Following his return to London, in 1954 Andrews, together with Eduardo Paolozzi, acted in *Together*, a film directed by Lorenza Mazzetti about two deaf mutes living and working in the bleak, bomb-flattened landscape of London's East End. The film's sparse, repetitive plot is unremarkable, although its evocation of the deaf-mutes' purposelessness – so that they passively experience the things that happen to them – is archetypally existentialist in outlook and mood. Andrews subsequently lived at a succession of London addresses, eventually taking up residence at the Digswell Arts Trust, near Welwyn Garden City, from March 1958 to June 1959. During this lean period Helen Lessore, the owner of the Beaux Arts Gallery (where Andrews had exhibitions in January 1958 and June 1963), occasionally sent him small supportive sums of money.

While living at Digswell he noticed a local gardener, apparently a retarded man, who passed Andrew's window on his way to work each day. From these glimpses, Andrews constructed a response in which observation, memory and a certain empathy combined to produce three *Digswell Man* portraits. Helen Lessore's observations about one of the paintings, which was then hanging in her gallery, are worth quoting at length for they convey vividly the capacity of Andrews's portraits to transcend physical description and to engage an imaginative response:

> Your picture ... has the most remarkable quality, that it convinces me that it exists, in the dark while I'm asleep, and that things happen in it which I don't see – that man has been somewhere else in the night – his past and future exist, it is only that it's just at the one particular moment he passes the point in the circle where I can see him. There is such a sadness in the way he is bogged down in that raw red earth, sunk in that landscape of thick acrid green trees, where he is condemned to pass his life[4]

As the striking *Self-Portrait* of 1959 shows (no.12, p.76), by the end of the 1950s, the ethos of directness advocated by Coldstream – involving an open, unpremeditated responsiveness to the subject – had matured in Andrews's work into a distinctive artistic vision. Whether working from imagination or observation, or a combination of the two, Andrews was now making paintings which evolved as a kind of dialogue between his subject and his response to it. Rather than imposing preordained ideas upon the motif, the work could have, as he put it, 'a life of its own'. In a notebook of 1964, he added: '[painting] can surprise you – extending your taste ... [it] can draw a unique pattern of form [and] line of thought from you'. As Andrews saw it, the purpose of such activity was the way that it revealed aspects of his own nature. 'The point is to know where one stands in relation to everything and then to get to know a bit more and then to get into a better relation, into right relation, with everything.' In this work, the artist confronts his own image without a hint of self-regard or false sentiment. It is the image of an individual appraising himself – not to flatter but to know.

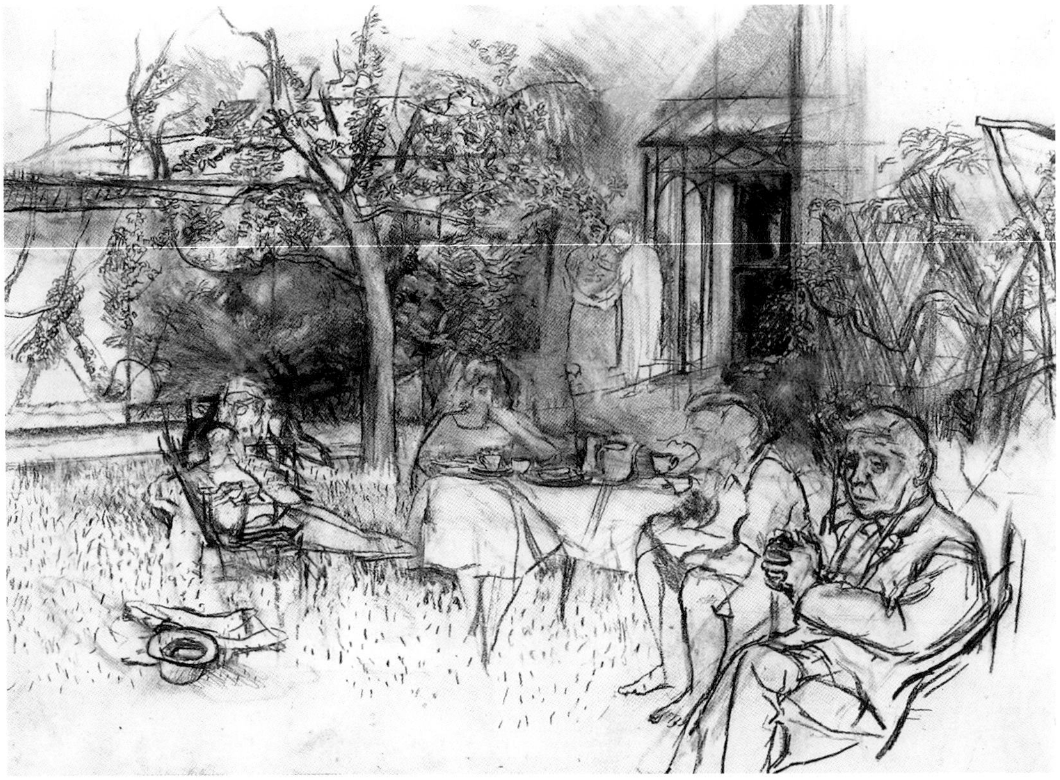

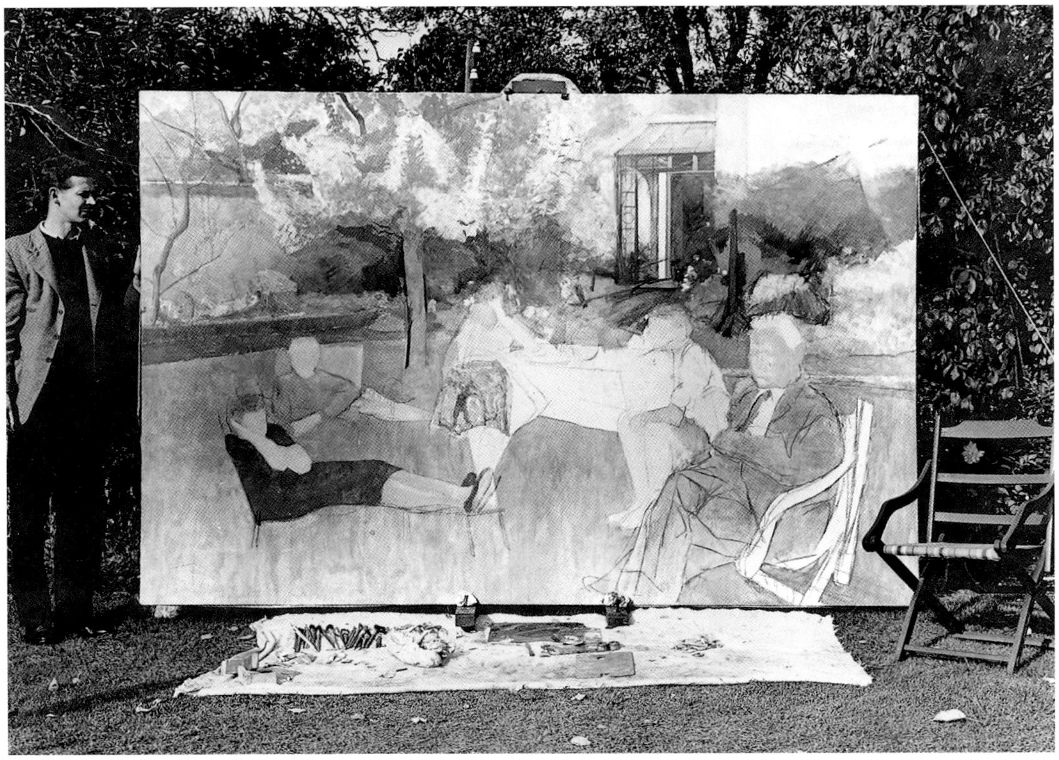

FIG.5
Study for *Family in the Garden I* 1960–2, charcoal on paper, 52 x 65
Private Collection

FIG.6
Andrews with *Family in the Garden*, in progress, Norwich, *c.*1960–2

Parties

During the 1960s Andrews's subject matter broadened by turning to the behaviour not simply of individuals, but to individuals behaving and interacting as part of a complex group. In part, this can be related to his growing confidence as an artist, and can be seen as the outcome of his desire to take on more ambitious figure compositions. Two early essays on this theme, *Four People Sunbathing* 1955 (no.7, p.70) and *Late Evening on a Summer Day* 1957 (no.10, p.72), are, in comparison to the subsequent party paintings, charming if somewhat tentative beginnings. While they succeed in suggesting atmosphere – a kind of idyllic languor invested, in the later work, with mildly erotic sensuality – Andrews's later ability to develop formal or psychological tension between the figures is at this stage relatively undeveloped.

Perhaps sensing the need to develop the way his figures relate to each other in order to create a more unified and more charged human situation, Andrews embarked in 1960 on what would be his first fully realised group composition. The largest painting he had then attempted, *The Family in the Garden* 1960–2 (no.13, p.75), took two years to complete and depicts Andrews's family: (from right to left) his father, brother, sister, grandmother and mother. Painted in the garden of his parents' house in Norwich, it was a work made, in Andrews's own words, 'in peace'. Certainly he found in this composition an order, and a contemplative calm, which contrasts with the heavily engaged brushwork of the *Digswell Man* paintings. Again, there is a sense that the image is as much a reflection of the artist's situation and his disposition towards the subject, as a record of the thing observed.

It is clear, however, that the development of Andrews's interest in painting the interaction of figures answered certain personal, as well as artistic, needs. His diary for 1964 contains the observation: 'I'm concerned with knowing what I feel – for moral confidence.' Living in Norwich, his routine differed markedly from the way of life to which he had become accustomed when he was living in London. An intensely shy person, Andrews was nevertheless highly sociable. In particular he both enjoyed and was fascinated by parties, seeing them not only as convivial occasions but as an opportunity to observe in all its diversity one of the things which most interested him: people behaving. He saw parties as

> an occasion when people are together on the whole by choice – to see each other and/or to be seen. They allow themselves to be and are judged. They perform. They succeed or fail. They increase in stature or flop. They put themselves to the test. So as a dramatic or theatrical device it's very exciting.

In now taking the party situation as the subject of his work, Andrews found a theme rich in implication – a melting-pot of human relations which he could both celebrate and contemplate.

Andrews began with a situation he knew well. Since 1954 he had frequented the Colony Room, Muriel Belcher's celebrated drinking club in Soho – small, shabby and the haunt of London's bohemia. The artists Francis Bacon, Lucian Freud, Frank Auerbach, John Minton and Rodrigo Moynihan were regulars; but Belcher's great talent was her ability to attract people from all walks of life. The mix of personalities generated the atmosphere. As Daniel Farson put it, 'Why did I and so many others make this place our second home? The answer is simple: we could be ourselves, and that is one of the hardest things to achieve in life.'[5]

The Colony Room I 1962 (no.16, p.83) responds precisely to this milieu: its confining, box-like space enlivened by an informal, yet keenly observed gathering of people – Bacon and Freud among them. In contrast to the more controlled Norwich painting of his family, Andrews's faith in letting the work evolve – so that he responded to, rather than directed, its progress – reasserted itself. The development of the image was guided by memory and, as these impressions accrued, Andrews sought to 'adjust and focus my concept at every signal of recollection'. Consequently, when areas of the painting were changed, Andrews embraced this, seeing the revised areas as being like memory traces. As such, while the image evokes a moment in the life of the Colony Room, it nevertheless arises from accumulated recollections and from the growth of the artist's imaginative engagement with his subject.

The difference between images that record literally the appearance of a subject and those in which appearance is combined with an interpretation of that subject is crucial to an appreciation of Andrews's art. This distinction is central not only to the party paintings which followed but, indeed, to the subsequent development of his work. Throughout his career Andrews constantly sought to clarify the nature and purpose of his activity as an artist and, in the copious notes that he made, the difference between illustration (as he saw it) and interpretation is recurrent. For Andrews, the point of addressing in paint his 'object of thought' – observed or imagined – was to reveal and define how he was 'disposed' to a particular subject. From this point onwards, engaging imaginatively with a subject became increasingly important to him for it enabled this process of definition to evolve. 'It's the way the subject impresses itself on your mind that must show.'

The radical changes in his work brought about by this resolve are apparent in the two party paintings which Andrews completed between 1962 and 1964. The starting point for the first of these, *The Deer Park* 1962 (no.18, p.81), was Norman Mailer's novel of that title, published in 1957. Mailer's book contained the following quotation from Mouffle d'Angerville's *Vie privée de Louis XV*:

> The Deer Park, that gorge of innocence and virtue in which were engulfed so many victims who when they returned to society brought depravity, debauchery and all the vices they naturally acquired from the infamous officials of such a place.

In a characteristic leap of imaginative association, Andrews made a connection between the world described in Mailer's novel and his own experiences of hedonistic Soho. It was, Andrews explained, 'a broadening of context'.[6] In making the painting he extended his method of combining disparate observed or imagined elements by referring to a much wider range of visual material, mainly photographs of film stars, celebrities, and models from magazines and other publications. These formed the basis of the figures in the imagined

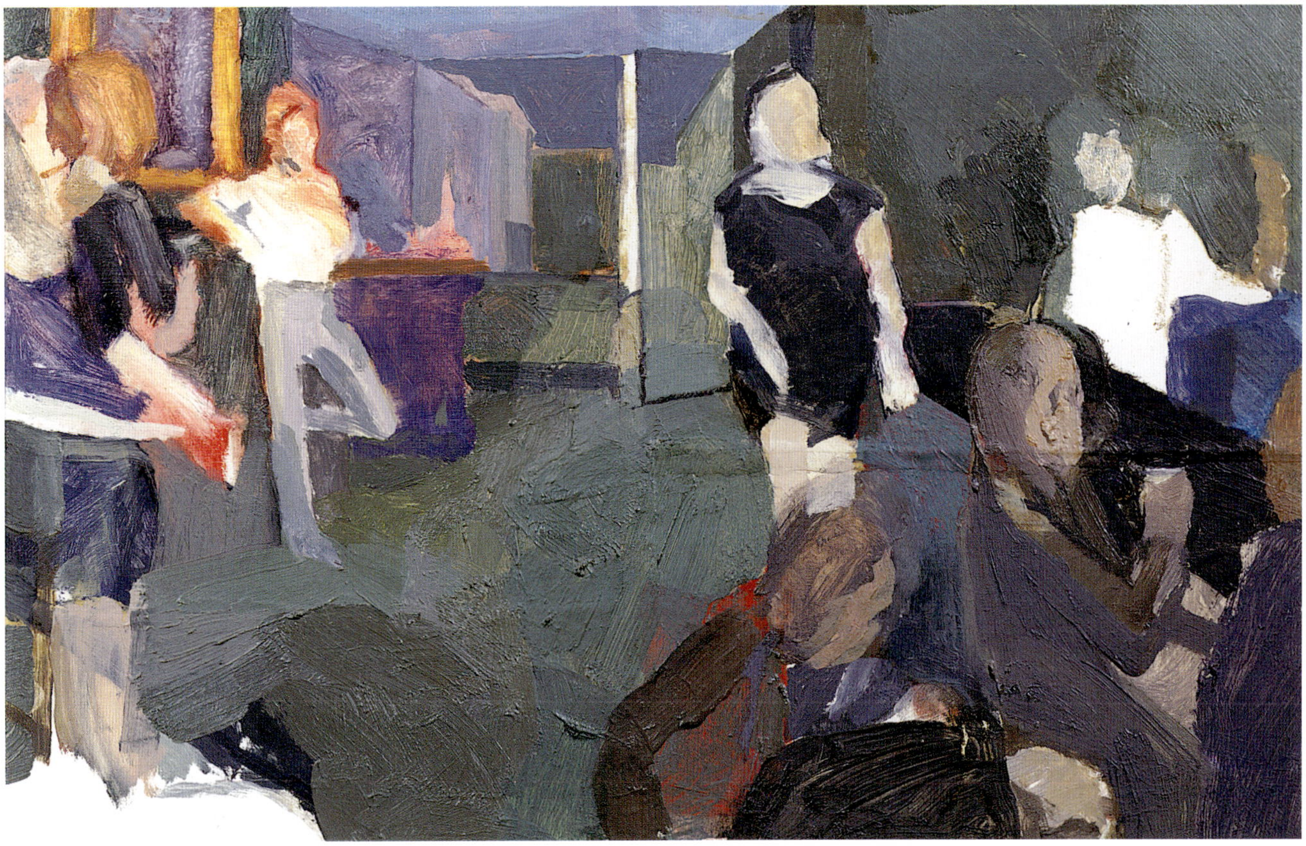

FIG.7
Study of The Colony Room
1962, oil on board,
31.4 x 48
Private Collection

FIG.8
Andrews with *All Night Long*, *c.*1962–4
Photo: Jorge Lewinski

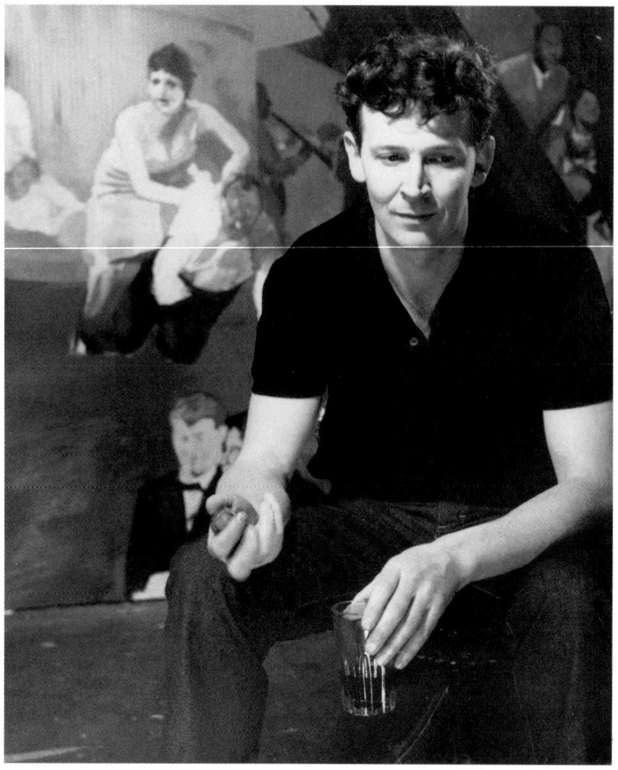

FIG.9
Andrews with *Good and Bad at Games* *c.*1964–8
Photo: Jorge Lewinski

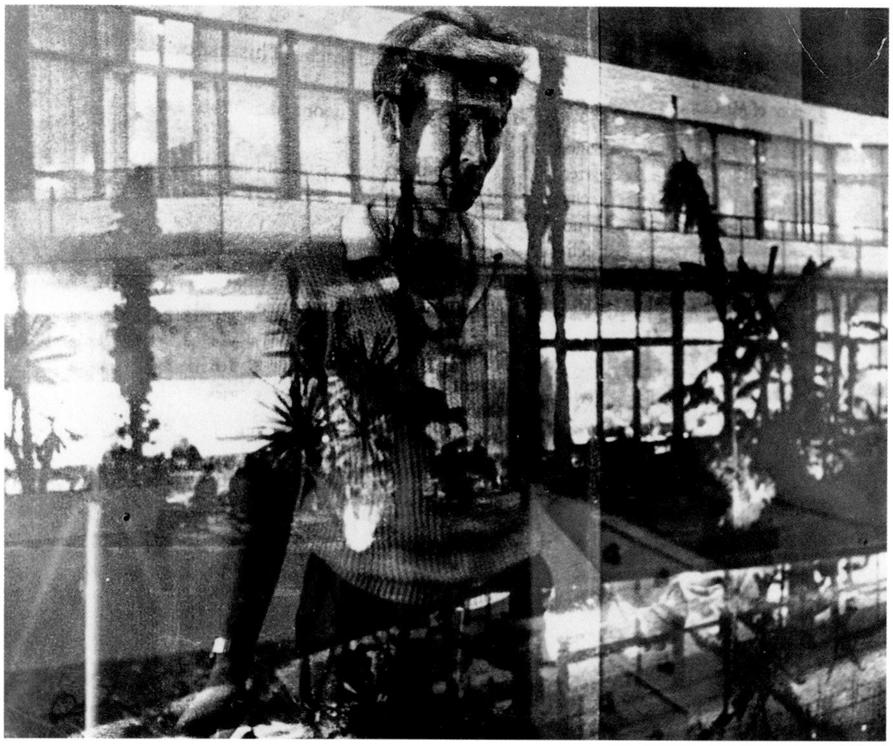

party which Andrews now staged. The poet Rimbaud, whom Andrews was then reading, appears at its centre.

All Night Long 1962–4 (no.20, p.86) which followed, proceeded by similar, if less urgent means. *The Deer Park* had been painted quickly, as if carried along by the momentum and liberating excitement of this new, associative way of working. *All Night Long* was conceived as a kind of sequel, in which he could stage another party, but take a slower, more measured look at what was going on. As with *The Deer Park* the party-goers were based on photographs, mainly advertisements, from *Vogue* and other magazines. Moving from the enveloping, film-set like space of *The Deer Park*, the party has now opened up and moved outdoors, the participants' behaviour exposed to the glare of harsh lighting. A string of nude girls at the left of the image (copied from a photograph of a Swedish sauna party) adds a risqué element, as does the pair of lesbian lovers on the opposite side. Even so, the presence of the dinner-jacketed men in the foreground signals that this is a different kind of party from the *The Deer Park*: sultry sensuality has been replaced by a cooler sophistication.

Andrews's party paintings offer views of fish tanks in which exotic fish have been replaced by people. We observe, instead, the swim of human behaviour – the predators, the performers and the observers, all caught in the currents and eddies of their fortunes. *All Night Long* is a spectacle and its theme is adaptation – behaviour in flux, influenced by the presence of other people. In the game of social interaction, adaptation sorts the winners from the losers – one prevails or one succumbs. From 1964 to 1968, Andrews worked on a final, large-scale party painting, *Good and Bad at Games* (no.21, p.88), which takes as its subject the way people, interacting, affect each other's behaviour. Some grow in confidence and stature; others shrink and whither. The three panels which comprise the work represent three moments in the course of the party; and, in a singular departure, Andrews suggests the changing fortunes of his party-goers by representing the figures as balloon-like shapes which expand and deflate according to mood. The painting was an advance in more ways than one. The adoption of the balloon metaphor suggested the rich possibilities of more symbolic forms of representation. And, in attributing changes in behaviour to fluctuations in a personal sense of well-being, the notion of self-consciousness – the idea one has of oneself – now began to exercise a fascination.

Lights

Throughout his career it was Andrews's practice to write notes to himself while he was thinking about a particular subject for a painting or meditating on a certain idea. Sometimes these notes took the form of extended observations as a train of thought developed; frequently they were written down as aphorisms – succinct distillations which encapsulate a feeling or perception. One such scrap of paper bears the words: 'To be released and unselfconscious how wonderful that would be.' This sentiment is the genesis of the magisterial series of paintings which preoccupied Andrews between 1970 and 1974, a sequence of seven large paintings he entitled *Lights*.

Andrews undoubtedly felt that shyness in certain social settings was a drawback, a barrier to spontaneity. Elsewhere in his papers he confided: 'I am more of a spectator than I am at most times prepared to admit to myself.' He admired and enjoyed the sense of confident, unselfconscious well-being that radiated from friends like Francis Bacon. 'He was,' Andrews recalled, 'euphoric.' Such perceptions undoubtedly coloured and influenced his fascination with behaviour and its causes. Towards the end of the 1960s, Andrews began to make plans for a series of paintings which would address the issue of self-consciousness and its influence, not only on the way we behave, but on the way we view the world.

Building on the methods he had developed in the party paintings, Andrews immersed himself in his subject – compiling information from a variety of sources and allowing connections and unexpected associations to develop. The phrase 'the skin-encapsulated ego', used by the psychiatrist R.D. Laing, caught Andrews's attention – capturing precisely, it seemed, the idea of self-obsession, self-watchfulness, which was beginning take shape as his subject. Around the same time, he came across in a newspaper a photograph of a manned balloon drifting across a rural landscape. He instantly made the connection with Laing's phrase – fitting the idea to its symbol. Thus launched, as it were, on his imaginative journey, he began actively to assemble other material – dozens of photographs and pictures of balloons, cuttings to do with air, sky and atmospheric phenomena, aerial views of different kinds of landscape, pictures of tower blocks at night, postcards of seaside resorts – the variety of source material is bewildering. Indeed, its volume and diversity suggest that Andrews was collecting these elements not simply for use as possible imagery; rather, he was feeding the growth of an idea.

As the notion of using the balloon as a symbol for the ego took shape, it became clear that the balloon's movements – rising and falling – and its passage through different landscapes could be used to suggest fluctuations in self-consciousness and their relation to external circumstances. As he continued to think around this subject, other perceptions and implications began to accrue. The ego, Andrews saw, is not simply the image one has of oneself, it is 'one's acquired disposition: prejudices, values' – in other words, a psychological veneer which colours one's view of the world. Andrews had been impressed by Henry James's observation, 'to live without any image of oneself'. And from Sir Charles Eliot's book *Japanese Buddhism*, Andrews copied out the following description of the state of Zen expertness: 'My observer self with all its burden of fear is no longer between me and my goal.' Pursuing a growing interest in Zen, Andrews understood that the elimination of self-consciousness was a desired state, for this enabled 'seeing things just as they are – reality as it is: unconditioned reality (i.e. not surrounded by or conditioned by ideas)'. In this strange echo of Coldstream's ethos of responding to the observed world without preconceptions, Andrews had arrived at the Zen idea of ego-loss as a prerequisite for seeing things 'as they are' – a state of illumination implied in the title of the series. The journey of the balloon is thus in one sense a personal odyssey; but at the same time it concerns the shedding of self-regard.

The series commences with *Lights I: Out-of-Doors* 1970 (no.36, p.97) and the painting immediately signals a radical departure. In the same way as Andrews had encouraged the

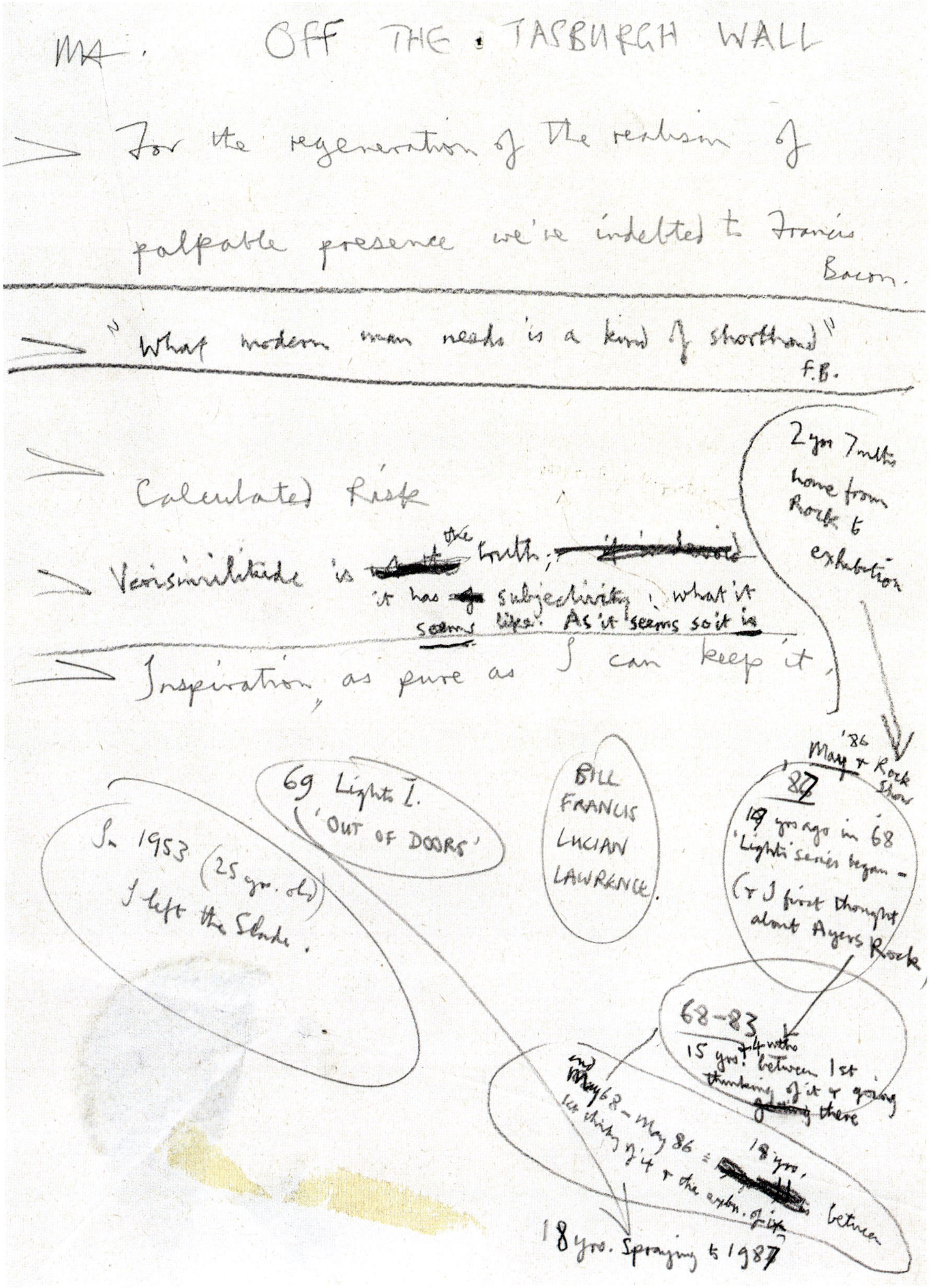
MA. OFF THE TASBURGH WALL

For the regeneration of the realism of palpable presence we're indebted to Francis Bacon.

"What modern man needs is a kind of shorthand" F.B.

Calculated Risk

Verisimilitude is the truth; it has subjectivity: what it seems like. As it seems so it is

Inspiration, as pure as I can keep it,

2 yrs 7 mths home from Rock to exhibition

69 Lights I. 'OUT OF DOORS'

In 1953 (25 yrs. old) I left the Slade.

BILL
FRANCIS
LUCIAN
LAWRENCE.

'86 May + Rock Show

87 19 yrs ago in 68 'Lights' series began – (+ I first thought about Ayers Rock)

68–83 15 yrs! 4 mths between 1st thinking of it + going there

end May 68 – May 86 = 18 yrs, between 1st thinking of it + the exbn. of it

18 yrs. Spraying to 1987

FIG.10
A sheet of notes by Andrews, 1987, an example of the hundreds of sheets of observations and aphorisms which the artist amassed during his career

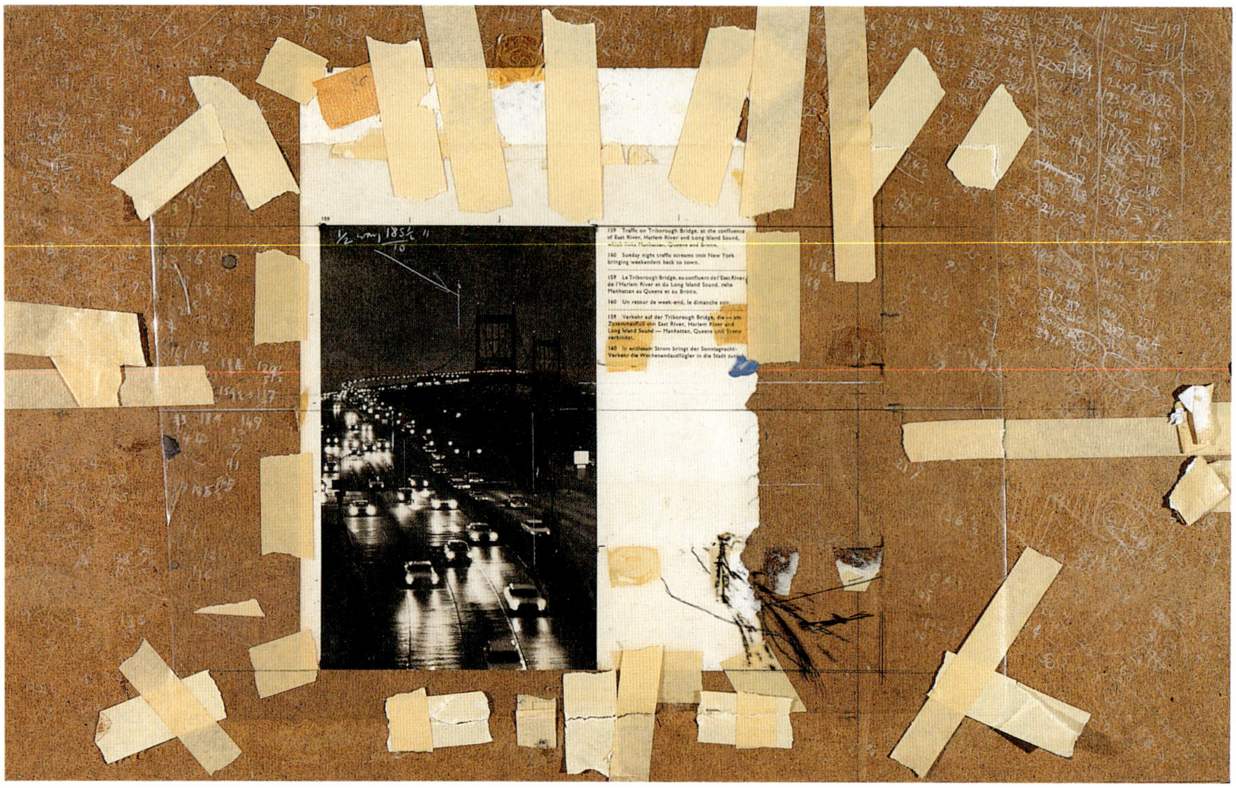

FIG.11
Collage for
Lights VI, *c.*1974
Tate Archive

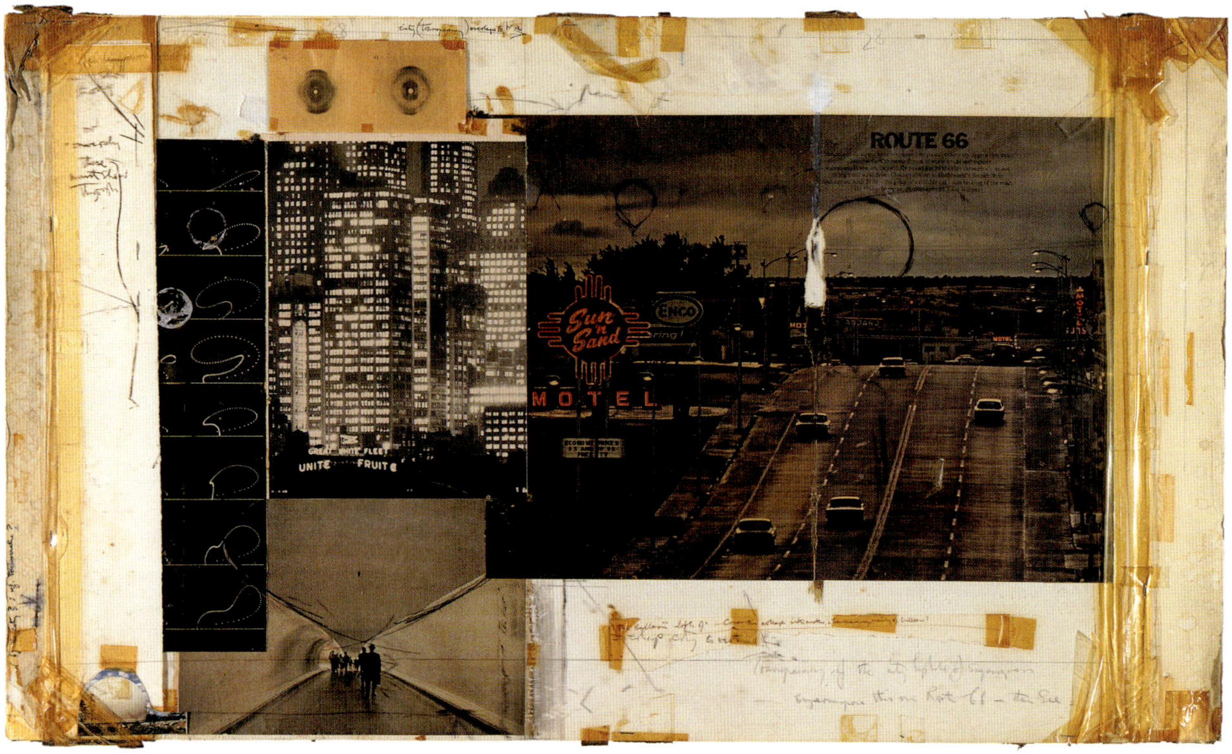

FIG.12
Collage for
Lights II, *c.*1972
Tate Archive

metaphorical association of ideas in his imaginative development of the theme, so in planning its execution he made a connection between the subject and his working method. The paintings were to be about flight, air, atmosphere and weightlessness and this should therefore be evident in the handling of the paint. Thus for the first time Andrews used a spray gun and in so doing he transformed his entire approach. From now on Andrews's use of spray would entail the progressive application of paint using a complex array of masking devices, stencils and templates. The adventure begins in the warm light of a country landscape as the balloon begins its ascent.

Almost immediately the game of adaptation begins. In *Lights II: The Ship Engulfed* 1972 (no.38, p.98), night has fallen and the balloon – now a dark, brooding presence – drifts through an urban landscape of skyscrapers. Significantly, Andrews has chosen to show the balloon silhouetted against the glare from hundreds of brilliantly lit windows. The city is apparently humming with life, yet not a soul is to be seen. In the midst of a vast urban populace the solitude of the balloon and its sense of isolation are tangible. This mood deepens in *Lights III: The Black Balloon* 1973 (no.39, p.99). The scene is now Waterloo Bridge, London. The balloon hangs over the Thames – black and eerily still; the manned basket beneath it is the only sign of life in a strangely deserted metropolis. Though dark, the scene is depicted with a sharp, even clarity. No detail dominates, nothing is obscured – a view of the world in which the process of expunging preference and prejudice has begun. Yet, at its centre, the vast balloon is still a looming, unavoidable presence.

During the course of working on *Lights*, Andrews continued to compile and to classify a growing archive of source material. Folders entitled 'The Balloon', 'Start Places', 'Flight and the evolving experience' and 'Places flown over or seen from above and the early experience' document the growth of his ideas about the journey and his exploration of different possibilities. At some point in the project he began to think about his destination – a place for the balloon to descend. A file bearing the title 'Landings, landing places and the full inner experience' contains assorted images in which various locations in Rome, Morocco, Spain, South Africa, Bermuda and Portugal appear to have been considered. Astonishingly, a large amount of documentation relating to the 1969 moon landing suggests that the lunar surface seems also to have figured in his thoughts. Finally, Andrews invented composite locations which incorporate elements from closer to home: Brighton, Yarmouth and Scarborough.

In *Lights IV: The Pier and the Road* 1973 (no.40, p.100), the Palace Pier at Brighton is combined with a detail taken from a postcard depicting a section of coast road near Rome. *Lights V: The Pier Pavilion* 1973 (no.41, p.101) depicts the no-longer existing Britannia Pier Pavilion which was destroyed in Edwardian times. *Lights VI: The Spa* 1974 (no.42, p.102) effects an even more radical imaginative juxtaposition by combining New York's Triboro bridge with a distant view of Scarborough. Why these particular locations – simultaneously 'real' and yet non-existent? Andrews's phrase 'the full inner experience' is notable, for it signals the particular significance he attached to his chosen terminus. His destination was not simply geographical but, in keeping with the theme of the series, carried metaphorical significance. Brighton, Yarmouth and Scarborough all carry pleasurable associations of holidays and crowds – ideal places to rejoin others, after a solitary journey. Indeed, Andrews planned (but never executed) a final spectacular party painting titled *Necessary Leaps*, which would have marked this kind of occasion.

It is, however, the way Andrews has interpreted these scenes that reveals his deeper purpose. Significantly, the view of the balloon has been replaced by views from the balloon. Andrews's symbol of the self-observing ego has disappeared. Instead we have open, expansive vistas whose treatment evokes a sense of unified evenness and calm objectivity. Within that vision, there is acceptance of the way things are – or appear. This objectivity evokes the Zen state of illumination which Andrews understood as 'a way of liberation which regards everything just as it is'. Without the presence of an interfering, value-laden ego, the interrelation of external things becomes apparent – and with that realisation, a new freedom. In imagination a bridge joins New York and Scarborough: such images are, as Andrews commented, 'my vision of the interdependence of things'.

Andrews's reading of books on Zen made it clear, however, that striving to eliminate self-watchfulness is, inevitably, in itself a symptom of self-regard. As Alan Watts observed in his book *The Way of Zen*, 'it is impossible to achieve nirvana or to intend to reach it, for anything desirable as an object of action is by definition not nirvana'.[7] Illumination is achieved only when one ceases to strive for it. This paradox is at the heart of the final painting in the *Lights* series. In it, the balloon drifts out to sea, continuing its journey. As in the preceding three paintings, the balloon is not shown. Instead, there is a view from the balloon of its own image, revealed now as a fleeting, ephemeral shadow – an image in which absence and presence are conjoined.

School

From May 1977 to July 1978, Andrews worked on a group of four large paintings of fish, a series he called *School*. At first sight, this subject appears like a surprising departure from his longstanding engagement with themes of behaviour, social interaction and, more recently, personal identity. In fact, the fish paintings are a continuation of these previous themes, combining various strands of his overriding concern with the way that people act.

By focusing on the idea of self-awareness, the *Lights* series had diverted Andrews's attention from the themes of behaviour and social interaction which had been a preoccupation prior to 1970. Interestingly, however, *Lights* had brought to the fore the idea of the interdependence of things – the sense of relation and connectedness between disparate external phenomena. The notion of interdependence in human behaviour now engaged Andrews's attention. He began to be interested in the ways that people form into groups and communities and the reasons for this. Of these developments, Andrews observed: 'I was thinking of social similarity, and difference (conformity, uniformity, upbringing) and so on and the fish images occurred – came to mind: School I, II, III, IV.' Whereas previously his work had centred on the patterns of behaviour arising from interaction, his thoughts now turned to the mechanisms or structures underlying the behaviour of groups. In particular his

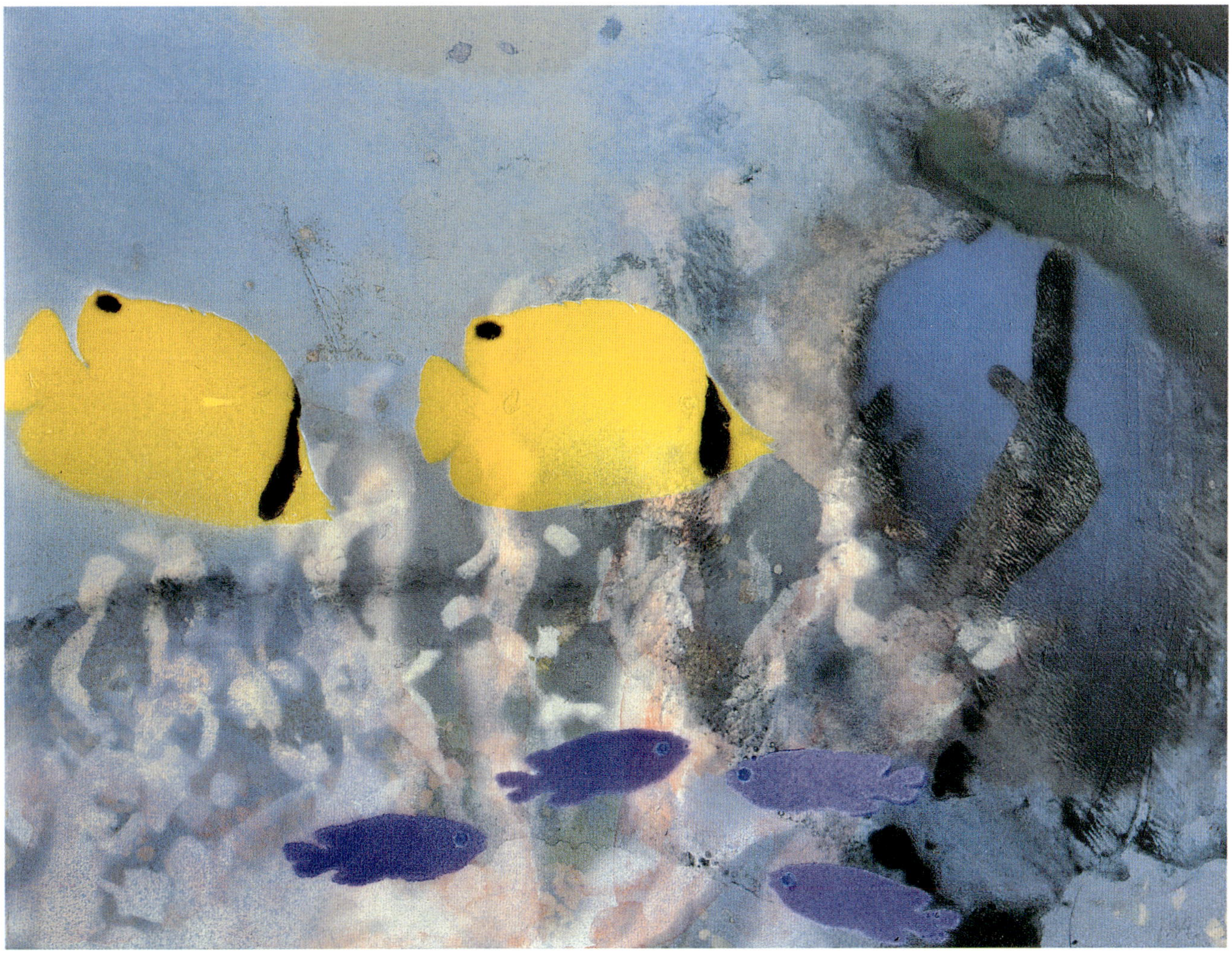

FIG.13
Study for *School III*
1978, watercolour
on paper,
19.7 x 25.4
Private Collection

interest centred on notions of similarity, difference, exclusion and opposition – the dynamics which draw individuals together or set them apart.

Developing his use of symbolism in *Lights*, in the *School* series Andrews's treatment of a complex theme also avoids literal illustration. It proceeds instead by a process in which observation and metaphor are combined. Having formed the initial idea, with characteristic attention to detail Andrews set about furnishing himself with further information about the appearance and behaviour of fish. He obtained an aquarium which he then stocked with neon tetra fish. These are the protagonists in the first painting in the series, *School* I 1977 (no.48, p.109). Numerous surviving thumbnail sketches, annotated with colour notes, attest the close observation which informed the development of the image. But it was the opportunity to observe the behaviour of the fish – in particular, the way they would suddenly form a shoal, moving almost as one – that fed the subject of the painting. In the resulting image the tetras cluster together, individual differences subsumed within a new group identity. One of Andrews's working notes, written while he was involved with this work, reflects: 'How alike we all are ... and our propensity to stick together.'

Of course, the notion of the group – the community – involves a drawing together, a closing of ranks. And with that dynamic follow ideas of difference, separation and exclusion. In the party paintings there are glimpses of individuals set slightly apart from the rest – Rimbaud in *The Deer Park* is in the thick of the party but seems remote, connecting with no-one in particular; and the seated figure, head cupped in hand, at the centre of *All Night Long*, seems immersed in his own thoughts. In *School II: Pike and Roach* (no.51, p.110), the relation of the individual to the group moves to the foreground. Depicted from above, as if seen through the surface of the water, a large pike stalks a shoal of roach. Here, the relation is that of predator and prey. Difference is perceived as threatening, and similarity is a defence – the group finds safety in numbers.

Immediately prior to commencing the series, Andrews had written: 'Identity and community – and identity in community; that's my prevailing preoccupation – my prevailing idea.' That a theme so apparently embedded in human relations should receive a form of interpretation so removed – visually – is startling; yet its suggestiveness is apparent and there is a relation between his treatment of the theme and his own situation. During the course of his work on the series, Andrews moved his house and studio to Geldeston, on the border between his native Norfolk and Suffolk. In transferring from an urban location to a rural setting, he and his family (his wife, June, and his daughter, Melanie) were themselves moving from one kind of community to a very different one. Andrews seized on the change to develop the growth of his ideas. In his new surroundings, he began to make watercolours of ponds and the marine life they harboured; local streams, the Old River (a tributary of the River Waveney) and the Waveney itself also became subjects, extending his engagement with the theme of water. These studies from life – depicting light effects, the appearance of water, fishlife and boats – were not intended as preparations for the *School* paintings; but they expanded the context in which the larger works developed.

The concluding paintings in the series, *School III: Butterfly Fish and Damsel Fish*, and

School IV: Barracuda under Skipjack Tuna (nos.57, 58, pp.111, 113), both finished in 1978, concern the relations between different types of community. In the first, two groups of fish are clearly differentiated by their respective 'uniforms'; in the second, this difference has deepened. The two communities do not simply co-exist – the difference between the groups has implications for both: 'Now it's two kinds of creature aggressive and peaceful.' Interdependence, it would appear, is not simply a passive condition. One of the implications of the *School* series is that the relations between individuals are in constant flux – the individual moves alone, attaches to a group, the group disperses and it reassembles elsewhere. Identity and community intersect continuously and the connection between the two must be constantly renegotiated.

The idea of leaving one group and moving to another community informs the subject of *Melanie and Me Swimming* 1978–9 (no.59, p.121). The painting is one of Andrews's most personal and affecting images and was completed immediately after the final painting in the *School* series. While it was conceived as the first work in the series which followed, titled *Holiday*, its connections with the themes of water, swimming and the relation of individuals are clearly apparent, so that it forms a bridge between the two series. The painting depicts Andrews and his daughter, Melanie, swimming together in a rock pool. The image was based on a photograph taken by a friend, Jean-Loup Cornet, in 1976 while the family was on holiday in Scotland. At that time, Melanie had started school and – like the fish Andrews had been observing – had acquired a uniform. The sense of her passage from the family to the wider community is evoked in the way Andrews holds his daughter: protectively supporting her, while helping her acquire the skills that will enable her, eventually, to swim away.

Holiday

From the late 1970s the focus of Andrews's concerns turned increasingly to the relation of the human figure to its context. This issue – 'the interdependence of figure and field', as he called it – was, on the surface, to do with the way individuals are affected by their surroundings. But, at a deeper level, his subject matter now also began to address the sense of connectedness that grows up between an individual and their environment. The roots of these developments can be traced to the paintings of the imposing formal gardens at Drummond Castle at Crieff in Scotland that Andrews made in the late 1970s.

In summer 1975, Andrews and his family stayed for the first time at Glenartney, near the Drummond Castle estate, while holidaying at the home of a notable collector of his work. The gardens there made an immediate impression. Laid out in front of the house, the expanse is carved into four parts by two long diagonal paths impressively echoing the St Andrews cross on the Scottish flag. A number of shorter linear and circular walkways subdivide the space further, threading through and around the topiary, hedging and flower beds. This enormous space, looking for all the world like a great stage – devoid of people yet inviting human occupation – evidently captured Andrews's imagination. This was, however, a reversal of his usual thinking, for the setting appears to have preceded the situation. What kind of human behaviour would be appropriate for its atmosphere of refinement, its formal symmetry and sense of history?

As the two paintings of this subject show, Andrews's response could not have been predicted. In both versions, painted in 1976 and 1977 respectively, the foreground is occupied by four figures whose status is ambiguous. Dressed in animal costumes they are both comic and yet sinister; apparently benign yet potentially threatening. In some ways they seem at one with the strange unreality of the place. At the same time, they appear like a modern intrusion, completely at odds with its history and dignity. Whatever their identity, a peculiar frisson arises from the relation of the figures to the setting and this is what makes these images both unsettling and compelling.

Andrews and his family subsequently returned to Glenartney each summer for their family holiday and, with growing familiarity, the unique character and history of the place began to exercise a fascination. During his second visit, Andrews was invited to go stalking. Here he found a new kind of party – individuals in the landscape, seeking out and shooting deer. It was the context for a kind of behaviour that was completely alien to him. Yet, at the same time, he was intrigued by this insight into another dimension of human activity: the rituals and patterns of stalking, the skills of the stalkers and their relationship with the historic landscape, and the experience itself – of tracking and killing. Perhaps the activity of stalking also suggested some analogy with his own activity as an artist – the sighting and stalking of the subject, the drawing upon and the honing of skills, and the effort to fix the subject in his sights. The motives for Andrews's engagement with this theme are complex; and, as before, the paintings he made of this subject can be seen as the evidence of Andrews making up his mind – making tangible his response to the issues before him.

Although Andrews made numerous smaller stalking paintings and studies of the landscape at Glenartney throughout the 1980s, the four large paintings he made between 1979 and 1982 form the heart of the *Holiday* series (nos.67–70, pp.126–9). The extent of Andrews's examination of his own behaviour is evident in the way that of these four paintings, three depict the artist himself in the act of stalking. In an inversion of the way that the *Lights* series had sought to eliminate a sense of self-watchfulness, Andrews now seems to have felt the need to know how the situation in which he was immersed appeared. Following the lead suggested in *Melanie and Me Swimming*, Andrews asked the same photographer, Jean-Loup Cornet, to take photographs during his various stalking trips. These images enabled Andrews to stand outside his subjective view and to appraise his position in the landscape, alongside the stalkers, with his prey in front of him – as an objective fact to which he could begin to respond.

Peter's Day; 3rd Stalk 1979 shows the artist huddled alongside the stalker, Peter Cramb, as a herd of deer flash past in the middleground. *Alistair's Day; 2nd Stalk* 1980 depicts Andrews again, this time with the head stalker, Alistair Work, in the immediate aftermath of having taken a shot at their quarry. *Alistair's Day; 2nd Shot* 1980 freezes the moment when the deer they had been tracking is finally dispatched. These are taut, dramatic images which concentrate vividly the tension of the stalk amidst the vast panorama of the setting. In purely

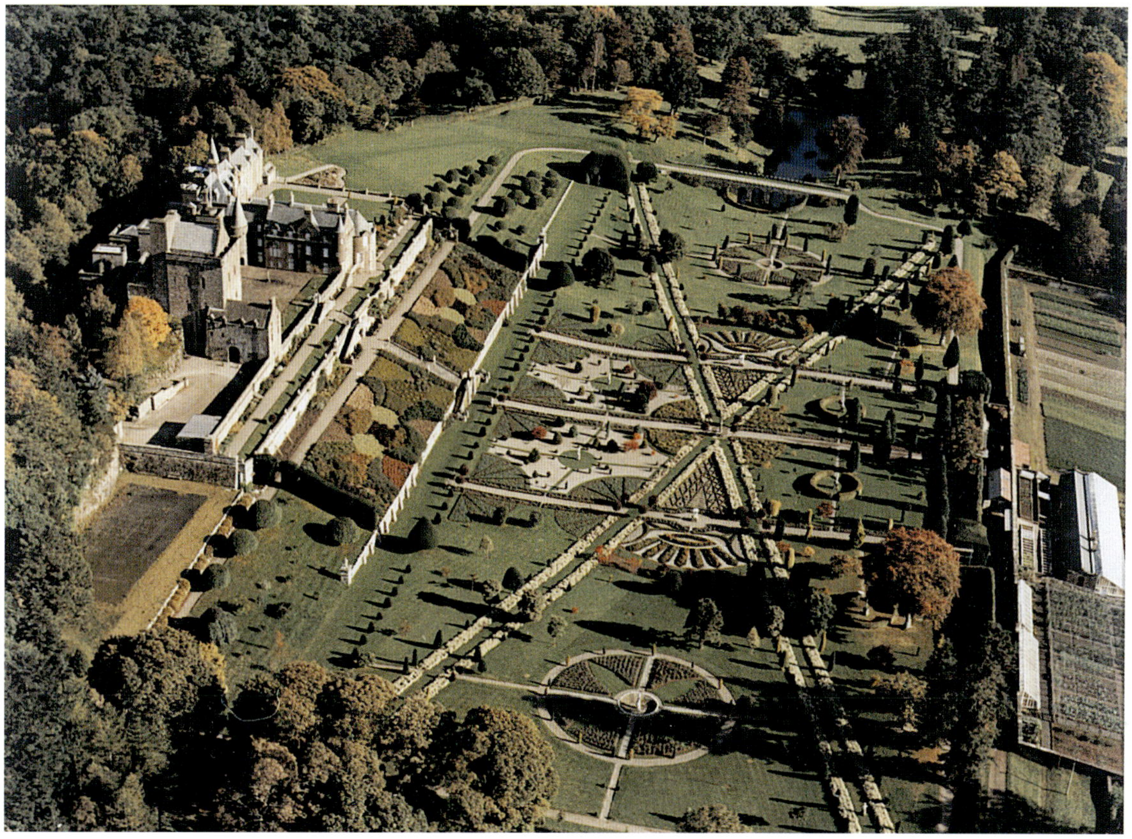

FIG.14
Drummond Castle

visual terms the subject posed considerable challenges concerning scale and light, and also in regard to such questions as how best to convey the vast stillness of the mountainous backdrop while evoking the darting movement of the deer.

Andrews was clearly aware of these issues, as his working notes reveal. 'Agitate the surface,' one such message urges, 'it should all be vibrant and alive – not stark and dead.' On a technical level, Andrews evolved for these paintings a new, wider range of means, both for descriptive and expressive ends. He deliberately exploits contrasts in scale – for example between the size of the stalkers and that of the deer – to reinforce an impression of distance and depth. It is clearly important that the viewer should be able to identify with and to feel the space of the image. And, as Andrews's note suggests, the surface of the painting is pitched in different ways. It moves from the diffuse, pale light of the sky, to the sharp focus fixed on the figures' jackets, to passages describing the surface of the landscape where paint applied with spray and stencils is combined with splattering and the evidence of much freer activity.

In this unlikely setting, themes evident in Andrews's work from the outset found a new resolution. In these images we find the individual, caught in the intensity of his own concentration, behaving in complete accord with another human being in close proximity. Bound by their shared experience they observe the movements of other living creatures, sensitive to their every movement, adjusting their own position to every change in their surroundings. Every action is attuned to the moment, and is acutely responsive to circumstance. Yet such actions are also part of a pattern of behaviour whose roots lie in the distant past, in the actions of predecessors, whose similar activities and lives are inextricably bound up with the history of the place. The perception that arises from the *Holiday* series is that human nature embeds itself in particular locations. This notion, and the resulting sense that certain places – in the absence of people – can evoke a human presence, is the dominant theme of Andrews's subsequent work.

Rock of Ages Cleft For Me

In surveying Andrews's career, one of the most striking aspects of his work is the extraordinary degree of continuity that unites it. This relates not simply to his practice of working in series, nor even to the way such series interconnect. The links are much longer. When in 1960 he observed that painting was a way of making up his mind, it might have been supposed that he was referring to particular subjects. It is only with hindsight that the true span of these thought processes is apparent. The ideas, preoccupations and values that were the catalysts for his work in the 1950s were, thirty years later, still drawing Andrews's work forward, yielding fresh insights and new subjects.

Among these preoccupations, one of the most prominent was the imperative Andrews felt for 'getting things in right relationships'. In engaging with this idea, his art functioned as a way of coming to a clearer understanding of the world and of the individual's place in it. By the early 1980s, his attention had fixed on the interdependent relation between man and

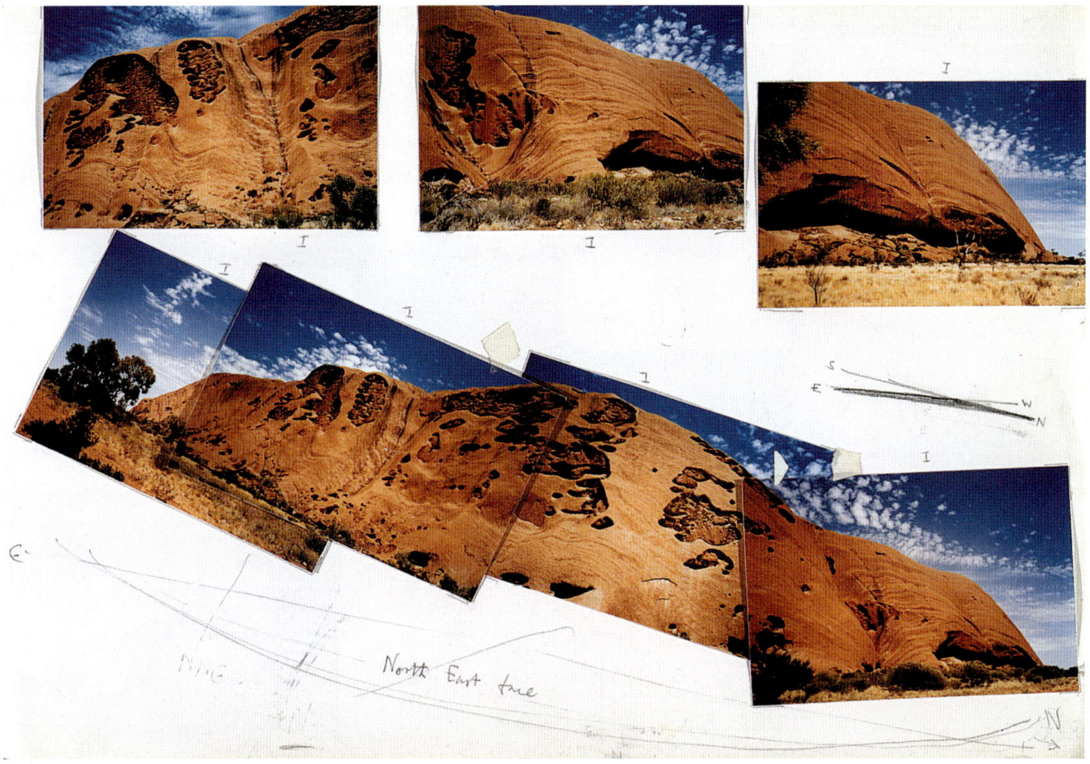

FIG.15
Collage of Andrews's photographs of Ayers Rock relating to *The Cathedral, The North East Face/Uluru (Ayers Rock)* 1985
Tate Archive

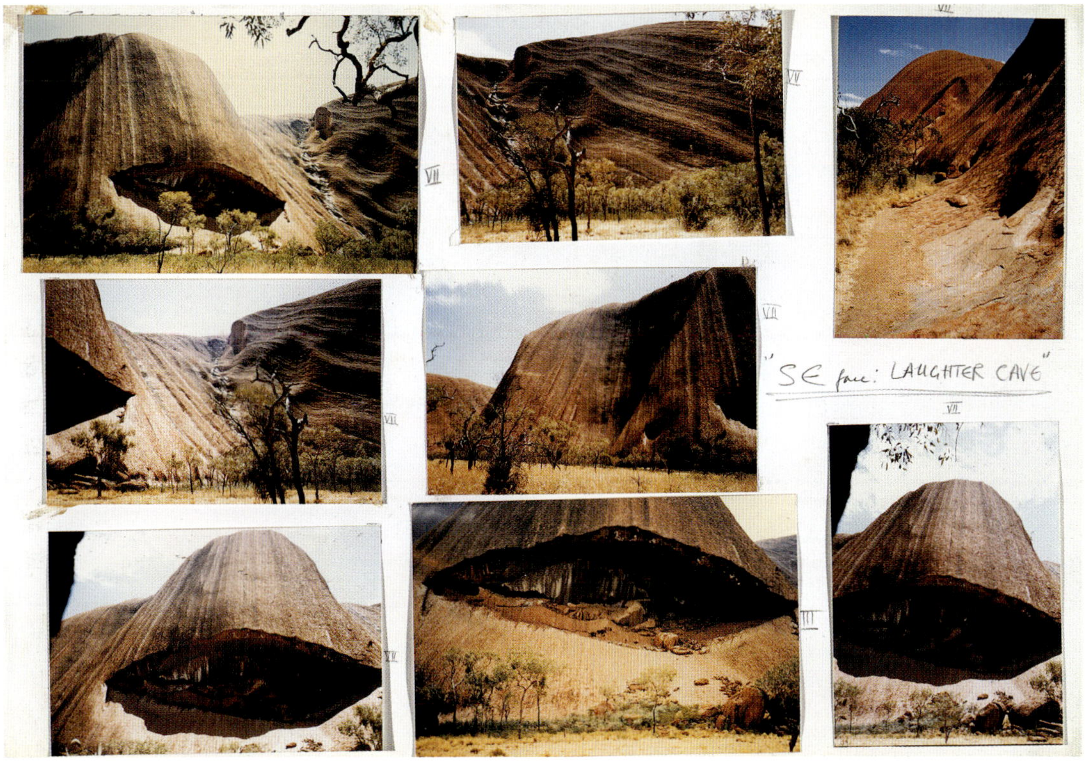

FIG.16
Andrews's photographs of Ayers Rock relating to *Laughter Uluru (Ayers Rock)/The Cathedral I* 1985
Tate Archive

his environment. It was thus with some intuition of its special significance in this connection that in October 1983 Andrews travelled to Ayers Rock, in the heart of central Australia, thus fulfilling an ambition he had held since the 1960s.

If this trip appears to have connotations of a pilgrimage, Andrews was not wholly unaware of them. Three of the nine large canvases that were the result of his visit include within their title the phrase 'The Cathedral'. For this is how Ayers Rock seemed to Andrews. Rising 348 metres above the flat, surrounding scrubland, this great natural monolith recaptures the medieval pilgrim's experience of seeing, say, Durham Cathedral, at the end of a long journey. It is an experience in which awe, reverence and an acute sense of personal insignificance are combined. The diminution of self-obsession which Andrews had evoked in *Lights* receives at Ayers Rock its ultimate confirmation. This realisation is contained in the second line of Toplady's eighteenth-century hymn whose title Andrew appropriated for his paintings of the mountain:

> Rock of Ages, cleft for me,
> Let me hide myself in Thee.

Andrews's visit to Ayers Rock lasted nine days. During that time, he made numerous watercolours and took hundreds of photographs. He climbed the Rock and he walked around its base – a journey of almost 9 kilometres. In circumnavigating the Rock in this way, its unique character and significance unfolded. Until the early twentieth century the mountain had been inhabited by aboriginal people, whose cave paintings survive, and almost every point on its scarred and cavernous surface has spiritual meaning for them. According to aboriginal tradition, Uluru, as the mountain is called, belongs to the dawn of time – 'the dreamtime'. For them, the evidence of the events of that time, when the beings and beasts of their mythology stalked the earth, are etched into the Rock's surface. The sacred meanings attached to particular parts of the mountain – the rock hole Mutidjula, known as Maggie Springs, and the mouth-shaped cave Lagari (Laughter) – impressed Andrews and they form individual subjects within the series. But as a whole it was the growing realisation of the way human life and nature had become inextricably fused that moved Andrews. '"Cleft" opened for me in revelation of a near perfect manifestation of interdependence [between] man and environment.'

The series of paintings that Andrews completed on his return to Britain express his response to this enormous subject. In an immediate sense, Andrews's concerns were, naturally, topographical. The viewer must know what the Rock looks like. The primary difficulty which thus confronted Andrews was that of conveying its sheer scale. The two paintings which show different faces of the Rock in their entirety tackle this subject head on. The first of these to be completed, *The Cathedral, The North East Face/Uluru (Ayers Rock)* 1985 (no.78, p.136), shows the mountain rearing up, as it were, from the flattened foreground. This is the longest of the Rock's faces and its strange, red, organic surface – smooth in parts, yet everywhere ruptured by fissures and holes – is revealed. The trees receding sharply from the foreground to the base of the mountain indicate that this is a distant view, yet its physical presence fills the entire picture space. Andrews states the mountain as an inescapable, overwhelming visual fact. This is an image about the otherness of the Rock – its strange, enormous immobility concentrated into a form that the viewer can perceive, but cannot fully comprehend.

The paintings are never simply topographical however. Andrews's response to Ayers Rock was, from the first, alert to the way its significance transcends the physical facts. 'The land abounds with being,' he noted, 'creatures actively alive or metamorphosed into rocks or trees imbued with the spirit, with the living presence of totemic ancestors.' It is this sense of absolute identity between living things and their surroundings, a fusion which connects the individual's experiences to the historic past, that most impressed him. This, for Andrews, was his real subject. Throughout the series, the Rock is seen as a living thing. Such images as *The Cathedral, The Southern Faces/Uluru (Ayers Rock)* 1987 (no.82, p.140) powerfully convey an impression of stillness, but the mountain is not presented as inert, geological matter. There is a feeling, rather, that it slumbers.

Such anthropomorphic qualities are at the heart of the aborigines' stories about the mountain and they permeate Andrews's images. The paintings are never, however, illustrations of aboriginal mythology. For example, the large cave Lagari, which is the subject of *Laughter Uluru (Ayers Rock)* 1985 (no.77, p.135), for aborigines is a Kunia man (an ancestral native inhabitant) laughing. Andrews's image preserves the connotation of a laughing mouth but at the same time there are suggestions of other sexual, female generative associations. Andrews's imaginative engagement with the Rock empathises with its symbolic significance for the aborigines. It was not, however, conditioned by those considerations. The paintings of Ayers Rock are about the relation between man and his environment but they arise from his identification with a particular, unfamiliar place. As such they are a personal response, manifesting a view of the world untainted by preconception. A view, simply, of how things seem.

Late Landscapes

In 1984, Andrews copied out the following passage from Janet Adam Smith's book, *John Buchan and his World* (1979), which quotes Buchan:

> Being equally sensitive to the spells of time and of space, to a tract of years and a tract of landscape, I tried to discover the historical moment which best interpreted the ethos of a particular countryside, and to devise the appropriate legend.

Buchan was one of Andrews's favourite authors and alongside this extract Andrews has written: 'it's marvellously clear this quote. I sympathise. It is deduction: Buchan's historical moment, for me is induced or suggested by landscape and its ethos. The ethos is the history. It's the ethos I try to paint.' The implication is clear. For Andrews, landscape and history are inseparable; and painting particular landscapes entails an engagement with their 'ethos' –

FIG.17
Photograph taken by Andrews relating to *The Source of the Thames*

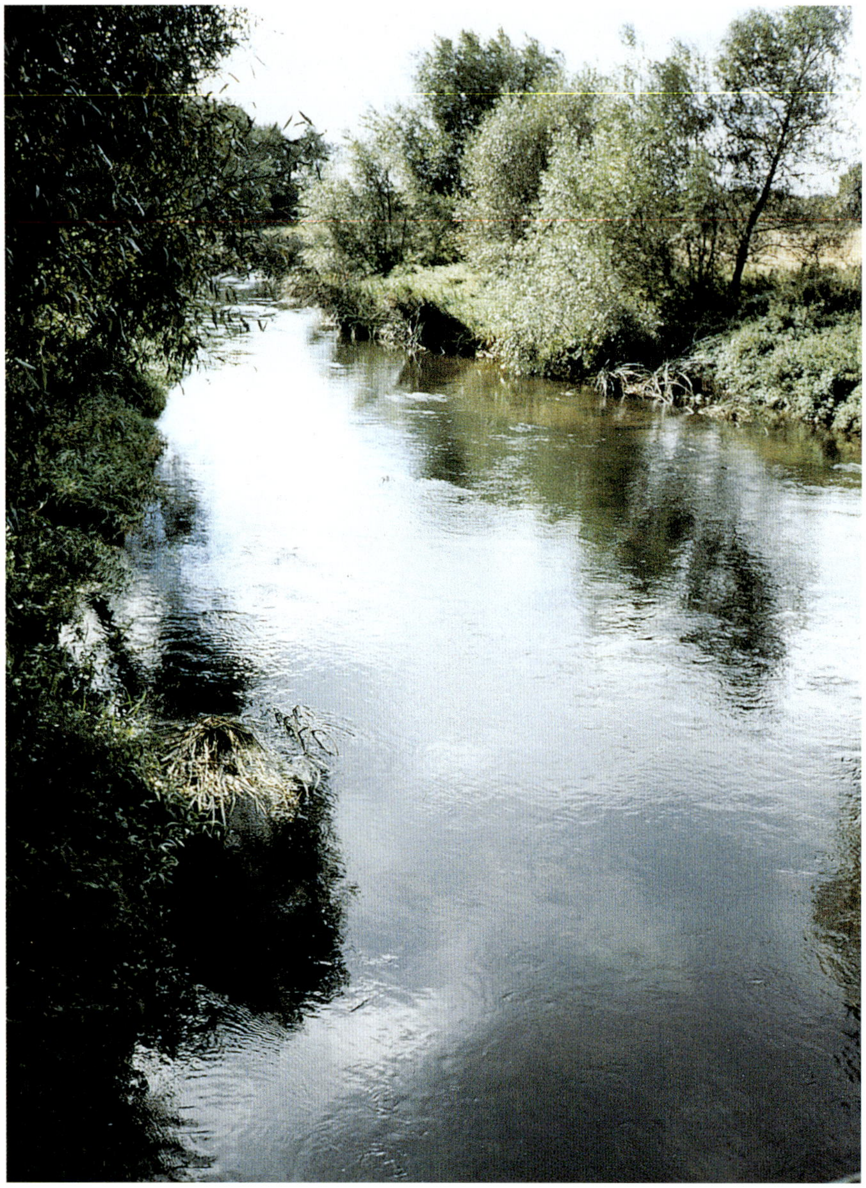

their history. In this way, Andrews's longstanding preoccupation with the figure, which to date had sustained his exploration of human nature, now increasingly translated into an absorption with the depiction of place. Certain landscapes, impressed with history and human experience, would now serve in the context of his 'search for the nature of being'. Although he did not cease to paint people in his final years – indeed he painted an impressive late series of portraits of himself, his wife June and friends – these ideas suggest reasons for the prominence which the subject of landscape assumed in the last ten years of Andrews's career.

Andrews's first 'historical' landscapes had been the paintings of the gardens at Drummond Castle. These were followed by two paintings titled *SAX A.D. 832* 1982 and 1983 (fig.32, p.168, no.83, p.145): views of Saxlingham, the seventh-century village near Norwich to which he and his family had moved in 1981. At the time of painting these works, Andrews's studio was in a rented former chapel and the experience of this historical setting was clearly conducive to the way his work was progressing. He also undertook a number of landscape commissions: *Lafite* (a view of Chateau Lafite) in 1981 and, subsequently, *Daylesford* 1983–4, and *Oare, the Vale of Pewsey* 1989–91 (nos.84, 85 pp.146–7). Significantly, Andrews's growing involvement with landscape subjects was underpinned by an increasing variety of painterly attack. In *Oare*, for example, the vast space depicted is enlivened by paintwork which combines taut drawing in paint with transparent washes of colour.

In 1990, Andrews returned to large-scale paintings of Scottish subjects with two works that provide further forceful demonstrations of this way of working, combining precise observation with a much freer and looser handling of paint. The first, *A View from Uamh Mhor* 1990–1 (no.86, p.150), is a panoramic 'prospect' depicting the mountainous landscape at Glenartney. The view was assembled from a collage of individual photographs and records the numerous stalking routes he had taken over the years. The second work, *Edinburgh (Old Town)* 1990–3 (no.87, p.148), presents a sharply contrasting historical perspective. It depicts the stark, dark mass of the ancient castle set against a bleached sky. The picture's viewpoint is the Grassmarket, a site of execution – as Andrew well knew – where numerous men and women were hanged during the late seventeenth century for their adherence to the reformed religion. During his work on the painting Andrews was much affected by a necessary immersion in his subject's historical significance and, at one point, progress ceased and the painting was turned to the wall. The final image presents a contemporary view of the Old Town, but it is a view through the lens of history.

In 1992, Andrews returned to London, taking a flat with June and Melanie near Albert Bridge in Chelsea. His thoughts in this new location naturally turned to his next subject and he considered various options. In February that year, he made his first visit to New York and for a while that subject remained a possibility. As he began to explore his surroundings, however, a new idea began to take root. Having set up a new studio in Sydney Close, his walk there each morning entailed crossing Albert Bridge. Pursuing this daily routine, the views of the river impressed him with its grandeur, changing appearance and – not least – the sense of continuity it implied.[8]

His impressions were, at first, specific. He began making trips along the river looking at particular views, making sketches and taking photographs. Gradually, however, the subject gained imaginative weight. 'I am interested in external appearances for what they reveal of what is internal'; his interest in the river grew as its significance burgeoned. His fascination with the Thames subject began partly because of its personal associations – bound up, as it was, with his own life and his present circumstances. But this interest was sustained by a developing perception of the river's deeper metaphorical significance. The river appeared to him not only as a source of life – emerging at some point into the world, gathering direction and flow, and eventually disappearing into the sea; it also seemed to him to encapsulate the very idea of history which he had been pondering: the river as a continuous stream of events.

In 1994, he commenced what he saw as an open-ended series of paintings of the Thames subject. The first painting, *The Thames at Low Tide* 1994–5 (no.94, p.157), depicts a couple of barges resting on mudbanks with the river, at low tide, alongside. The picture presents no specific location and it brings together impressions based on a surprising range of material: thumbnail sketches from life, colour photographs of the surface of water at Venice, photographs of the Thames, a newscutting from the *Evening Standard* about the neglect of the Thames and – perhaps – distant memories of footage of the Thames in *Together*, filmed almost forty years earlier.

In late September the same year, Andrews commenced a further two Thames paintings. The start of this activity followed a period of convalescence; earlier that year, in June, he had undergone an operation and cancer had been diagnosed. Andrews had wanted to trace the source of the Thames – to begin again where the river emerges gently – and the week before recommencing in the studio he and June had travelled to Thames Head. He realised that to paint the source itself was not possible as it was then dry, the flow only being apparent in winter. However, around three miles further along, he found a point where the river became 'a clear and gentle stream'. The water there was crystal clear and reminded him of the rivers he had seen in Norfolk as a boy. The second, unfinished painting, *Source of the Thames* (no.96, p.158), forms the beginning of his response to these impressions.

The third picture, *Thames Painting: The Estuary* 1994–5 (no.95, p.159), depicts what Andrews described as an 'ideal' estuary. Again, the image combines observation and invention. On 14 October he and June visited Canvey Island in Essex and Andrews took a number of photographs. Back in the studio, these visual references connected with images of the Thames taken over a hundred years earlier (using modern prints of the photographs titled 'The Thames from London to Oxford' taken by Victor Prout in 1862); with aerial views of the mudflats at St Brieve, France; and with images of Florence, flooded. While working on the picture, Andrews's methods echoed events in the landscape he was depicting. Often the painting was laid flat and, wanting to evoke the movement of water and mud, turpentine was poured on to it direct. Ashes were mixed with the paint. Sometimes the results were 'disastrous' but, at some point, the figures on the jetty were added (based on a newscutting of a photograph taken in 1893). With these additions the image was reclaimed and a window into the past opened. It was his final painting.

'We are what has happened to us,' Andrews wrote in 1984. A note dated the following year adds: 'Each of us is a historical fact.' In these observations there is a sense that, as his art progressed, Andrews's search for the nature of being became inextricably bound up with a deeper appreciation of the importance of history. Behaviour, he saw, was just the tip of the iceberg. Human nature is not only about the way people act, or even what they feel. Rather, it is the accretion and interpretation of experience, and a sense of relation with their surroundings and with the past, that shape the individual's nature and his view of the world. Andrews's art engages with human nature in all its diversity and, at times, its dark complexity. But it is essentially affirmative in spirit – a consoling vision that defines and confirms, thereby offering the prospect of renewal.

Notes

1 Unless otherwise indicated, all statements by Andrews are from an uncatalogued collection of the artist's papers belonging to June Andrews.

2 'Notes and Preoccupations', *X – A Quarterly Review*, Mar. 1960, vol.1 no.2, p.141.

3 Letter dated 16 July 1958 from MA to Mary Chamot, Assistant Keeper, Tate Gallery, in reply to her cataloguing enquiry (Tate Catalogue file).

4 Letter dated 2 July 1960 from Helen Lessore to Michael Andrews (Tate Archive).

5 Daniel Farson, Soho in the Fifties, London 1987; third impression 1988, p.44.

6 Quoted in catalogue entry on *The Deer Park* in *Tate Gallery Illustrated Catalogue of Acquisitions 1974–76*, London 1978.

7 Alan Watts, *The Way of Zen*, p.71.

8 For information regarding Andrews's work on the Thames paintings I am indebted to Richard Morphet's report 'Information given by MA to Nicholas Serota and Richard Morphet during their visit to 11 Avenue Studios on 28 February 1995'.

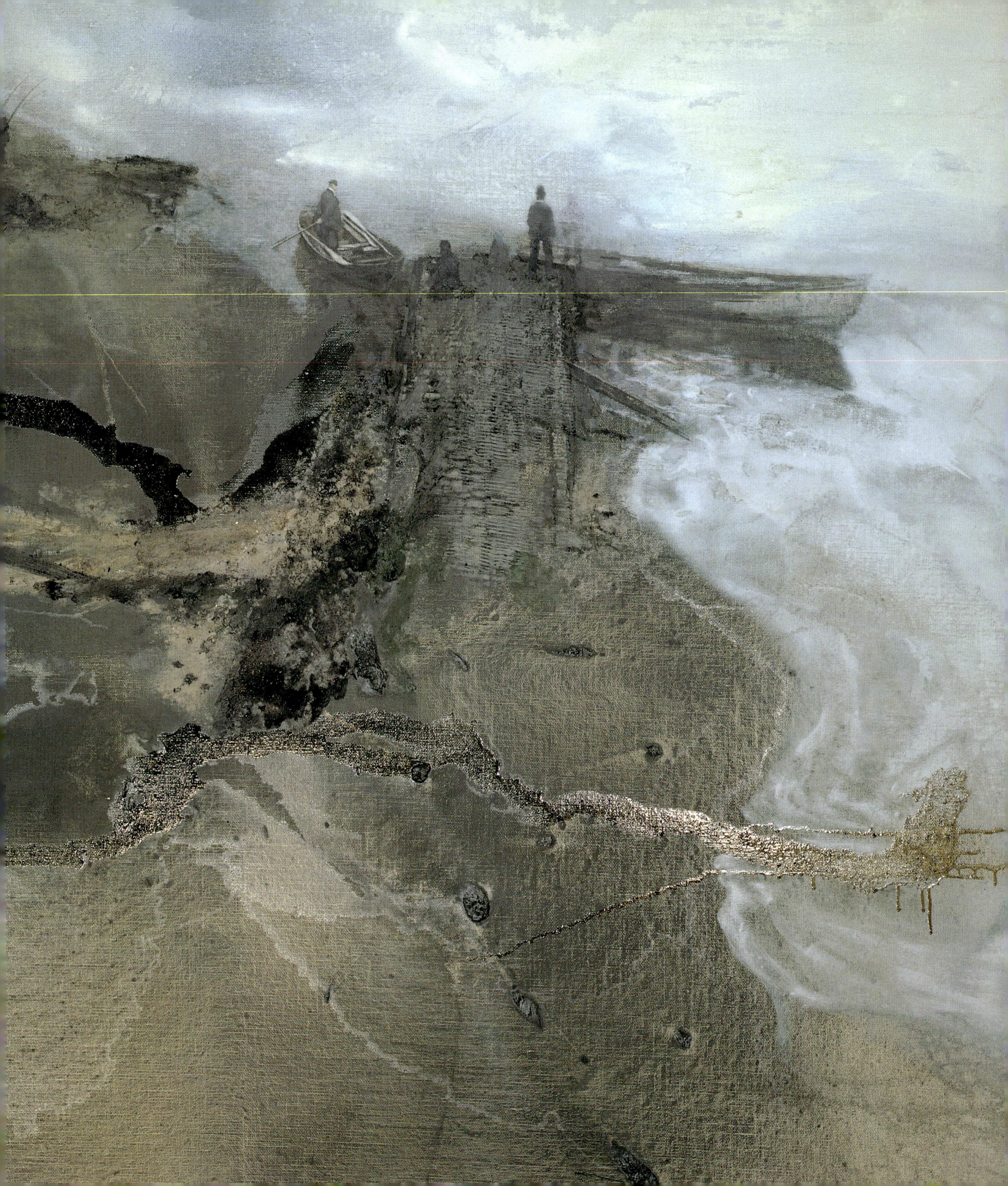

An Actual Present Atmosphere

William Feaver

Apprehensive about what he had let himself in for, yet pleased at having arrived on time, Michael Andrews sat down and looked around at the studio's padded walls and baffle boards and at the microphone poised to catch his every word. A freestanding door – a sound-effects door elaborately encumbered with locks and bolts – caught his eye and he was just about to remark on its futility when suddenly, from an intercom, came a voice asking him for level. Say anything, the producer said. What did you have for breakfast? This being his first radio interview – indeed the only radio interview he ever did – the question surprised him but he answered carefully. Next thing he knew a green light flashed and I was asking him why there were apt to be few, if any, people in his landscapes.

'Um um I think I'm probably very conscious of of ... of of of of there being an onlooker there, er,' he ventured. 'In other words whenever there isn't somebody in my picture you can assume there's a visitor um looking at, at ... whatever the picture depicts.' All tape transcripts have lapses, but not epic lapses: page after page of conscientious vacillation. 'I thought the hesitancy almost destroyed the interest – it certainly would "live",' Judith Bumpus, the BBC producer, wrote to me the next day as she set to work on the recorded material.[1]

Eventually, after weeks of editing, clarity prevailed and the interview went out in March 1991. Some ums and ers remained; rightly so, for Mike teetering was like a tightrope walker advancing, the trick being not to look down. So too when painting. He worried at things, hesitated over distractions, acutely conscious of not knowing until perhaps too late which thought would advance him and which would land him in confusion. He became more definite once he was committed, trying, as he said, 'to make the credible plausible. Trying to make the believable persuasively believable.'

Towards the end of our conversation that afternoon he came up with a fine distinction, an illuminating one, to do with the divide between art theory and painter's actuality. 'There's such a marvellous difference between ideas and imagery. I mean you can't paint ideas; you really cannot paint ideas. Pictures which are based on ideas are the ones that founder.'

The microphones were switched off and Mike lit a cigarette, euphoric once the ordeal was over. ('Poor old Bill,' he said to June, his wife, when he got home. 'I'm such bloody hard work.') We chatted on and I said something about how, to a hardcore modernist, illusion could only mean false pretences. He laughed and waved his cigarette at the sound-effects door. Convincing illusion: that was what he aimed to achieve, no matter how. Come to think of it, he had said as much in his 'Notes and Preoccupations', published in *X* magazine thirty years before: 'I want an actual present atmosphere in my painting. I don't mind how I get it.' Michael Andrews's paintings are about illusion, about being there or, to be more precise, about the sense of being there. The traveller alights, the stalker inches into position; the scenes are come upon, overflown, descended into, disclosed, each a prospect with potential.

FIG.18
Detail of *Thames Painting: The Estuary* 1994–5 (no.95)

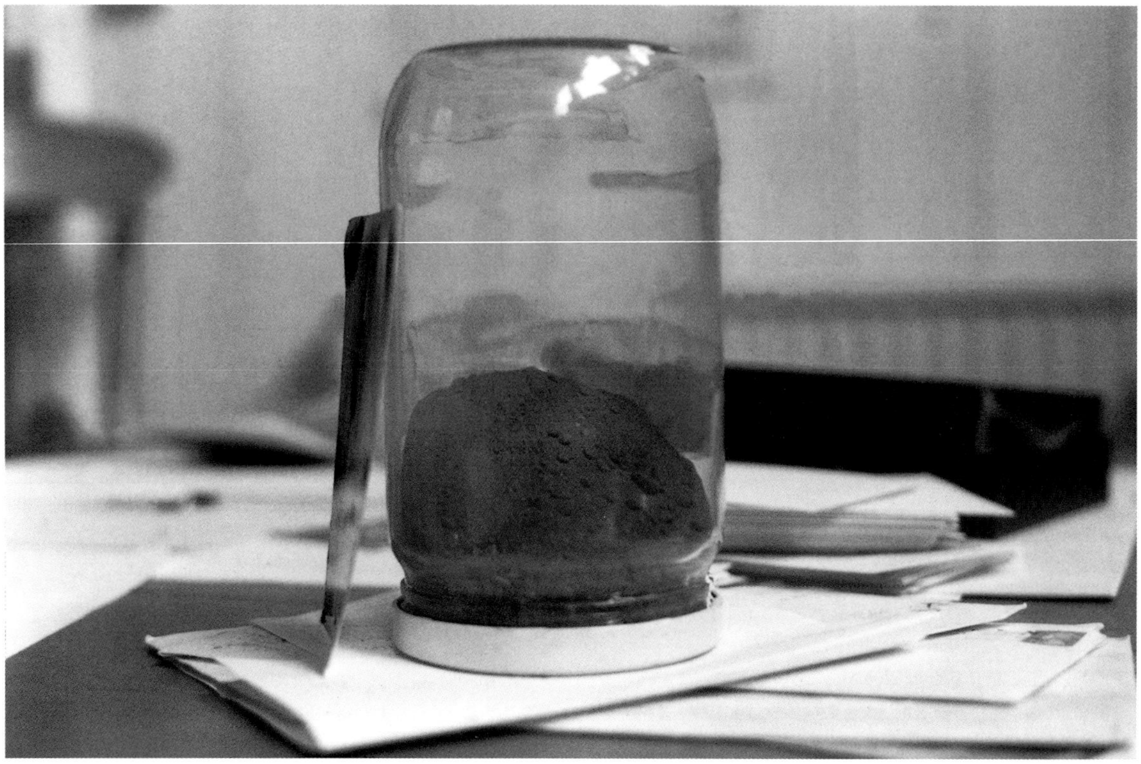

FIG.19
Jar of soil from Ayers Rock in the Sydney Close studio, September 1995
Photo: William Feaver

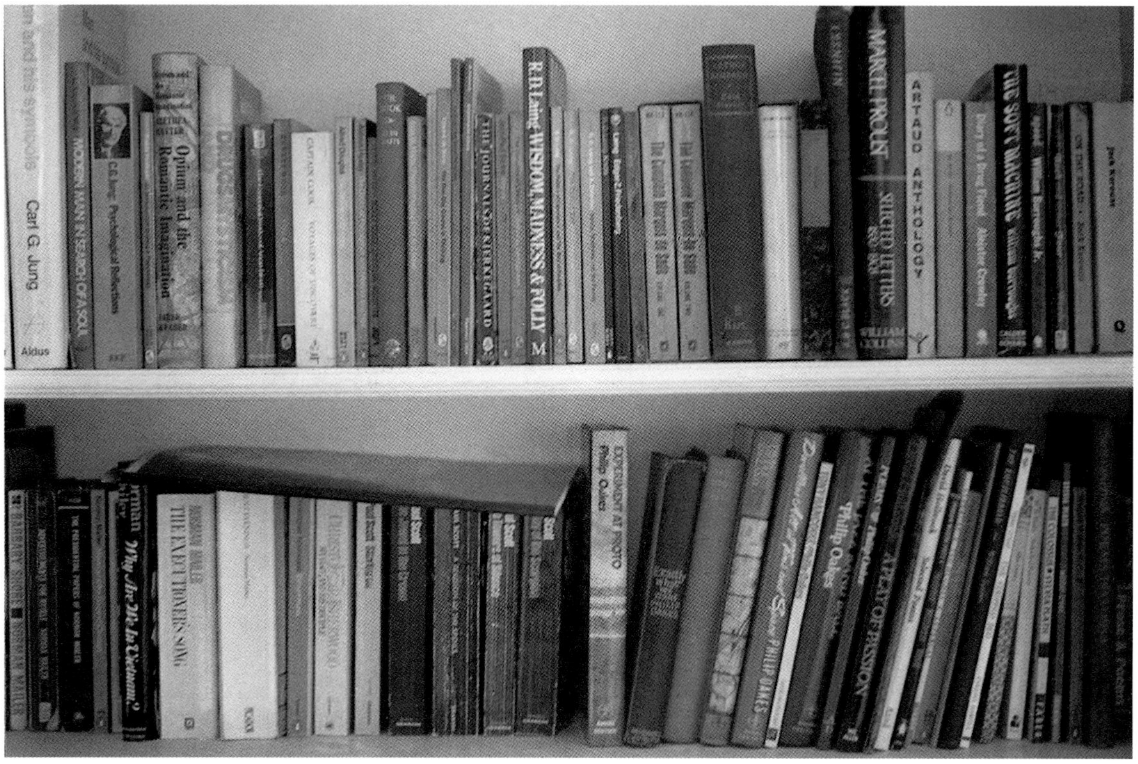

FIG.20
Bookshelves in the Sydney Close studio, September 1995
Photo: William Feaver

The occasion may be a family gathering, a student party, a civic reception or a personal mishap. Whatever. Each is an illusion floated, an image sustained; tantalising ideas submerged in the actual present paint.

'Once one is launched on a subject everything you pick up seems to apply, and not at all remotely so,' Andrews remarked to Lawrence Gowing in 1980. Fearing confusion, he went to elaborate lengths to avoid it. The worry that dogged him was how to differentiate between stimulus and distraction. Or, more subtly, how to negotiate between temptation and seduction. He loved to hit on serendipitous connections. Running boy, running deer; falling man, family man; rock, hill, pavilion, sea. Images that occurred to him (the Spa Hotel, the Spanish Steps, the Great White Fleet) became vehicles for his persistence and his exquisite touch. He was, as we can see, a consummate painter, progressively inventive, an achiever of pictorial feats, not least an intimacy of panoramic proportions. His are illusions that go the distance.

When taking stock, as he compulsively did for reassurance, Andrews often doodled down relative distances, relative sizes, relative life expectancies. He worked numbers into symmetries and ratios: how long it had been since he started at the Slade; his exact age when he first stalked at Glenartney ('47 yrs 9 and a half months') and how old, compared to him, his father had been at some point. Measurements and calculations helped sustain his idea of congruity. If one thing led to another then patterns, surely, would emerge; and from pattern there could arise the beauty of resolution. 'The kind of image I valued,' he said to his friend Victor Willing in a conversation they recorded in 1964, 'was one that worked musically like a chord.'

The tics and checks were marginal, of course, to the true concerns of the painter. Absorbed as he was in the demands of painting, Andrews measured his time in what he had managed to complete; as for the months he took prospecting for images attuned to his impulses, he regarded that as time invested. Anxieties, panics and shifts in routine primed him, as did the Sunday supplements. 'Think in images,' he urged himself. Illusion depends, he decided, on 'right orientation, disposition, atmosphere'. It may in itself constitute experience.

In 1952, when he was still a student at the Slade – regarded as the most promising of his year – he set himself thinking about how to depict a startling moment, a splat of unexpectedness dashed against the mind's eye. *A Man Who Suddenly Fell Over* 1952 (no.4, p.66) represents a shock so abrupt that, beyond cupping her hands to her chin, the woman looking on hasn't yet reacted. The man himself, a split second from impact, is in no position to consider the formal aspects of his fall in relation to Henry Moore reclining figures, say, or indeed to those citizens of ancient Pompeii overwhelmed, vanished into lava moulds and reconstituted in plaster centuries later. He looks ridiculous, as grown-ups do when they go arse over tip, particularly bald ones in Monty Burton suits. As he hits the grey London pavement he loses proportion; gross in relation to the woman, he is a pathetic great lump with hands stuck out uselessly, like tyrannosaurus claws come the Ice Age.

Clambering around on Ayers Rock, early one morning thirty-one years later, Andrews himself slipped ('nearly heart stopping') and almost fell. Picture it: the hat dropped and grabbed at, the instant, reeling, panic as the world – red-shouldered slope, blue sky, endless distances below – slews sideways and he scrabbles for a grip on the abrasive rock face. As he righted himself, okay apart from a few grazes, he thought how stupid of him. 'The idea was to breakfast in this cave and I took a shallow line up the slope, got into this shadow and began to slide.' The vertiginous sensation haunted him, on and off, for the rest of his ten-day stay.

'You should not be blasé about climbing the Rock,' the *Uluru National Park Guide*, 1983 edition, advised. 'There are so many skylines that appear to be the end of your journey so don't be deceived and quicken your pace because of this illusion.'

A couple of years afterwards, when he began a painting of the scene of what could well have been his last moments, Mike still felt the alarm. By then it was something to relish in that it had given him a more intimate sense of the bruising shadows and curved heights. 'I thought of a title "Where Gosse Clambered Up and I Fell Down" and I thought fuck that.' (William Gosse had been the first white man to scale Uluru, as the aborigines named it; he renamed it Ayers Rock after a premier of South Australia.) The painting, he decided, would be called 'Permanent Water', after the pool, Mutidjula, or Maggie Springs, a wink of blue at the foot of the ravine.

The Andrews Christmas card for 1983 was a photo of himself in front of Ayers Rock, ostensibly alone there. (His cousin Michael Ramsden took the photograph.) He wrote 'Happy Xmas May Your Dreams Come True'. For him, knee-high in bristling spinifex, the Rock was a dream materialised.

He had imagined it to be so remote as to be inaccessible. 'I came in a light plane from Alice Springs. So I saw the Rock gradually from the air, coming closer and closer to this wonderful motif.' The Uluru Motel, where he stayed, was about to be replaced by an Uluru complex a bit further from the Rock, offering the sort of resort facilities that he had featured twenty years before in *All Night Long* 1963–4 (no.20, p.86). Ansett holiday brochures were already urging 'Spend Seven Wonderful Nights with Australia's Greatest Rock Star'. Plonking though the analogy was ('the Bruce Springsteen of monoliths') it had a resonance for Andrews, whose transcendent images of idols Eric Clapton, Jimi Hendrix, Mick Jagger and Frank Zappa, derived from *Melody Maker* photographs, had featured prominently, though abortively, in the evolution of his *Lights* series in the late 1960s.

Ayers Rock was the actual present apparent mirage, so to speak, towards which Andrews had been working for at least fifteen years, ever since he saw in one of the Sunday colour supplements a Come Down Under advert consisting of a series of photographs showing the Rock in distant profile altering theatrically through the day. 'I imagined this would happen as a rapid transition, rather like a Wurlitzer in a cinema with its lights changing,' he said. Ideal, he thought, as 'a possible rendez-vous', by which he meant somewhere heavenly, an 'Enchanted Ground', not so much the Sixties Eel Pie Island or Watteau's Isle of Cythera, more the consummate destination, a redemptive place, the finale of the dream voyage represented in *Lights*. The ultimate illusion.

One morning Mike gasped his way, past many a false horizon, to the flattish top of the Rock. 'I was followed up by some pilots who were working on the airstrip and we were so thirsty we drank the watercolour water out of a bottle. Faintly tinted.' The Pom with his sketchbook and tepid pink painting-water – 'Me as Gulliver describes it very well' – became an eager initiate. He learnt the markings of the hot rough surface. Uluru, he now realised, is a narrative monolith, a repository of legend, the site of dreamtime feuds, battling dingoes and garter snakes. When he posed for the Christmas card photograph he stood directly below what the Pitjantjatjara tribe call 'the Brain'.

In his imaginings the thing that he had crossed the world to see revealed itself to be a cathedral, a mother church, a Jungian domain displaying sores and scars ('Good lord, there's vermilion when you look into those recesses'), a granite body shedding its skin periodically like a snake. A hymn, remembered from childhood, ran through his head:

Rock of Ages, cleft for me
Let me hide myself in Thee

'What was there was a radiant incarnation of Toplady's hymn,' he wrote in the foreword to the catalogue of the Ayers Rock paintings. 'It exceeded analogy.'

Bronze plaques mark the places where tourists have fallen to their deaths or died of heart attacks. While appreciating the desire to commemorate lives lost and holidays ended with sudden grief, Andrews saw that to tag Uluru was to treat it as an accident black spot. Whereas the paintings that he envisaged were to be exaltations, reified exaltations, of the natural wonder and unique resort. He sought transcendency: something approaching the beauty of holiness. 'The mixture has to be a blend of fact and interpretation. Expressionsim is all interpretation.'

With his haul of watercolours and photographs, bundles of spinifex grass and jars of red soil, Andrews returned home, to the redundant chapel that he used as a studio. There (and to do so in rural Norfolk was partly the point) he reasserted the sensations of heat and boundlessness and simmering silence a world away from the familiar fields and lanes that he cycled through each day from home in Saxlingham Nethergate to the chapel at Tasburgh.

The phone box, the telegraph poles, the wintry tussocks and ivied elms of *SAX A.D. 832 – Second Painting* 1982 (no.83, p.145), in which his house can be seen at the top of what in Norfolk counts as a hill, were elements rich, for him, in supererogatory meaning. Here is history: 1150 years, as village signs and the title of the painting declare, since Saxlingham began its recorded existence. For centuries the lane meandered muddily over the broad verges until, within living memory, a steamroller came, and lorryloads of tarmac, to render it permanent. The raking light of a cold afternoon sends shadows trickling across a frosty cultivated landscape; whereas the antipodean sun beating down on Ayers Rock gilds the primordial.

Near the studio-chapel door, on a box marked 'Free Will Offerings', he placed a photograph of the raked gravel and rock arrangement of the Zen garden in the Rioanji temple in Kyoto and, on a ledge above, fourteen spent cartridges, souvenirs of stalking in Scotland. Beneath the photographs of his Ayers Rock watercolours, the 'scaffolding', he said, of pictures to come, he wrote 'KEEP IT BIG KEEP IT SIMPLE BE BOLD'.

For the two *SAX* paintings, views in opposite directions, he used oils. For the grandeur of Ayers Rock the spray gun was indispensable. 'Like a studio assistant. Works very very fast, but it's almost less intelligent than the artist; one's working blind so there's a great deal of backtracking required; you make a mistake very quickly.' Whiffs of sky blue and red rock stained the end wall, marking the perimeters of ethereality: the azure and parched grasses in successive pictures. For pitted rockfaces he mixed handfuls of Australian soil into the paint. 'There is something slightly magic about using the materials that the rock is actually made of,' he said. Spinifex was used to mask foregrounds as he sprayed, hazing the apparent scrub. He did not approve of the Anselm Kiefer technique of bulking out pictures of ravaged German heartlands with straw and debris. It was befuddlement: 'unacceptably contradictory idioms, tending to make the whole thing implausible. The substance of the picture has to be appropriate.'

Andrews was aware that by appropriating the image of Ayers Rock he could be charged with committing cultural trespass. For him, though, the paintings were personal, not – as some took them to be – pictures investing the great outdoors with travel-poster banality and cinematic shine. Their lucidity was an expression of delight; their strangeness was sublime. That he employed the flawlessness endemic in advertising photography was bold in painting terms and riskier than churning out urgent expressionistic slurry. He was deliberately outdoing cliché, staring it down. 'I've always been interested in "discredited" subjects, almost in a slightly perverse way. But I don't think that's why I was interested in Ayers Rock. The point is the potency of the place and the power of the place.'

In the process of enlargement, from sketchbook and enprint to big-screen scale, painting considerations took over. 'As often as not it is the circumstantial marks on the drawing which actually have the structural significance in the picture. It's not the ones you think should be important that turn out to be; it's really the little odd things which point your attention to the important things.'

Andrews wanted not synthetic concoctions but immensities and convincing distances. 'From start to finish the canvas, as far as I am concerned, is a space; it's not a surface.'

> I literally have to feel that I'm there, that the photograph is the place in my mind's eye. There's a minimal but very important transformation in the photograph as it sits on the table.

Valley of the Winds 1985–6 (no.80, p.143), set in the Olgas, a day trip away from Ayers Rock, was particularly difficult to resolve. At one point two people were set walking into the middle distance, then he removed them, only to find that the going became immeasurable and close to being decorative. He wanted to establish an unexplored look. 'It's very much about glare and tangle and the possibility of getting lost; but I don't want it to be Max Ernsty.'

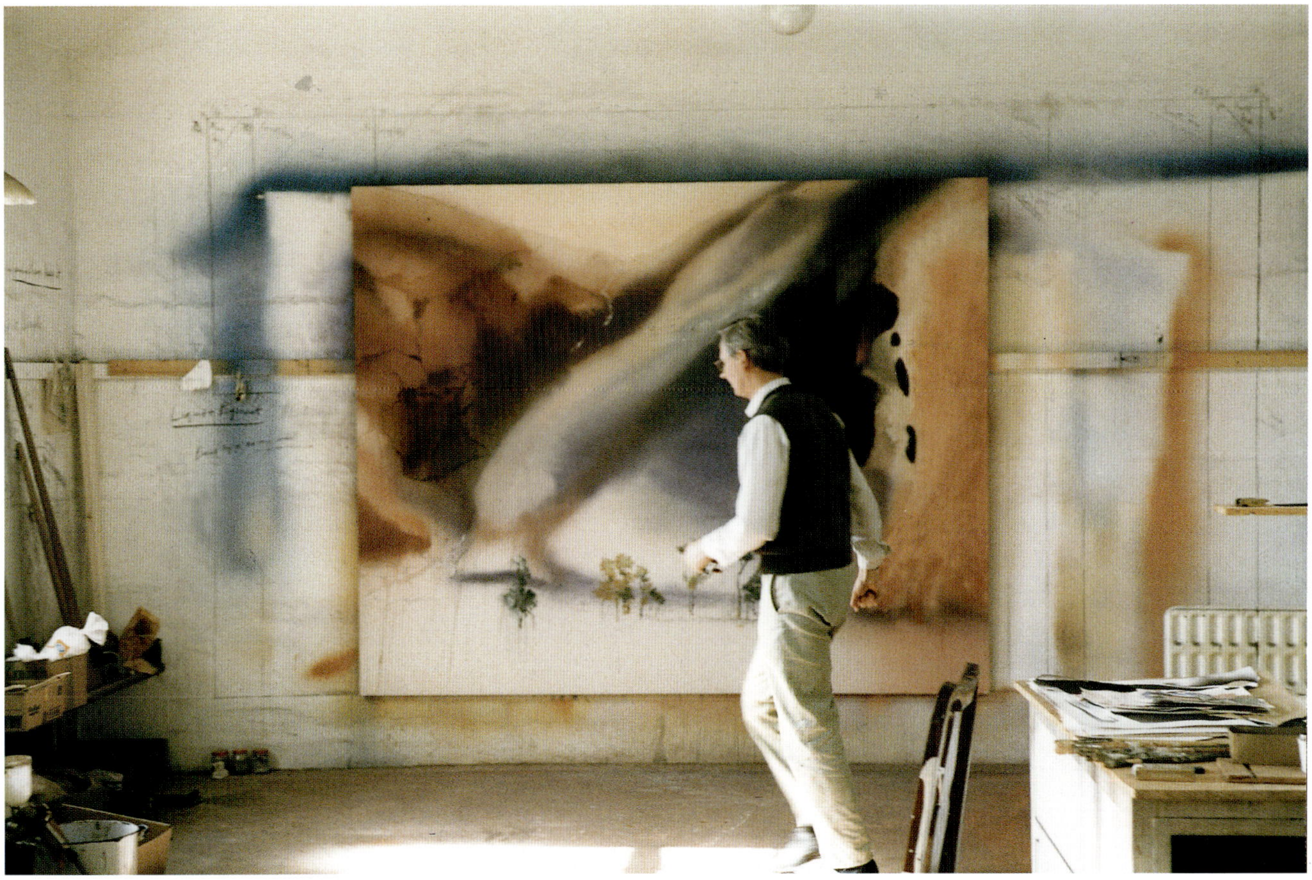

FIG.21
Michael Andrews with *Permanent Water Mutijula*, in progress, Norfolk, 1986
Photo: William Feaver

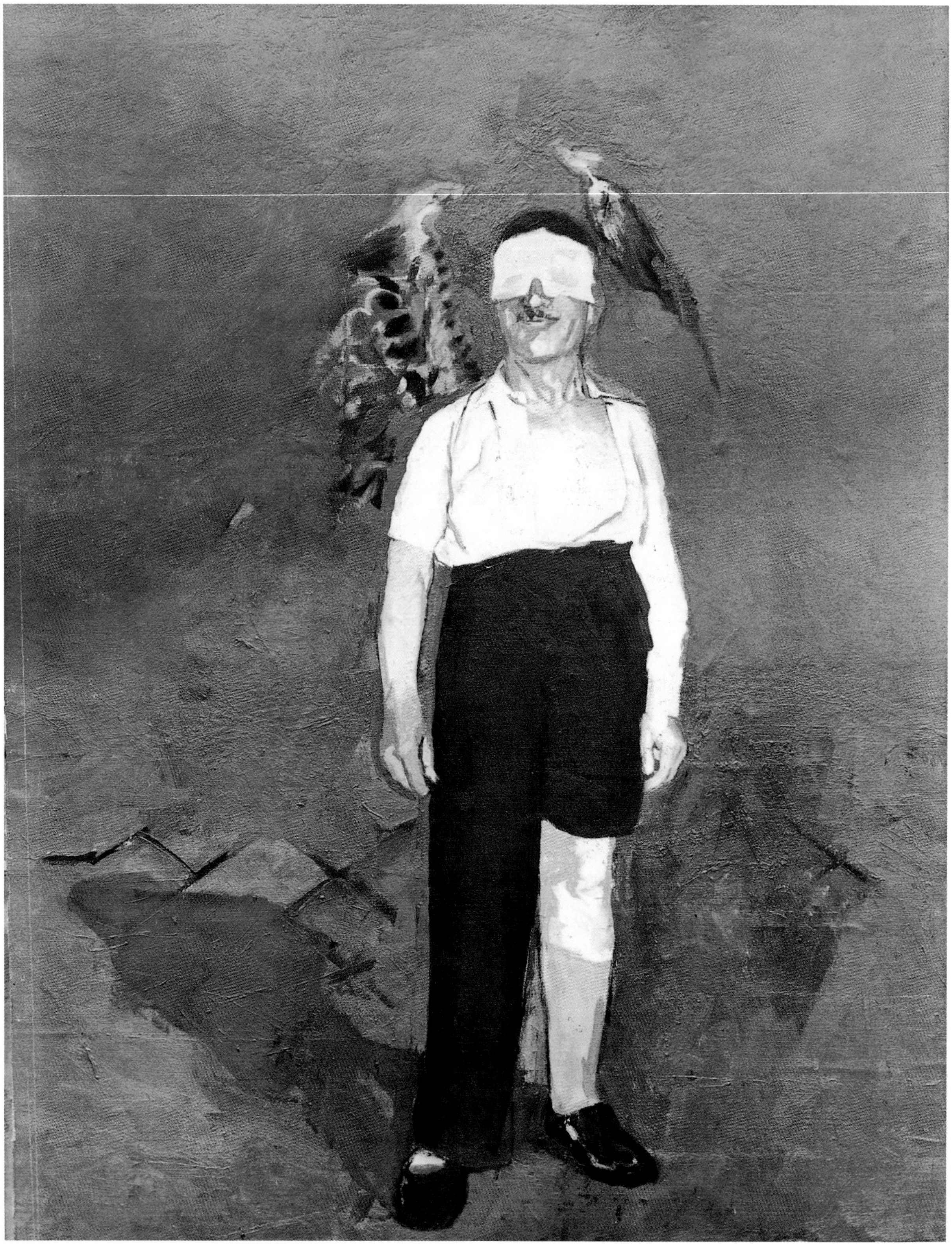

FIG.22
Mason 1956
(destroyed)

Not for him surrealistic complications generated from blottings and doodles. Stimulus came from specifics, from phrases that attached to images, insights fished from the flow. 'Rock of Ages', for one. 'As a boy I sang this hymn often but never liked it. The metaphor seemed too inert to identify God as I had been encouraged to believe in him.' Yet even a hymn could be redeemable.

Let the water and the blood,
From Thy riven side which flowed,
Be of sin the double cure,
Cleanse me from its guilt and power.

If preachers and psychoanalysts see eye to eye about anything, they agree about the primacy of guilt and power. Brought up on conscience, and on certainties set to stirring tunes, Andrews never lost the taste for a reassuring moral timbre. 'Lusty old Methodist hymns ("My chains dropped off"): I used to be very disparaging about them in my teens but at Ayers Rock I thought again of the frowning providence and smiling faces bit.'

Every Sunday as he grew up, after morning service at the Methodist chapel, Mike's parents kept open house at 13 Park Lane Norwich for as many as nine uncles and aunts and others, among them a friendly Captain from one of the nearby USAAF bases. 'They'd come home from chapel and all get together, laying up a meal in the dining room and cups of tea after,' June Andrews remembers. 'And then high tea.'

August for the People 1951 (no.1, p.64), a 'summer composition' from his time at the Slade, is a young man's view of family holidays dulled in the memory. The beach at Sheringham. Sky pasty, slumped figures, a solitary bikini, the odd umbrella. A father figure stands out from the crowd, refusing to admit that suits are inappropriate with bare feet. What's he waiting for? An aim in life? Soon, surely, the pubs will open.

This man, Andrews Man, reappeared in a painting from 1956, standing similarly but blindfolded, one trouser leg rolled up, shirt undone, and wearing a slipper and a shoe. He was 'Candidate prepared for initiation' from a Masonic handbook, identified as a Neddy Seagoon type and transformed into a cult figure with traces of wings from the Bircham Cope, a fifteenth-century masterpiece of East Anglian embroidery, inserted like laurels behind his head. Andrews could only speculate as to the sacrificial sheepishness. What sort of person volunteers to be ridiculous out of respect for a secretive code? Was there a connection with Francis Bacon's slurred men in suits? Probably. The painting was photographed but not exhibited. Norwich Man intervened in the person of the greengrocer who delivered vegetables to 13 Park Lane and was so appalled by the picture that Andrews flinched. He had not quite appreciated that the absurdity was, to some, a serious practice. The ritual model could have been the greengrocer himself, or a colleague of his father's at the Norwich Union. He shoved the picture behind a door and later destroyed it.

Another character about whom Andrews entertained illusions was a retarded man, a jobbing gardener who, most mornings during Andrews's residency at the Digswell Arts Trust in Welwyn Garden City, shuffled past the window. He painted him several times, treating him as a serial motif, like Bacon's Van Goghs, dishevelled in a green landscape. Knowing nothing about him except that he lived with his mother, he named him first 'The Gardener' then 'The Happy Man' then 'Digswell Man', by which time he had at last met him, if only the once.

'Mrs Happy Man hailed me on my way to paint out-of-doors,' he wrote to Jeffery Camp in April 1959. 'She and (get this) Cecil (that's the H.M's name!) were looking at this bubbling pipe not knowing what to about it. I must say I thought it might be a frog – or an old bottle – but I put my hand in the puddle and it was a pipe.' Digswell Man was, he found, not quite as he had thought him. 'I looked closely at Cecil who, though not loquacious, is quite articulate and said he could smell gas.'

Andrews's paintings of the anonymous bubble with speculation, whereas his self-portraits – such as the one he did in 1958 with the Phaidon 'Rembrandt' open beside him – are interrogatory (Who am I? How do I compare?) and those of his painter colleagues, John Lessore and Tim Behrens, are affirmations of painterly ambition. These aspects merged in *Lorenza Mazzetti in Italy* 1954 (no.6, p.68), a painting that he abandoned at the British School in Rome when, missing the life, he bolted back to London after a few months of his Rome Scholarship. His fellow-student, for whom a year earlier in 1952 he had played man-into-cockroach in her film of Kafka's *Metamorphosis*, smiles complicitly against the escalating baroque of the Spanish Steps. For good reason: the model was her identical twin sister.

Lorenza Mazzetti cast him again, in *Together*, in which he was required to learn a smattering of sign language, the illusion of fluency of gesture. 'A poetic fable' as Anderson described it, a first expression of 'Free Cinema', *Together* was awarded a prize at the 1956 Cannes Film Festival. Andrews walked each morning from South Kensington to the East End locations to save bus fares, and then walked all day for the camera as his role largely consisted of wandering with his co-star, Eduardo Paolozzi, from docks to pub to street market to digs, the pair of them playing deaf-mutes unable to relate to the sound-track. Mike's expressions of bewilderment and longing, smiling sweetly and – in his dreams – getting a girl, amounted to a portrait in reaction shots of the artist as a young man.

Cycling up the Great North Road through Hatfield on his way to Digswell in 1958–9, he was drawn to some blocks of flats, a pre-war development with lapsed pretensions to chic. The lettering of the sign, 'Altham Court', he noticed, had been eaten away. *Flats* 1959 (no.9, p.71) is a location seen from the point of view of a passing cyclist, pedalling slowly, imaging himself a cameraman securing a travelling shot, hardly noticing the rebel spirits (bikers astride Lambrettas rather than Triumphs) intermittently revving up. A For Sale board came and went on the wasteground beside the Altham Court fire escapes. 'The bloody builders,' Andrews complained to Jeffery Camp, 'have levelled my entire middle distance.'

Behind the facades of *Flats*, I suspect, is the 'mysterious conventionality' that Andrews talked of in the 'Notes and Preoccupations' that he compiled at Digswell. The baleful conventionality of Alfred Hitchcock, the Islington greengrocer's son in his trademark tight suit, and the dotty conventionality of Jacques Tati's M. Hulot. Guilt and power, religious and sexual and never satisfied, are the lurking urges. In *Late Evening on a Summer Day* 1957 (no.10, p.72), a painting that reads like an Iris Murdoch storyboard, the drab afternoons on the sands at Sheringham are long ago and far away from the suburban setting where, life imitating idyllic Bonnards, couples snog, among them a pair from a nineteenth-century Japanese photograph: two geishas clasped together like an amorous netsuke.

At Digswell, or in Norwich where he painted *Late Evening on a Summer Day* and the ceremonial tea-time of *The Family in the Garden* 1960–2 (no.13, p.75) (for which, challenging himself, he decided to order a stretcher the same size as Seurat's *Bathers*), Mike talked of six o'clock as being 'a difficult time of day'. Oh to be in Soho. Six o'clock: happy hour for him at Muriel Belcher's Colony Room in Dean Street. Stuck in 'Pigswill' as he called it, he yearned for the ready loss of inhibition under Muriel's direction, the illusion of cheerful harmony, spiked with sarky comment, as afternoons waned and evenings wore on. The Colony Room regulars in his conversation piece of 1962 are bunched, flush with drink, engorged by raillery. These are known characters: Jeff Bernard on the left, elbow cocked against the mantelpiece; John Deakin facing an indignant Henrietta Moraes, poised to deflate her; Bruce Bernard listening respectfully to Francis Bacon; and Muriel turning her sallow face to Ian the barman and ordering another round on someone's behalf. Lucian Freud, looking levelly out of the picture, serves as the one who knows what's going on: that, under the guise of a group portrait of friends and acquaintances, Mike is combining echoes of Manet (*Music in the Tuileries*: Bacon in place of the fat lady on the curly seat) with dashes of the Bonnard mural that he had painted at the top of the stairs four years before and mirrorings of Velazquez.

Where *The Colony Room I* 1962 (no.16, p.83) is recognisably a low-ceilinged *Las Meninas*, *The Deer Park* 1962 (no.18, p.81) is *The Colony Room* socially advanced beyond the parochial. 'Soho writ large,' Andrews remarked. The setting was an ameliorated Colony Room, the stairs grander, the mural become more a picture-window giving onto Velázquez's *The Boar Hunt*. And what a swell party it is. Marilyn Monroe clinging to Jose Balanos, Rock Hudson enjoying a joke, Rimbaud glowering and at the other end of the sofa a sprawling Norman Mailer.

In February 1962 the *Sunday Times* launched its colour section, the first in Britain, and to attract readers, published in it a complete James Bond short story, 'The Living Daylights', set in Berlin. Familiar territory: 'Bond walked hard for two hours along the leafy path, then chose a restaurant with a glassed-in verandah above the lake.' In *The Deer Park*, part brothel, part killing field, the bored man seated at the right, one eye on the wiggling cleavage, is Ian Fleming himself.

For Andrews, the Sunday magazines became a ready resource, their topicality priming him, their contrasts prompting him, their advertisements bringing to his attention new carpeting, new decors, new brands, new resorts: Pyrosil, storage units, Bri-Nylon, Ayers Rock. In January, 1963, he himself was the subject of a *Sunday Times* colour supplement article by David Sylvester ('Michael Andrews: Mysterious Conventionality') for which Lord Snowdon photographed him, cigarette in hand, squeezing between *The Deer Park* and *The Colony Room*.

All Night Long is *The Deer Park* colour-supplemented, the stairway and mezzanine rosewood-veneered like the QE2, the scene extending across three panels to Vistavision proportions. The period is circa 1963, between the Beatles' first LP and the start of *Goldfinger*, when Bond thwarts a cardsharper in Miami and a girl ends up coated in gold paint. Here, where jet set meets demi-monde, scandal brews. Christine and Mandy are the names under the beehive hair-dos and the clarinet bleats melancholy as dinner jackets are discarded and romps commence. Soon there will be official enquiries; meanwhile the night is long, the skinny-dippers frolic in the midsummer darkness (actually 'All Steamed up to Romp in the Snow', the source headline said) and the sapphic geishas from *Late Evening on a Summer Day* again embrace.

'An image gets weight as it goes along,' Andrews said. 'It snowballs.' Illusion. Allusion. He must have been the only Colony Room habitué to have read *Pilgrim's Progress* and made use of it. 'It's something I find er terribly interesting but uncomfortable reading. I'm reluctant to find Life and Progress quite such hard work as Christian found it.' In the Colony Room's Vanity Fair were latter-day sinners to match Bunyan's Mr No-Good, Mr Live-Loose, Mr Love-Lust, Mr Heady; John Deakin, photographer and scrounger of genius, his skin so dry that he rubbed butter into it when he sat for his portrait, was an obvious Mr Malice. Andrews was no Bunyan disciple; he appreciated nonetheless the virtues of an emblem-strewn narrative hugging the moral high ground. Fortified with themes and motifs and soaring assurances, he could concentrate all the more inventively on working the paintings.

A bird's-eye view of Vanity Academe was commissioned from the Norwich Museums Committee when Andrews was asked to commemorate, at £20 a square foot, a Lord Mayor's reception in Norwich Castle Museum for the Chancellor of the newly founded University of East Anglia. Here was an opportunity to blend his longstanding themes of initiation and social gathering. It was, he said, 'the chance to crystallise my feelings about Norwich people'. He engaged a wedding photographer to take shots from balcony level of town and gown mingling in twos and threes. These he collaged, transferred to canvas and progressively retouched, picking out floral decorations, posh frocks. The painting is a civic alternative to the collage-tableau devised by Peter Blake for the Beatles' *Sergeant Pepper* album cover, though the nearest thing to a celebrity is the bishop in his purple cassock. Guests are strung along the foreground like the front line of courtiers in *The Boar Hunt*, bifocals glinting at pleasantries, sherry glasses stiffly held. A chorus of waitresses awaits the signal to issue forth with canapés.

The three panels of *Good and Bad at Games* 1964–8 (no.21, p.88) parade a cast of variously connected characters, among them Craigie Aitchison, Vic Willing and Paula Rego, his wife, Paula's parents Jose and Maria Rego, Mike, his aunt and mother and brother. Dramatis personae, staked out by the pool of a Portuguese hotel, they are sized according to their billing, as it were. Some are mere extras, like the bikers in *Flats*; others – Vic Willing particularly – are blooming personalities, bigheads in several cases. As for Mike at parties: 'I begin well,' he said, 'and then I kind of dwindle after about the middle of the evening.'

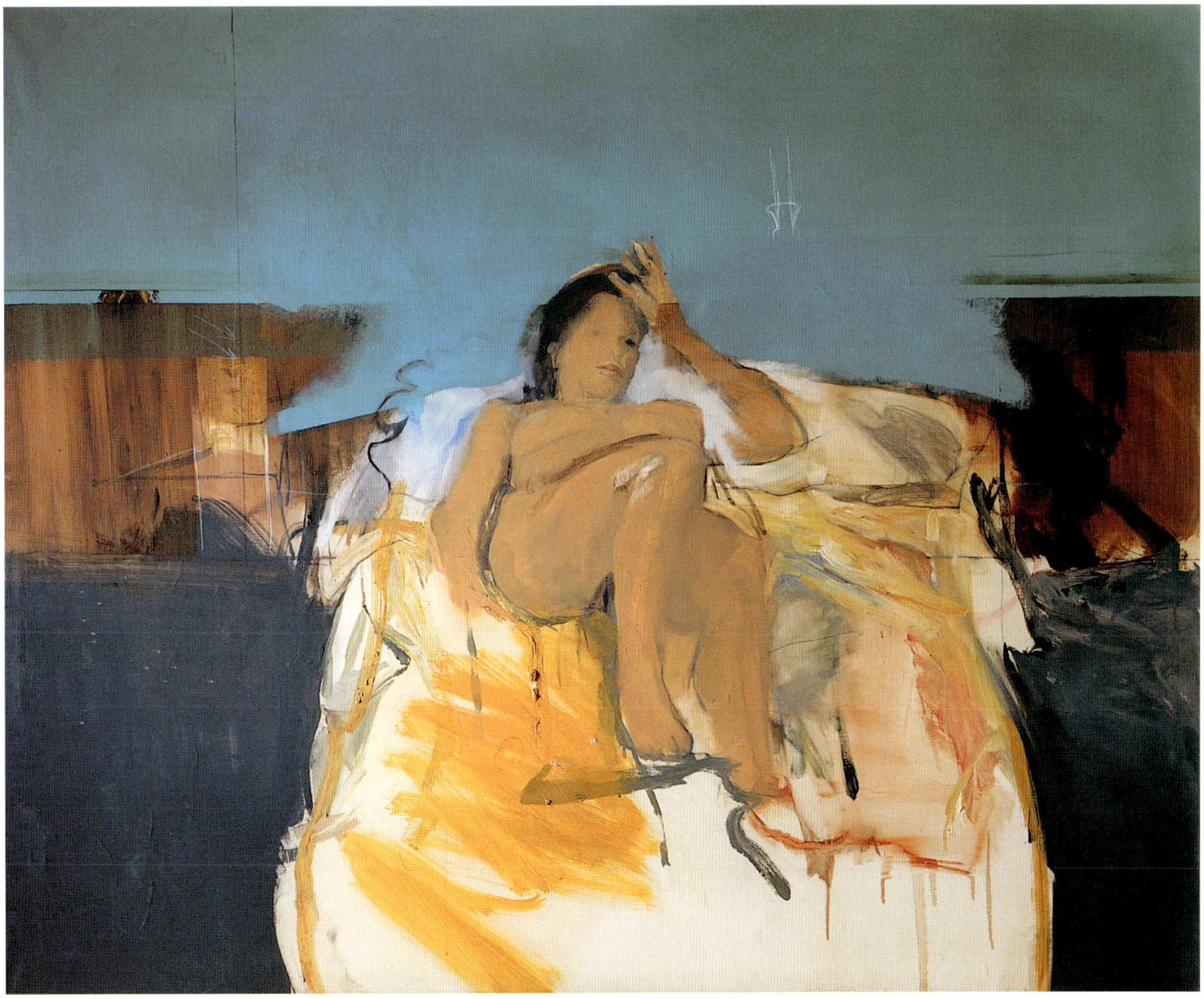

FIG. 23
Portrait of J.K.
1968–9, oil on canvas, 150 x 183
Private Collection

June Keeley (far left in the first canvas of *Good and Bad at Games,* then shifted to the right) first saw Mike at a Freud party in 1958. She was working as head girl in Churchill's, a West End club. Mike was running along Delamere Terrace beside the canal in Paddington, arms outspread, pretending to be an aeroplane. Not her sort at all. 'He had to have so much dutch courage when he hit London and discovered booze. Later he'd go into his head at parties and not leave the room.' The 'lanky diffident young man', as Lawrence Gowing described him, remained acutely self-conscious though far from taciturn. He himself talked of his 'mixture of greed, embarrassment and hapless polite bad manners'. June dealt with the haplessness and in 1963 they began living together.

June transformed his life with her ribaldry and warmth, her protectiveness and – directed at others – her powers of derision. Their daughter Melanie was born in 1970. When Mel was splashing one day in a plastic bath in the garden, June heard their neighbour muttering to himself about 'some people breeding like rabbits'. It was Frankie Howerd, star of *A Funny Thing Happened on the Way to the Forum*: Plautus Man, squawking outrage through pursed lips. June answered back and a loud two-hander developed over the wall. Overhearing them as he worked, Mike cringed. Preoccupied with his *Lights* series, he could not stomach distraction.

'This is a note I carry around,' he wrote to me.

> Zen is active meditation (painting in my case) leading to sudden enlightenment which is unself – or selfless – consciousness which is realising things just as they are: interdependent. (For example hold your breath and keep holding it, and see how long you feel independent – it's quite enlightening in itself.) You don't lose individuality or identity by dropping your idea or concept of yourself (your ego) or by acknowledging the fact of interdependence; on the contrary it becomes subtle and unrestricted. That's my understanding anyway.

Where *Good and Bad at Games* represented the fluctuation of egos in successive phases, *Lights* was metaphor extended way beyond the motivating image. 'The expansive thing is practically always right,' Andrews told himself. A balloon would serve as vehicle, a thinks bubble pursuing the theme of 'sudden enlightenment', a spiritual steeplechase, a Zen take on that shining seventeenth-century metaphor 'the voyage of the soul'.

Liner 1971–2 (no.37, p.104) (Philip Larkin's 'lit shelved liners') and *Cabin 1975* (no.47, p.107), in which the final descent of a charter flight into a Spanish resort tests confidence in wings and turbo-thrust, are ships of fools: containers of illusions about getting somewhere in life. In this they relate, perceptibly, to disaster movies. The seven *Lights* paintings from the early 1970s (nos. 36 and 38–43, pp.97–103), on the other hand, progress beyond schedules and scenarios. *Lights VII: A Shadow* is, supremely, an end in itself.

Illusions of scale and void and dreamy familiarity come into play. The balloon in *Lights I: Out-of-Doors* is seemingly immobile, a pearly bulb in sultry air, the woods and fields of Gloucestershire slipping by, defocused into camouflage. The balloon of *The Ship Engulfed*, wafted into Toronto, almost disappears into the glare of the office buildings. *The Black Balloon*, approaching Waterloo Bridge, passes over street lamps and fairy lights,

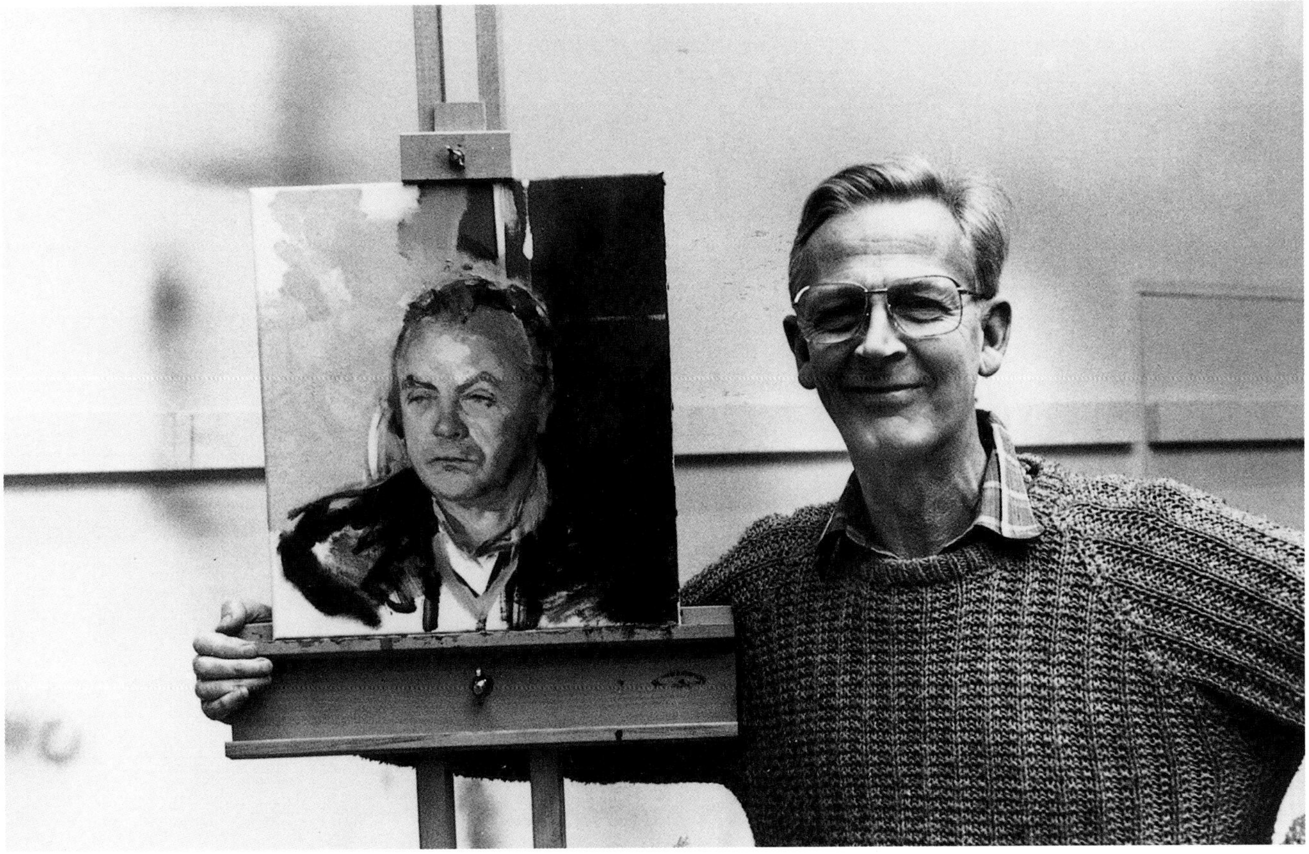

FIG. 24
Andrews
with *Portrait of Bruce Bernard* 1990
Photo: Bruce Bernard

immeasurably aloof. The balloon then disappears. Possible landing sites glide into view: one of the Brighton piers transposed to an Italian coastal strip, and the old Britannia Pier at Yarmouth, burnt down in 1909 and ethereally restored, resting on clouded shallows in a state of exquisite unfinish. *The Spa* – Scarborough approached over Triboro Bridge – is Old World twinned with New World, a harmony of grey on blue on deeper blue in which shadows are more substantial than the six-lane highway where advancing headlights weep. The final image, of the balloon shadow on the sands, staining the rough canvas, suggests the possibility of drifting on, out to sea. The sand is close below now, judging by the size of the shadow, and there may well be no more ballast sand to pour onto the beach. Not to panic; not in a painting that maintains so beautifully the illusion of calm.

After *Lights* the quest continued for an ideal place in which to touch down. With *A Shadow* he almost made it, synchronising thought and touch, reconciling several kinds of actuality: seaweed trail, photo-negative silhouette, saturate horizon. But pilgrims need progress and Andrews needed plans to advance, projections to follow through. Each sequence or series was exploratory, none more so than the *School* paintings, most of which were painted at Geldeston on the Suffolk border in a former maltings, a dark tank of a building at the end of a path thick with brambles. I remember him sitting there, sifting through fish photographs, pointing out the near-invisibility of the skate on the seabed and the stony markings on the wicked old pike caught by villagers. He talked about the hairiness of the reversed canvas and the dispersant he used to soften the paint, about getting choked by not wearing a mask, or letting the one he used become clogged up and having to rush outside for fresh air.

School was *Lights* under water, *Lights* without soul and without purpose, beyond the imperatives of feeding, spawning and not being caught. Fish display no visible emotions. Creatures of pattern, they blend and glint, flickers of silver from predators rising to their prey. Their perfection looks balletic. As it happened, Mel was starting school when he worked on the series, about to wear a uniform, learn school rules, school timetables. Mike talked about how this affected them. Suddenly school holidays appeared on the calendar and, for Mel's sake, holidays had to be taken. Hence Scotland, where their friend Jane Willoughby, a committed buyer of his paintings, urged them to stay. A theme suggested itself: *Holidays*.

A Design: The Garden at Drummond from Higher Ground (no.63, p.124), painted in 1976, is more to do with point of view than with landscape garden. The carnivalesque figures, birdy, doggy, amphibian, have come cross-country, presumably, and as evening shadows lengthen they stare at the man-shaped intricacies of a hidden valley suddenly revealed. Andrews considered the foursome to be found images, his to deploy, and was vexed when, of course, they were identified as the Beatles in 'Magical Mystery Tour' outfits chanting, 'I am he as you are me and we are altogether.' We as he as they become latecomers to the cinema, pushing along the front row, dwarfed by the prospect on the screen; souls alighted, that is, coming upon a place not topographic or geographic but marvellous: out of this world.

August for Glenartney. Holidays, from the mid-1970s onwards, were spent at Glenartney, a few miles beyond Drummond, in the Perthshire hills. There, in a majestic environment,

Andrews came to appreciate preoccupations very different from those that he addressed all the rest of the time in his studio. Cautiously, hesitantly at first, he joined in.

Melanie and Me Swimming 1978–9 (no.59, p.121) is a painting of the prime reason for being in Glenartney. August for Mel. The eight-year-old splashes happily, showing off to the photographer Jean-Loup Cornet crouched beside the dark pool of Ruchill Water, the best swimming place in the glen. Mel has surfaced from school; she kicks out, Mike steadying her. His white body and sunburnt face and neck are measures of fine weather and unaccustomed hours outdoors. He concentrates, she frolics. The poignancy of the painting is all the stronger for being derived from a holiday snap. Much of what the camera recorded is, to our eyes, rippling abstraction. A moment takes on untold depths.

The stalking pictures of 1979–80 are recollections of Glenartney, of landscapes in which every stretch of ground is known, each inch of cover. To Andrews, a day on the hill, being guided, gradually, to within range – downwind – of the stag to be culled was an exercise of nerve fraught with dilemma. He assured himself that for him, a meat eater, to shoot a stag was better than passively consuming abattoir produce; and he appreciated that stalking skills, undoubtedly the most ancient skills acquired by the human species, are peculiarly demanding and ritualistic. The stag selected by the stalker would be starving, injured or old, and his fear was that if he did not kill it cleanly it would suffer. He asked Jean-Loup Cornet to crawl behind and photograph him, tensed for the shot, and the herd grazing, unconscious of threat. *Peter's Day: 3rd Stalk* 1979 (no.67, p.126) is a day of failure; *Alistair's Day: 2nd Stalk* 1980 (no.68, p.127) is the instant before a stag drops; in *Alistair's Day: 2nd Shot* 1980 (no.69, p.128) the wounded stag is reapproached and despatched; then, returning to an old theme, *Recollection of a Moment in October 1989 – The Tobasnich Burn: Glenartney* (no.76, p.130) from 1992 shows him slipping, scrabbling, and having to swing himself around where the bank has caved in to grab the stalker's outstretched hand.

'Actually what I'm painting is historical landscape, that's to say landscape relating to the chain of events. It's time and landscape that interests me. The way it's been affected by the people living in it.' In *Daylesford* 1983–4 (no.84, p.146), the portrait of a country house built by the nabob Warren Hastings and owned by Baron Thyssen, lawns and lake are an intensively cultivated picturesque survival; in another commissioned painting, *Oare, the Vale of Pewsey* 1989–91 (no.86, p.147), the hillside has been contoured by a thousand generations of sheep. Each landscape that Andrews lit upon (he was flown one morning over Oare) was an historic composition, one that deserved chaste handling. Particularly Ayers Rock.

'To critics who thought surfaces "dead", not expressive, in Ayers Rock series: it is a mixture of balance and resonance that tells me when to stop,' Mike wrote to me. 'The painting should be definitive.' None more so than *A View from Uamh Mhor* 1990–1 (no.86, p.150), his return to the motif of Glenartney after six years of Ayers Rock. 'There was this colossal time spent among the reds in the spectrum and I began to long to move into the complementary colours; it was a great relief to move back to the greens in Scotland.' He worked downwards from sky to *tour d'horizon* to the broad and reassuring green hump around which the stream squiggles, gradually realising the many places with memories for

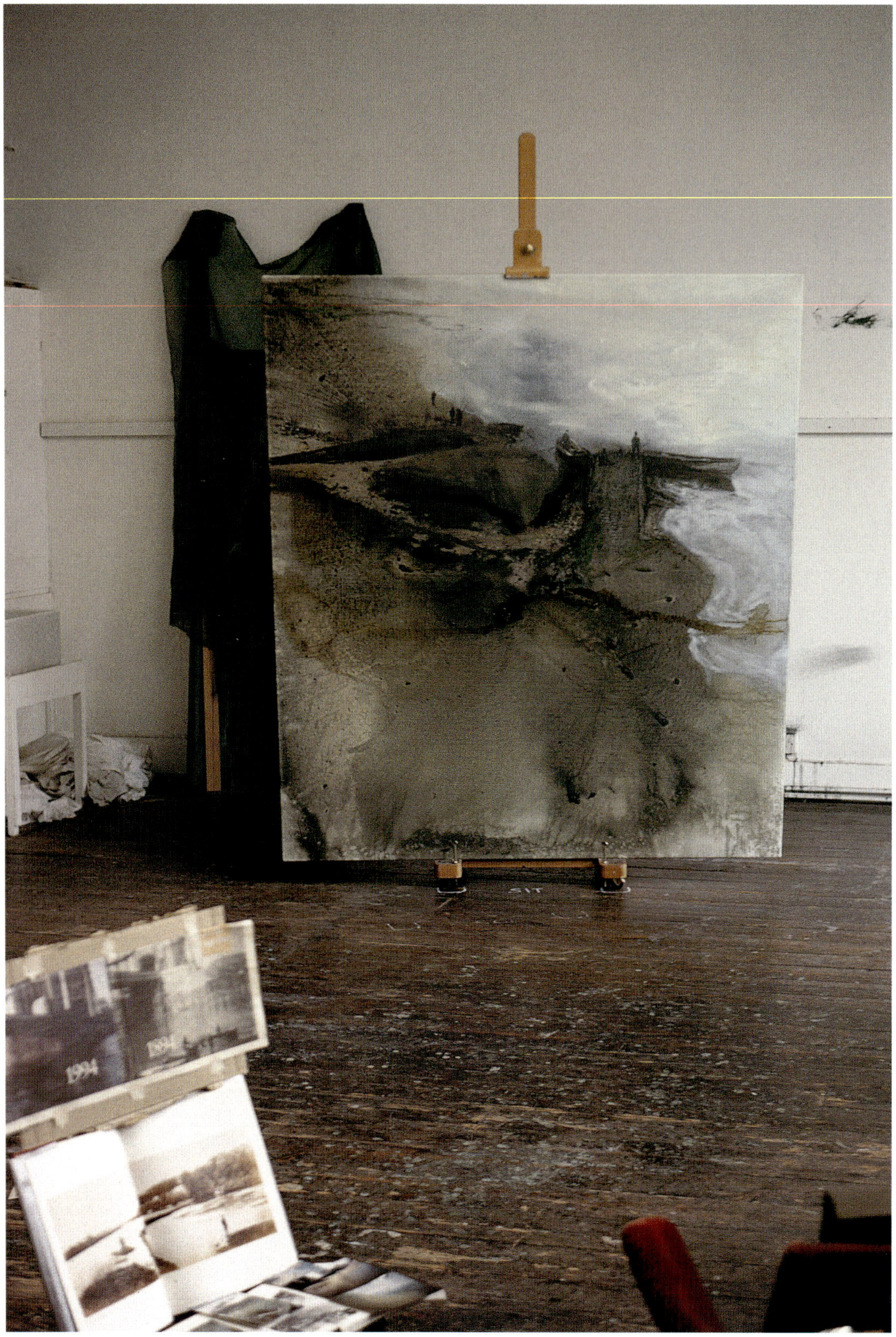

FIG. 25
Thames Painting: The Estuary in the studio, April 1995
Photo: William Feaver

him. 'There should be stalkers on the hill. I am very much aware that once upon a time there were many people lived in those hills and in these glens.' He marked the drovers' road to Callender. He was delighted to discover that it was roughly here that David Balfour and Alan Breck, on the run in Robert Louis Stevenson's *Kidnapped,* spent a day recuperating. 'The happiest ten hours of sleep in a fine, breathing sunshine and on bone-dry ground, that I have ever tasted.'

While working on this great sweep of Highland lore, he began *Edinburgh (Old Town)* 1990–3 (no.87, p.148), the sheer opposite: the rock fortified, blackened tenements on acid green slopes, skyline busy with turrets and spires and the ribs of the grandstands for the summer Tattoo. Edinburgh, to him, lay in the past: 'It looked like a smoky old engraving.' More present to him than tourist hordes were the heavily-etched characters of Sir Walter Scott's *The Heart of Midlothian*, set in the period of the Porteous riots and the climactic struggles of nonconformist against episcopalian in the 1730s. He considered re-erecting the gallows in the Grassmarket, a valid anachronism he thought, but then changed his mind. Too literary. Too obvious. The dour atmosphere of the painting, the grim associations that he read into it, depressed him. Here was Bunyan's Doubting Castle, the abode of Giant Despair and his wife Diffidence, a place 'nasty and stinking to the spirits'. He turned the picture to the wall and left it for months. 'It's all ideas and that's wrong,' he said. 'So I've got to wait til it all begins to become an image; I've got to be as mobile as the view.' In the time it took him to resolve it, several gift shops on the anamorphically squeezed street leading up to the Royal Mile closed down and the phone box vanished. History overtook him.

Having devoted himself for more than a decade to landscape, reclaiming the genre from scenic backdrop and cinema, not to mention endemic impressionism, Andrews decided to produce a series of straightforward portraits. Living witnesses. 'I had this terrific urge to be among people again, painting them: people with whom I feel no generation gap.' He remarked that *Late Evening on a Summer Day* had featured people the same age as him; and so it was: thirty years on ... where are we now? First a self-portrait, less resolute perhaps than he had been in 1959, certainly wiser and more self-aware. Then June, Serena Rothschild, Bruce Bernard and Jane Willoughby, followed by Jane Willoughby's uncle David Astor, former editor of the *Observer*, and Colin St John Wilson, eminent architect and collector who resolved, as he sat, to make a comparative study (*The Artist at Work* 1999) of the working methods of Mike and of his preceptor, William Coldstream. A portrait of Anthony d'Offay, the dealer, was begun.

In 1992 the Andrewses moved back to London and took a flat on the south side of Albert Bridge. Mike bought a studio, formerly Rodrigo Moynihan's, in Sydney Close, off the Brompton Road: no. 11 in a long corridor, opposite no. 12 where Sargent had worked and no. 10, where Baroness Orczy was said to have written *The Scarlet Pimpernel*. There, once he had at last completed the Edinburgh painting, he began what he intended to be a series of paintings on the theme of the Thames (nos.94–96, pp.157–9).

Twice daily, cycling to his studio and back, Mike crossed the river, seeing it in all lights and at different states of the tide. *The Thames at Low Tide*, beside Albert Bridge, is more mud than water, a tract of foreshore exposed, wet paint blown with a hair-dryer across the canvas, the literal an undertow upon which stranded lighters and sluice gates are superimposed: images obstructing the flow. 'It's delightful to discover that paint will do more things than you thought it would do, and so of course you indulge it a bit. I feel that where I painted thick and occasionally very thick and then allowed the turps to carry away in lumps which I've checked and stopped and altered.'

In June 1994 Andrews was operated on for cancer. Afterwards he made three drawings of his predicament. Himself horribly wounded, himself the stricken stag clambering instinctively upstream, himself eviscerated. Three months later he and June went looking for the source of the Thames. The weather was hot and the meadow at Thames Head in Gloucestershire was dry and dull. Three miles away though, there was enough of a stream to give him his image. The painting, *The Source of the Thames*, developed substantially enough to be a coming together of light and space and heavy foliage. He left it at that, resolving to return in better circumstances the following spring. Meanwhile, downstream, past St Mary's Battersea, past Butler's Wharf and the Tower and Traitor's Gate, all subjects that he had in mind, he went reconnoitring for *The Estuary*. It proved difficult finding a place with a view out and over the river's end. He tried the Isle of Grain, then he and June tried Essex – train to South Benfleet, taxi to the sea wall on Canvey Island. 'We sat up there on a seat,' June said. 'Watched the tide go out and men with shovels and margarine tubs dig up worms. There were dead rats.'

Again he began the painting on the floor, marking mudbanks 'wet wet wet wet', puddling turps, stranding sediment. Beside him as he worked he had a Constable catalogue open at *Chain Pier, Brighton* (marvellous foreground) and Bacon earholes, exemplary in terms of swirl and trickle. Watching figures from a photograph of Tower Bridge when it first opened in the 1890s were gathered on the jetty, contemplative little men, possibly morose. Though, remembering *August for the People*, who can tell? They look out at water so clouded it could be sky. The painting is an elegy to dissolution.

'Accept the flow and flux of things through the mind, the continual change, disappearance, and reappearance,' Andrews wrote in his 'Notes and Preoccupations'. 'Accept it, let it happen.'

He pinned up in the studio an *Evening Standard* headline: 'No Such Thing as Hell says Bishop.'

In March 1995, two days before he finished *The Estuary*, Andrews severed his connection to the d'Offay gallery. The relief exhilarated him. 'It's like an adventure for me, going to sea,' he said. 'I'm not tied down by anybody.'

In *Together*, back in 1954, Andrews and Paolozzi had been filmed trundling barrels down a slipway at Butler's Wharf. He now talked of *The Last Party*, a painting of people walking down to the inlet, one of the few nooks on the river recognisable from Dickens's *Our Mutual Friend*; that painting would have been, as so often in his work, a sort of re-enactment. Towards the end of *Together* the local kids, mischievous as ever, creep up behind Mike as he sits on a dockside wall and tip his hat off. Having heard nothing, being deaf, he is startled, slips over the parapet and disappears, presumed drowned. Writing to me about *The Estuary*, about what he 'hoped would be there', he added as a postscript a sketch of a hat afloat. I did not get the connection then.

The Thames paintings, two completed, one begun (at least three more were contemplated, including one of St Mary's Battersea where his funeral was held), are ravishing in terms of paint and rich in Andrews's unique blend of the exploratory and the apprehensive. They feed into one another. When he talked about paintings based on ideas being the ones that founder he added: 'You either abandon it or you have to be a bit more patient and the ideas dissolve, reassemble and come up as a mental picture. It's rather like digestion, I think.'

Among the illusions to which we cling is the notion that we can retrieve, make good, start again. In painting, of course, this can be done. The illusion is sustainable: an actual present atmosphere permanently attained. *Little Boy Running* 1953 (no.5, p.67) heads into a scumbled painting ground where the landscape ahead may be pictorial space or an inserted representation of a painted landscape. This was the illusion, the vision, that Andrews pursued. Norwich to London to Edinburgh, shore to shore, from Uamh Mohr to Ayers Rock to Canvey Island and beyond.

> Some years ago there was a very good French yachtsman who was competing in a round the world yacht race. He was thought to be the leader but he just didn't bother. He just sailed on. I sometimes get this picture of this man going on and on.
>
> The same thing happened when I went stalking. And at Ayers Rock. Gosh, I never expected in adult life for this to happen at all, let alone twice, that sort of superb exaltation you get as a child when, in the happiness of a holiday, you could run for ever.

Notes

1 Except the Third Ear recording, all statements and remarks by Michael Andrews quoted in this essay come (unless otherwise mentioned in the text) from letters to, and conversations with, the author between 1974 and 1995. Further material has been published in the catalogues *Rock of Ages Cleft for Me* (1986), *The Thames Paintings* (1998) and *Michael Andrews: Luces/Lights* (2000).

early works

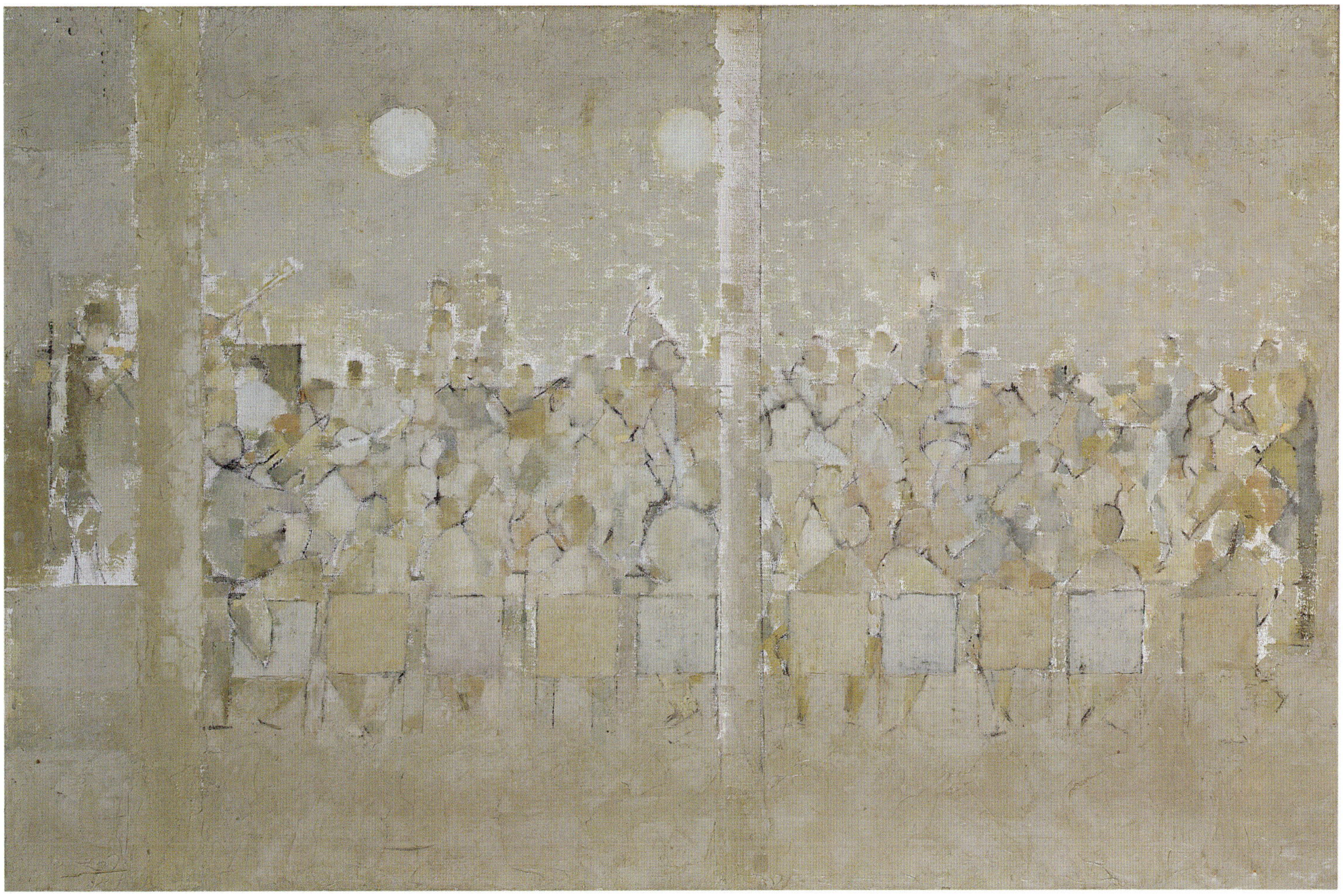

2
London Jazz Club/100 Oxford Street
1951–2
Oil on canvas
50.8 x 76.2

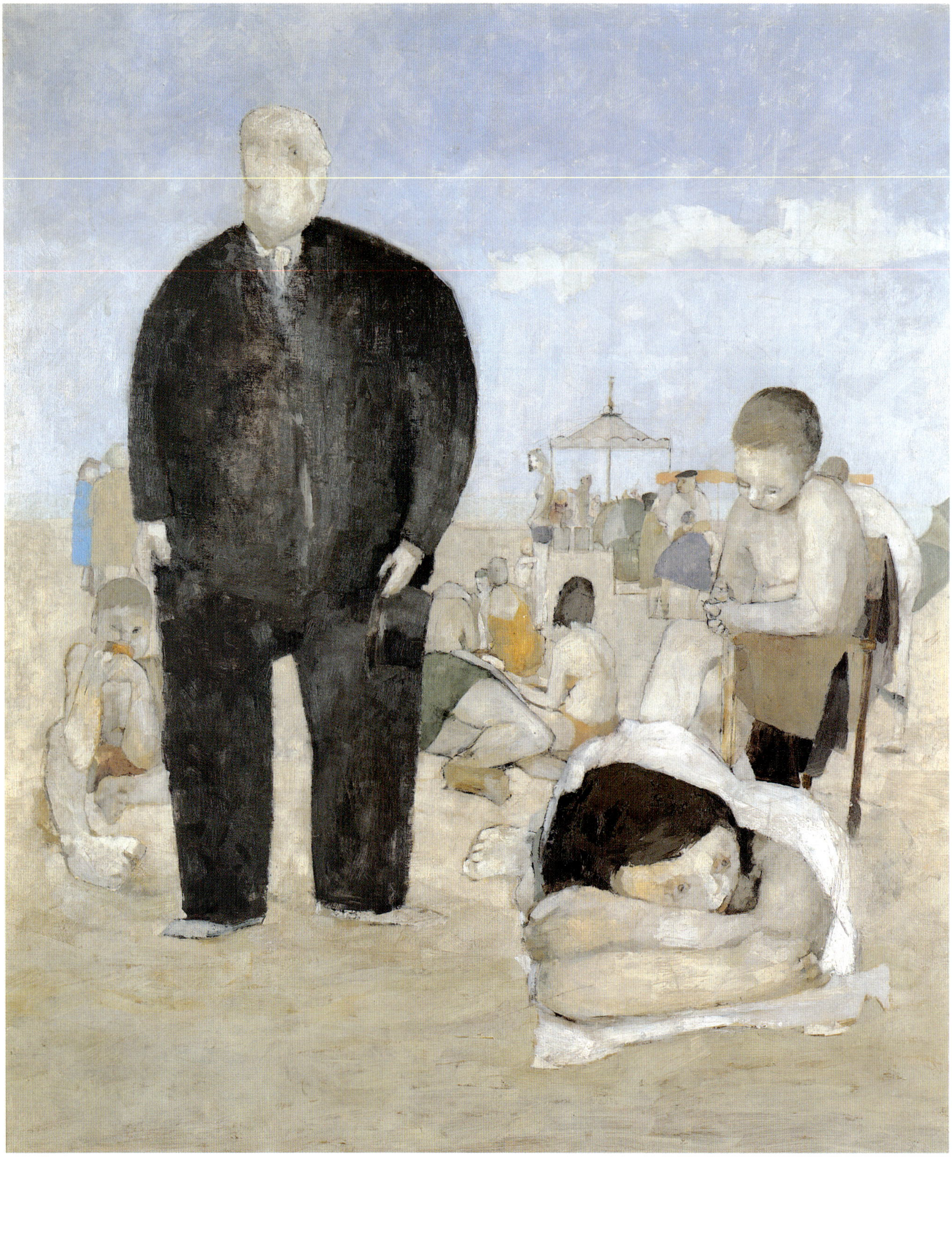

1
August for the People
1951
Oil on board
143.5 x 122

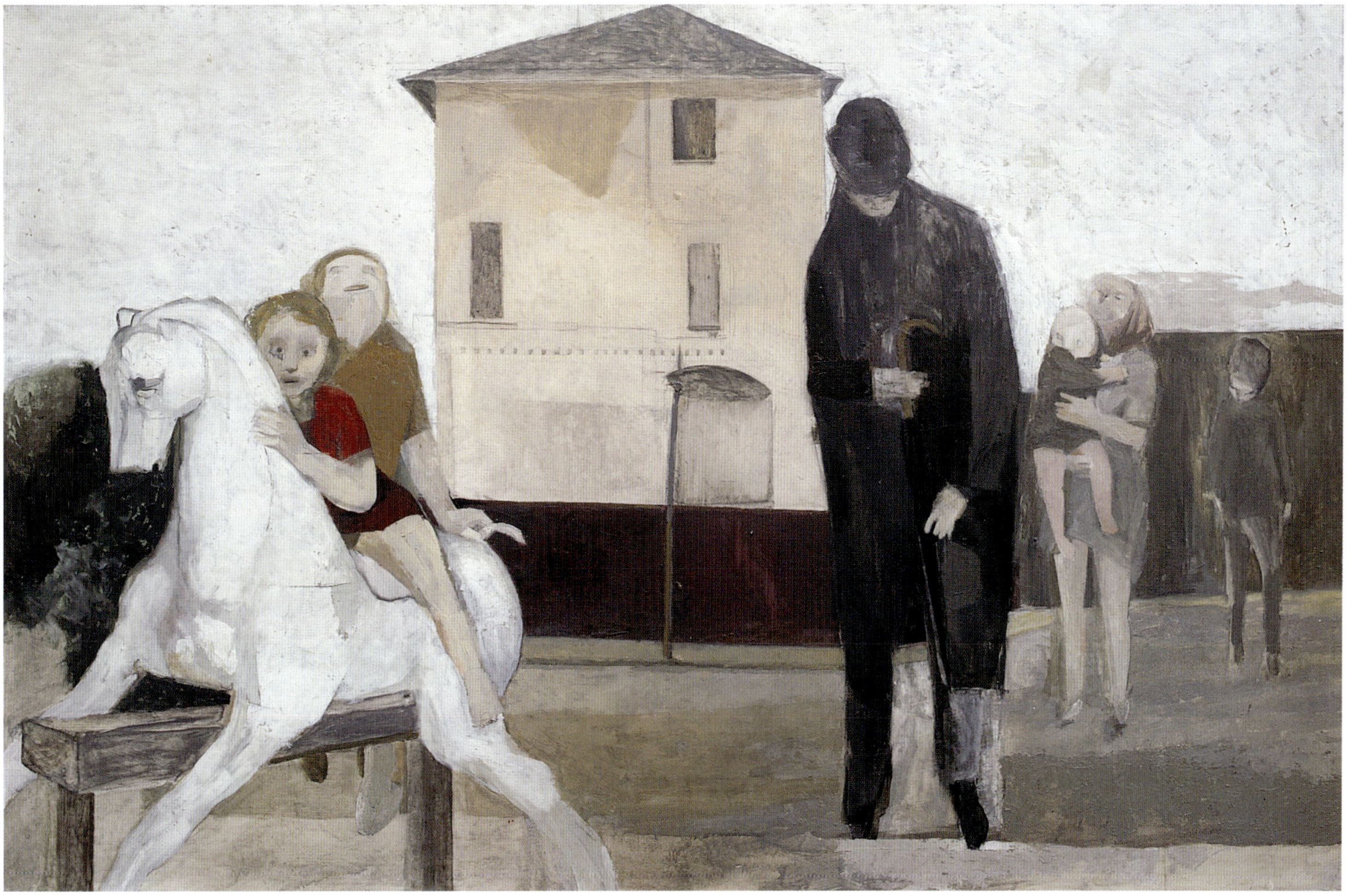

3
The Rocking Horse
1952
Oil on hardboard
122 x 182.9

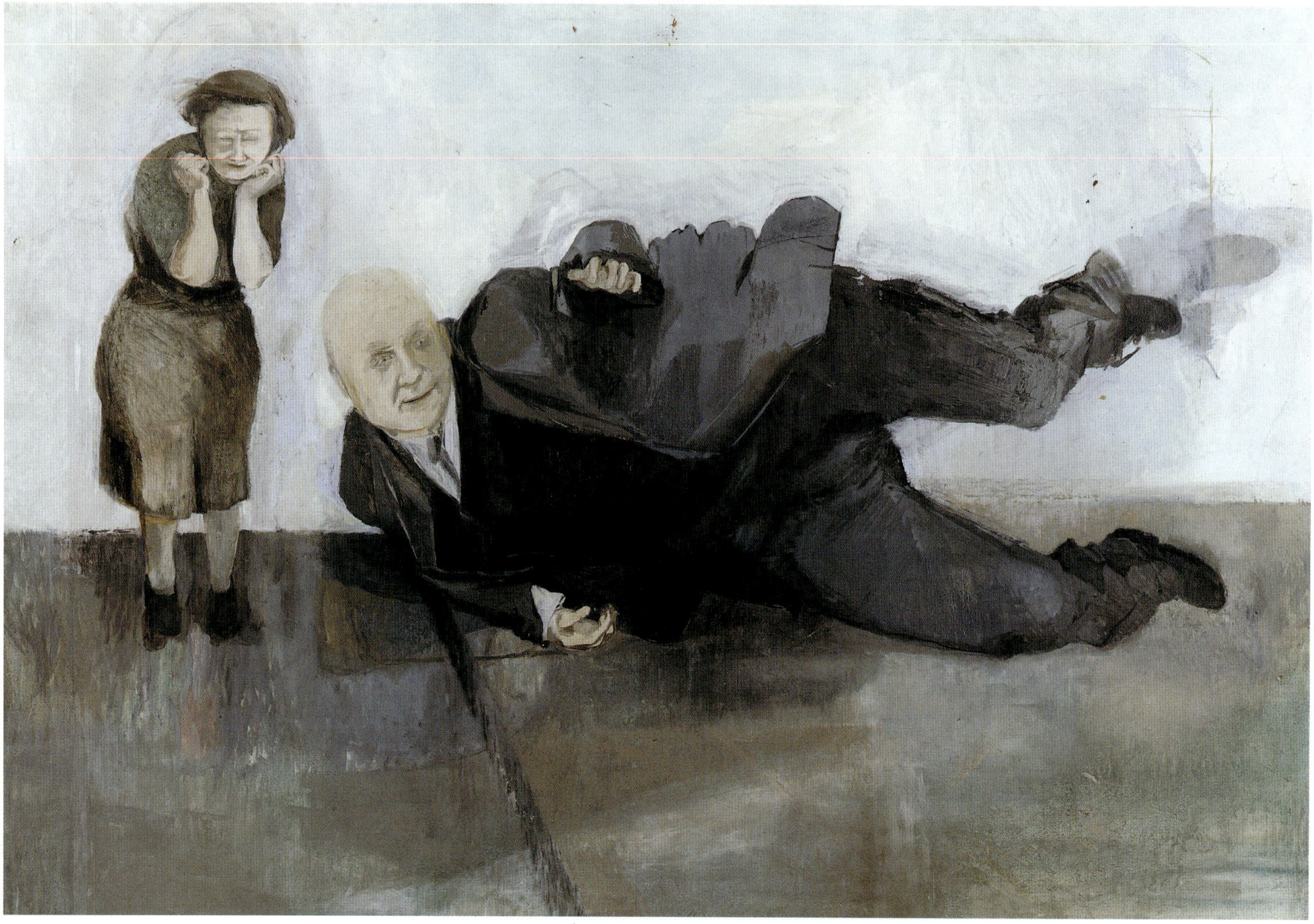

4
A Man Who Suddenly Fell Over
1952
Oil on hardboard
121 x 173

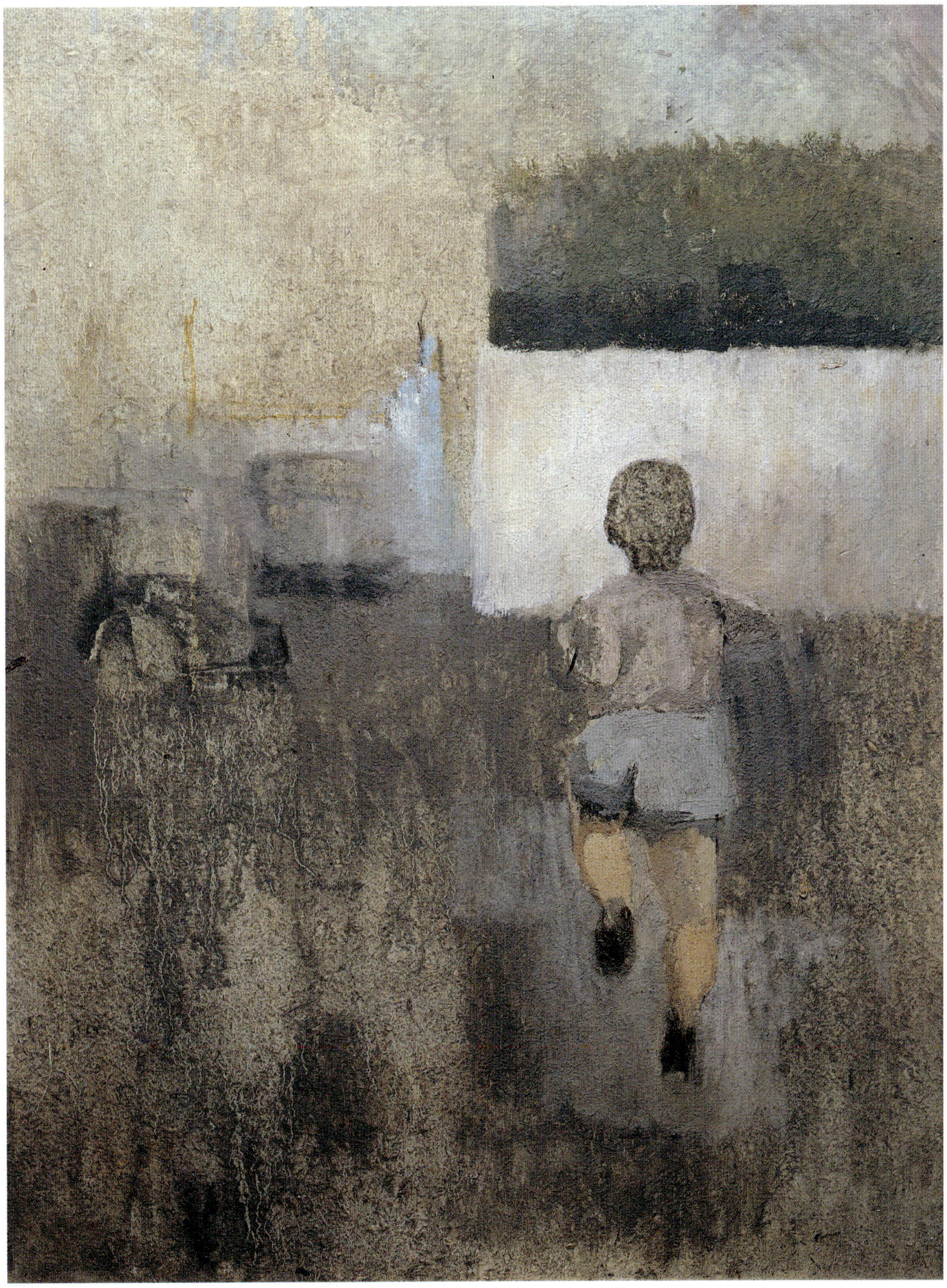

5
Little Boy Running
1953
Oil on board
51 x 38

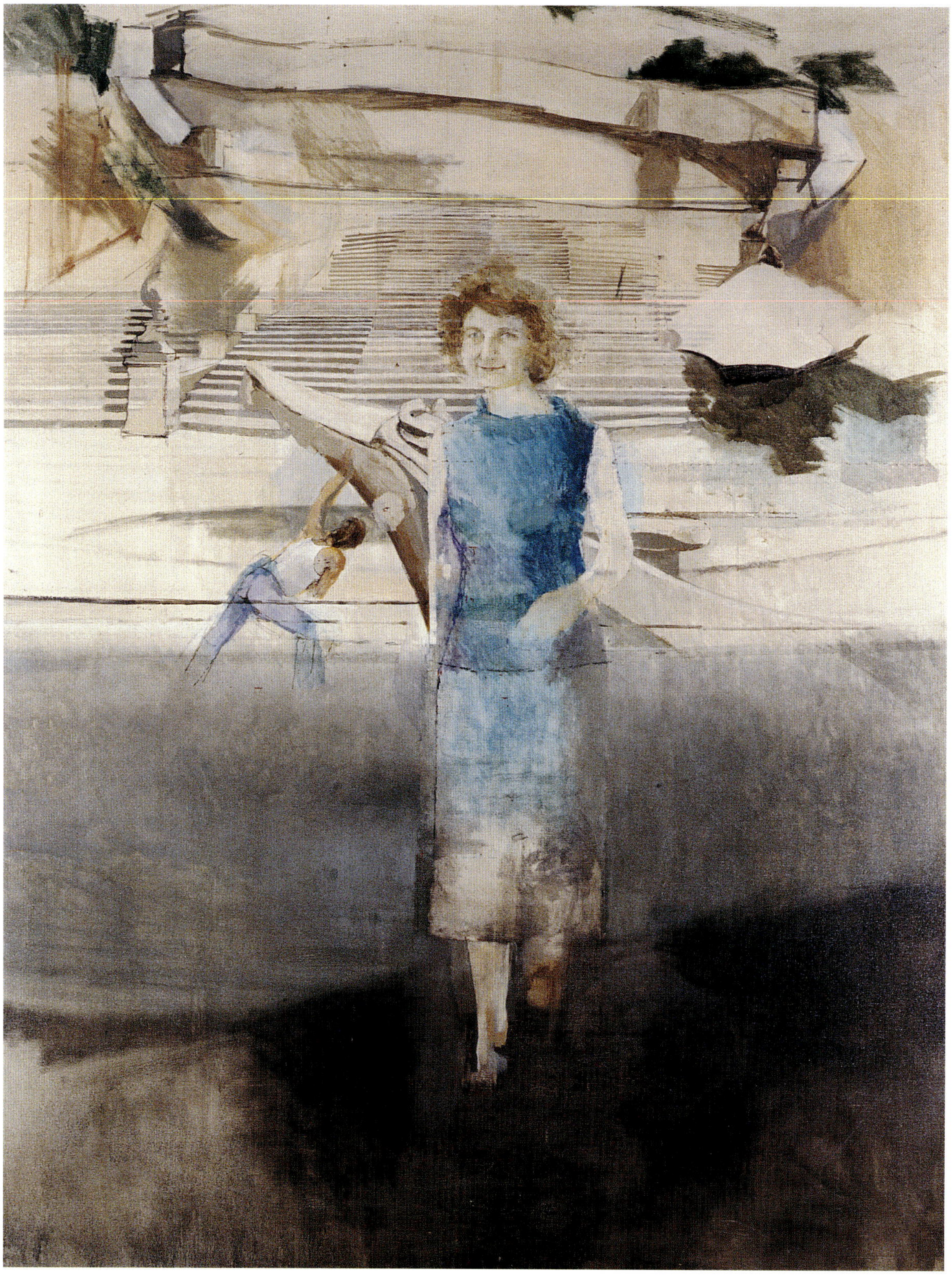

6
Lorenza Mazzetti in Italy
1954
Oil on canvas
196.3 x 145.3

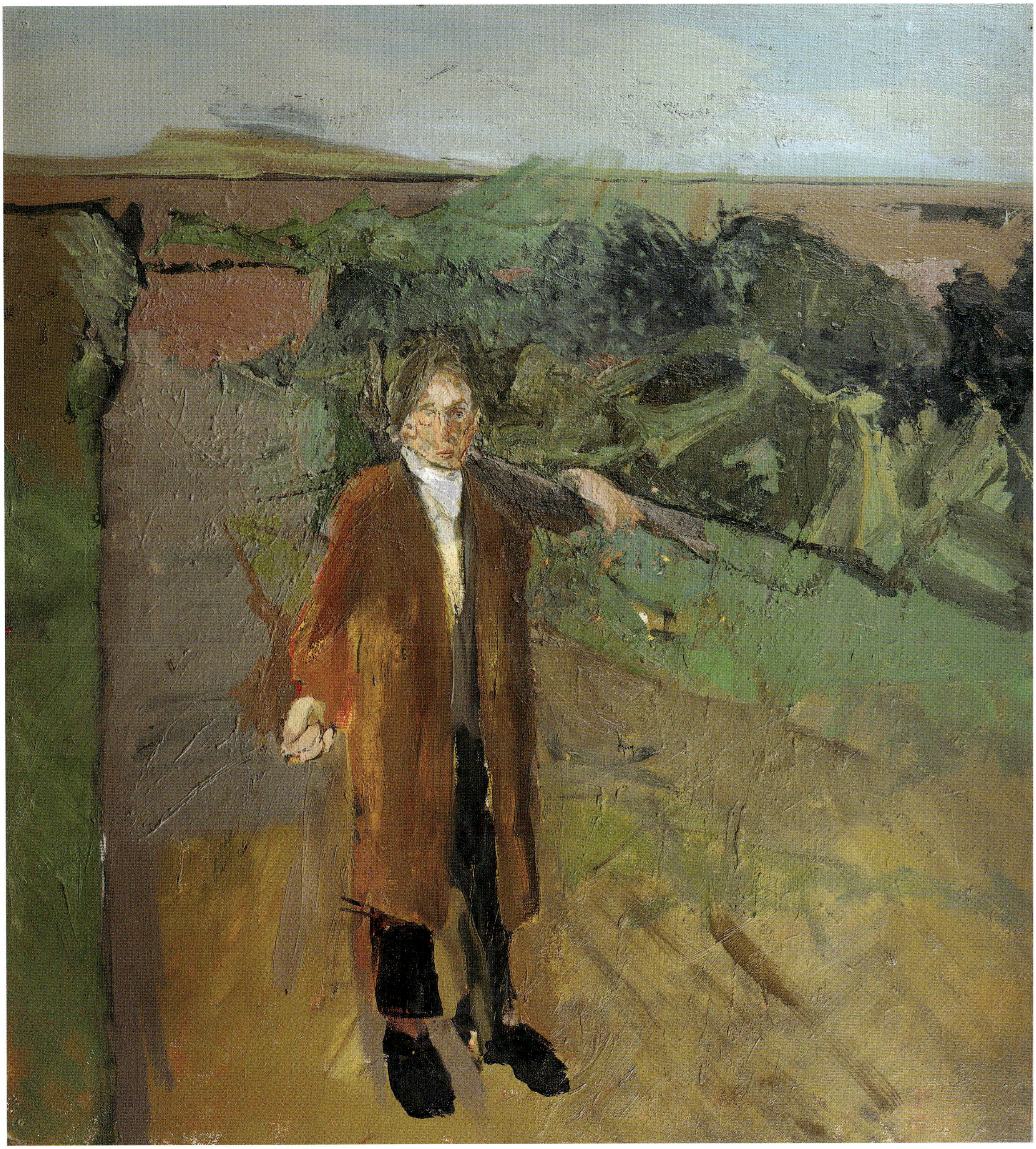

8

Man in a Landscape (Digswell Man II)

1959

Oil on canvas

135.5 x 119.5

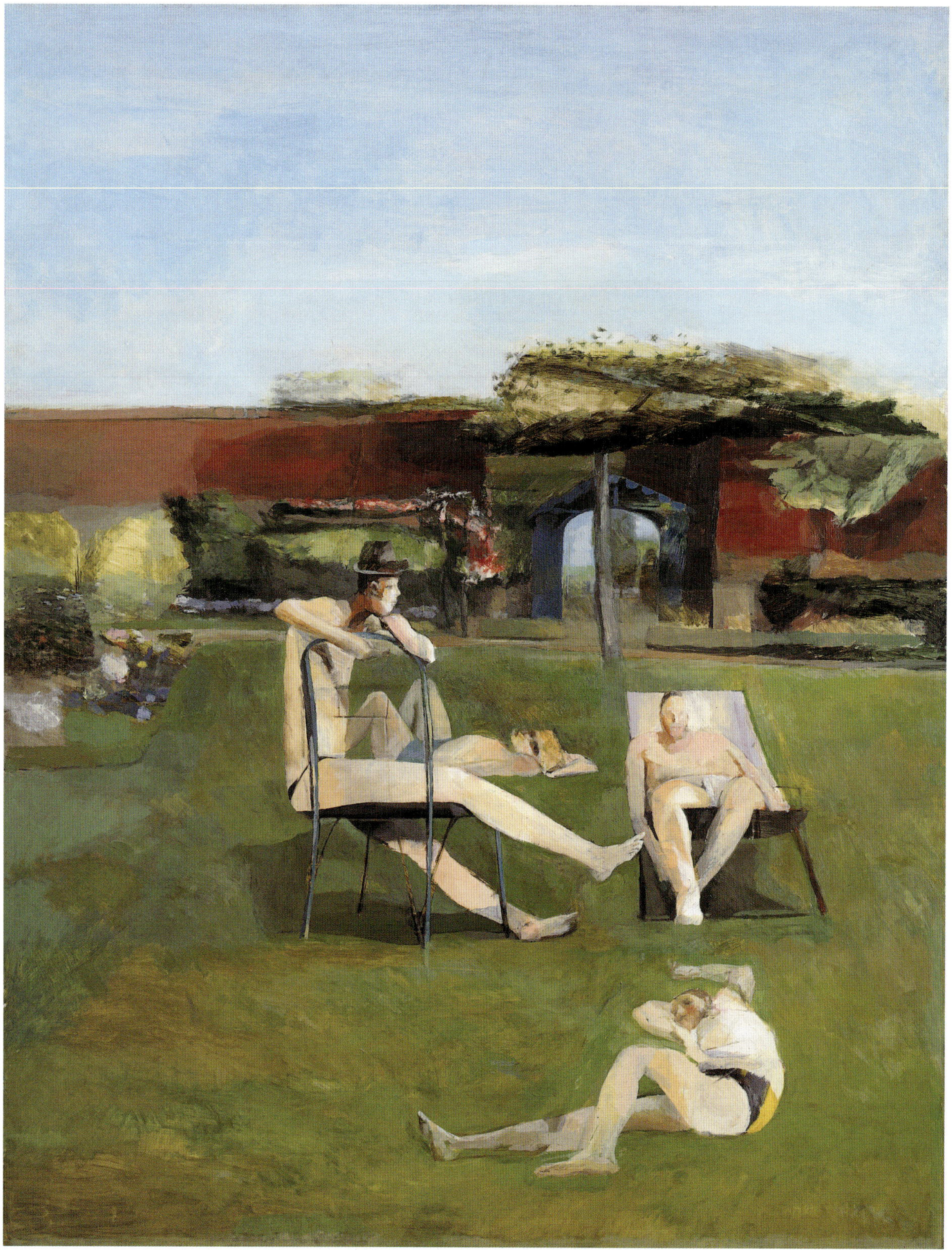

7
Four People Sunbathing
1955
Oil on board
122 x 95.5

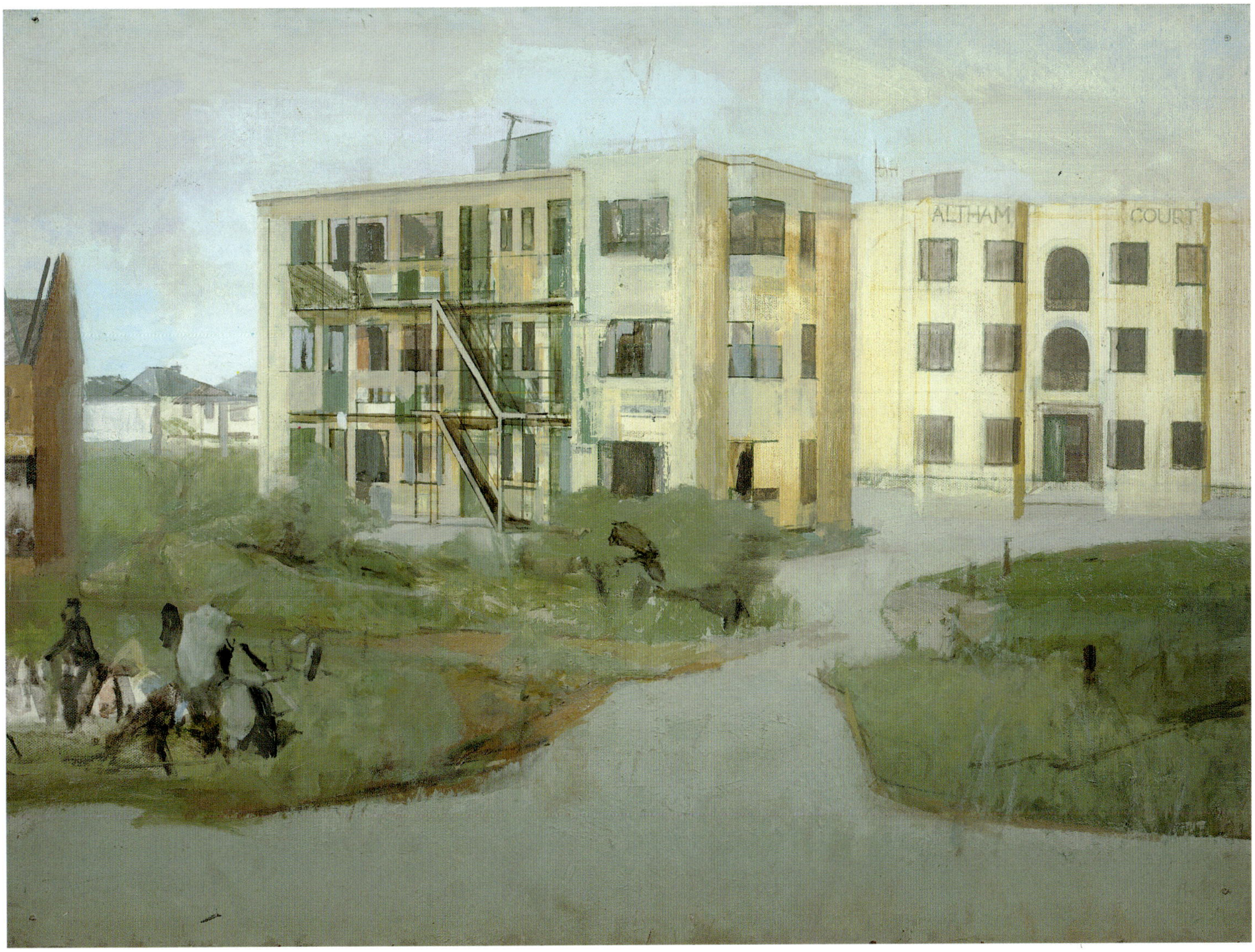

9
Flats
1959
Oil on board
105.5 x 139.7

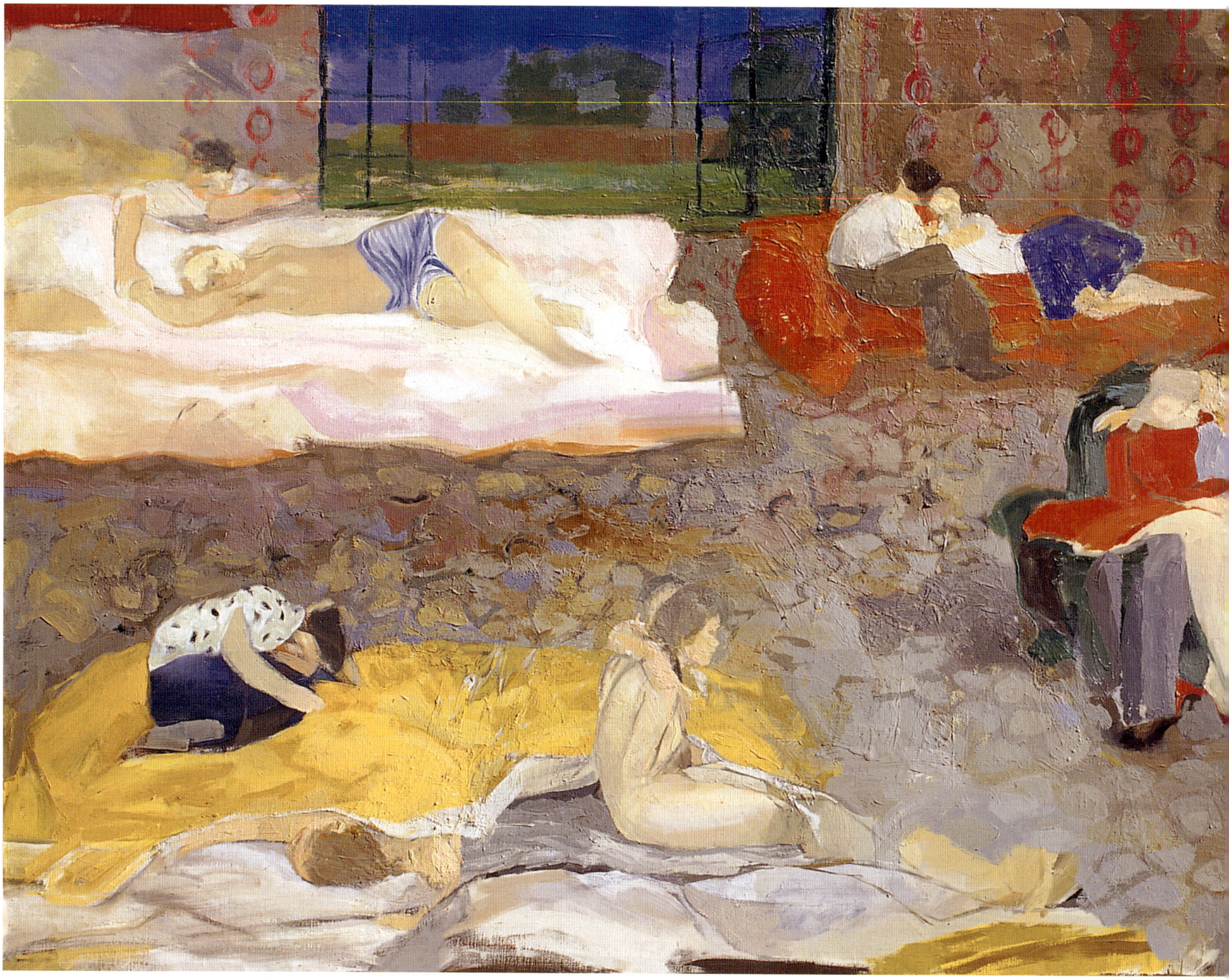

10
Late Evening on a Summer Day
1957
Oil on canvas
137 x 344

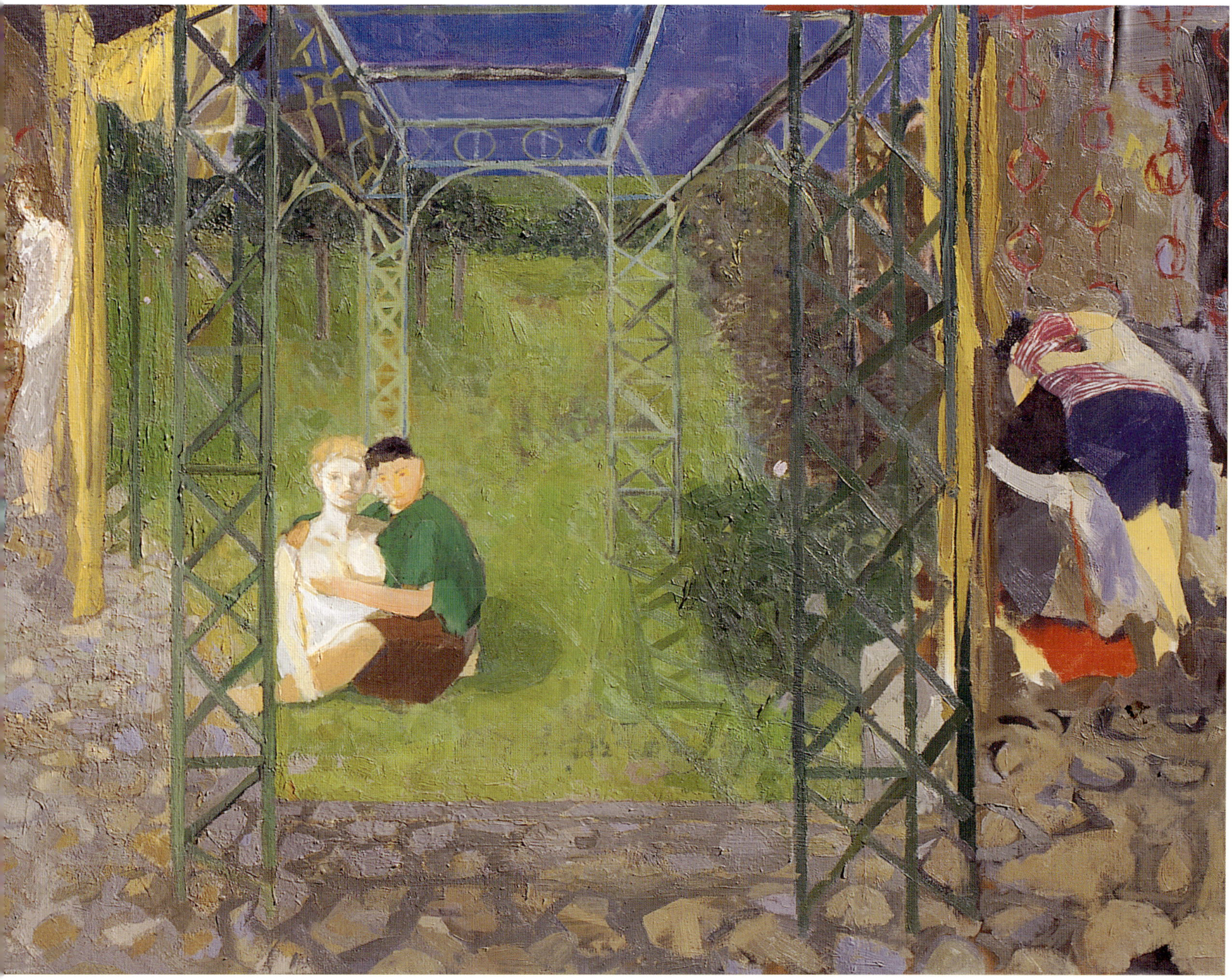

portraits

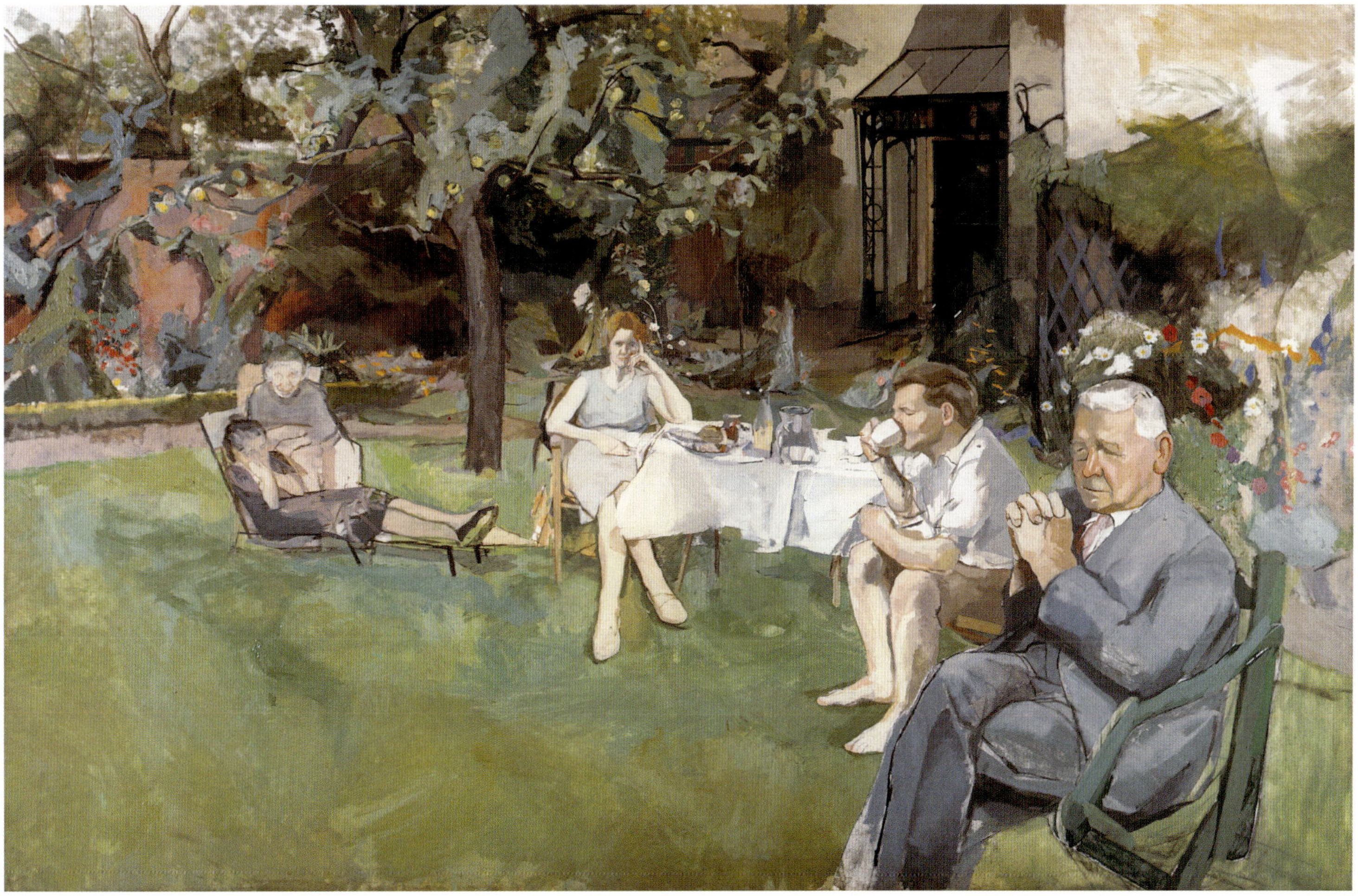

13
The Family in the Garden
1960–2
Oil on canvas
198.2 x 299.8

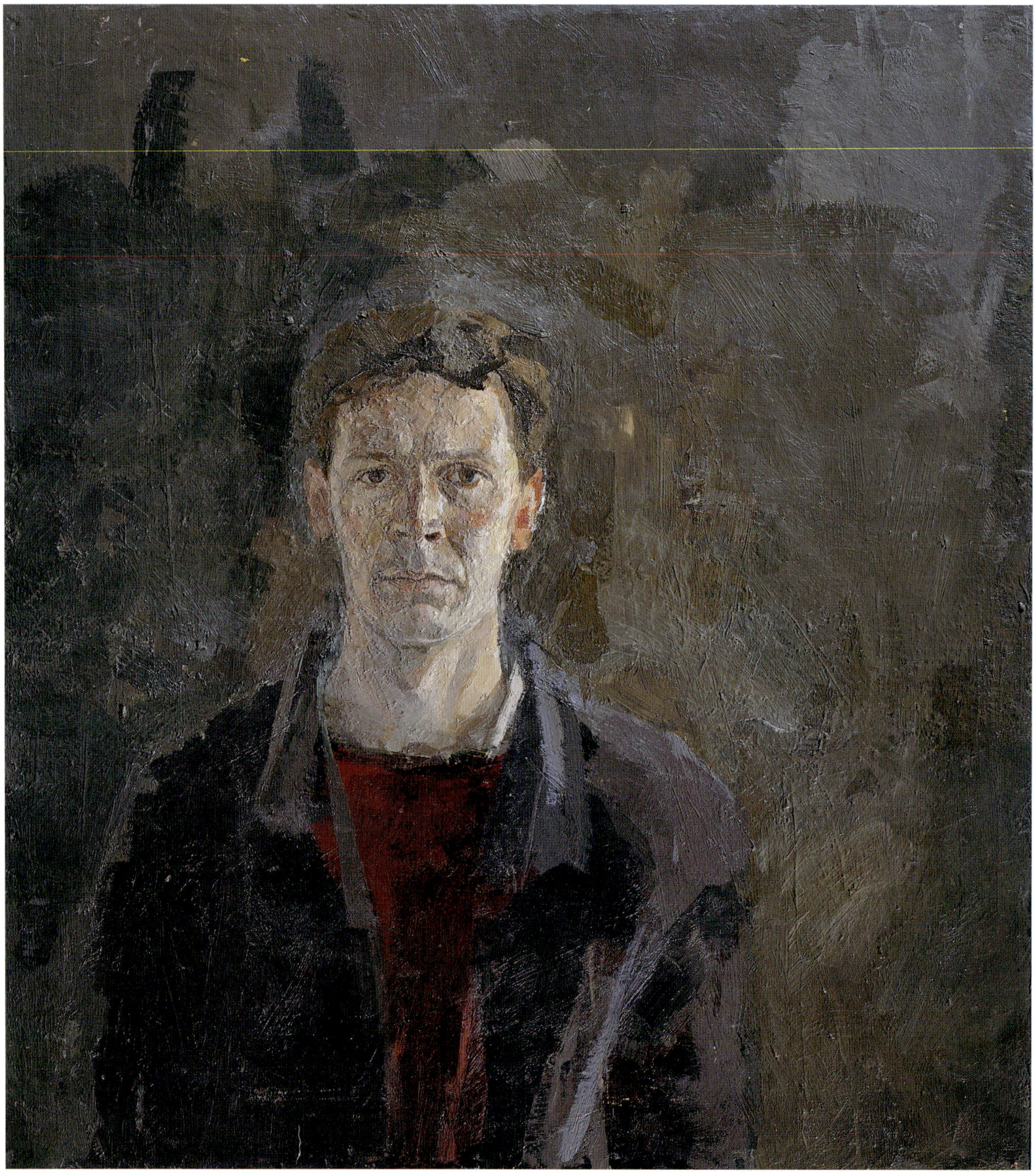

12
Self-Portrait
1959
Oil on hardboard
76 x 66

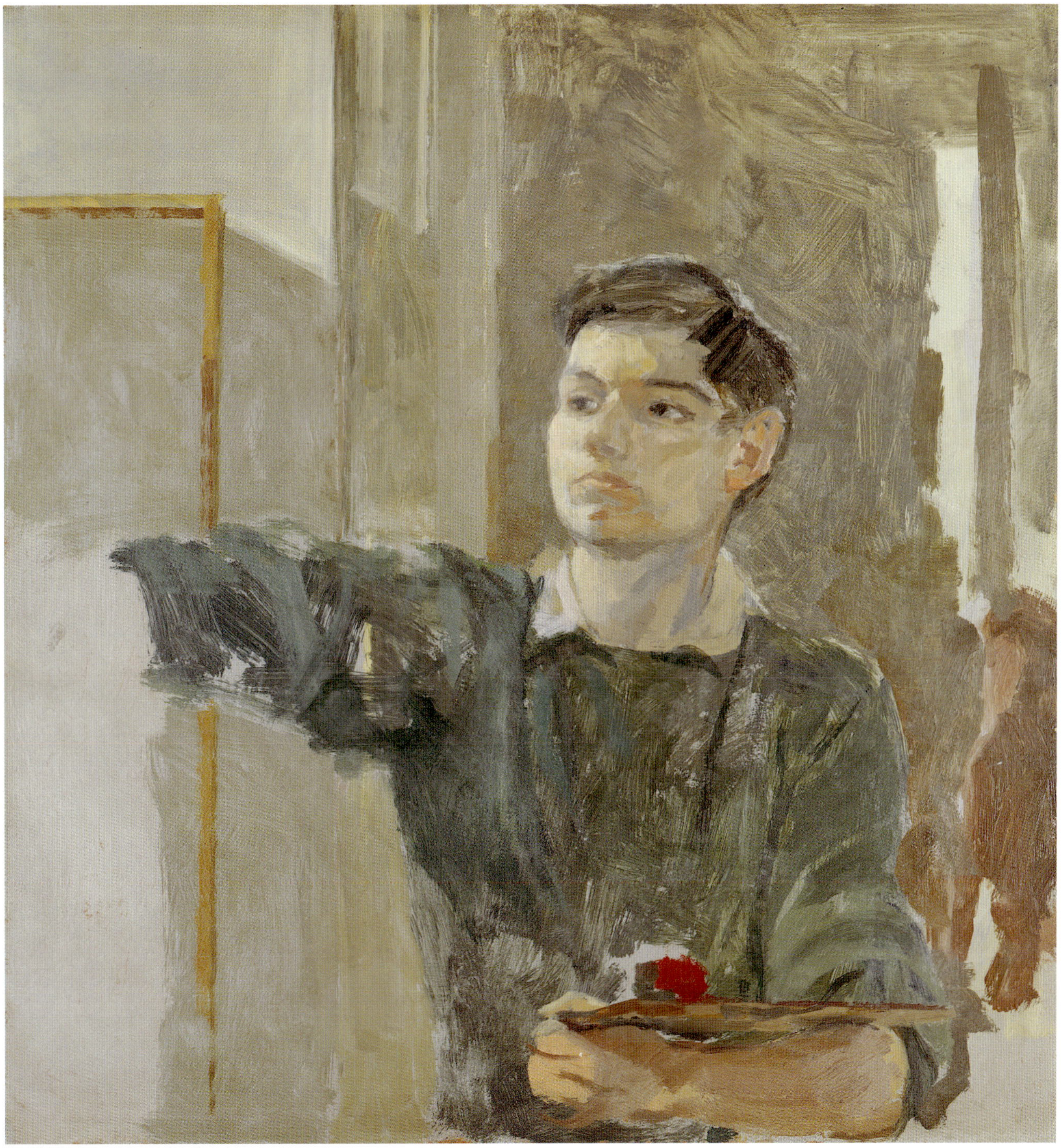

11
Portrait of John Lessore
1958
Oil on canvas
61 x 56

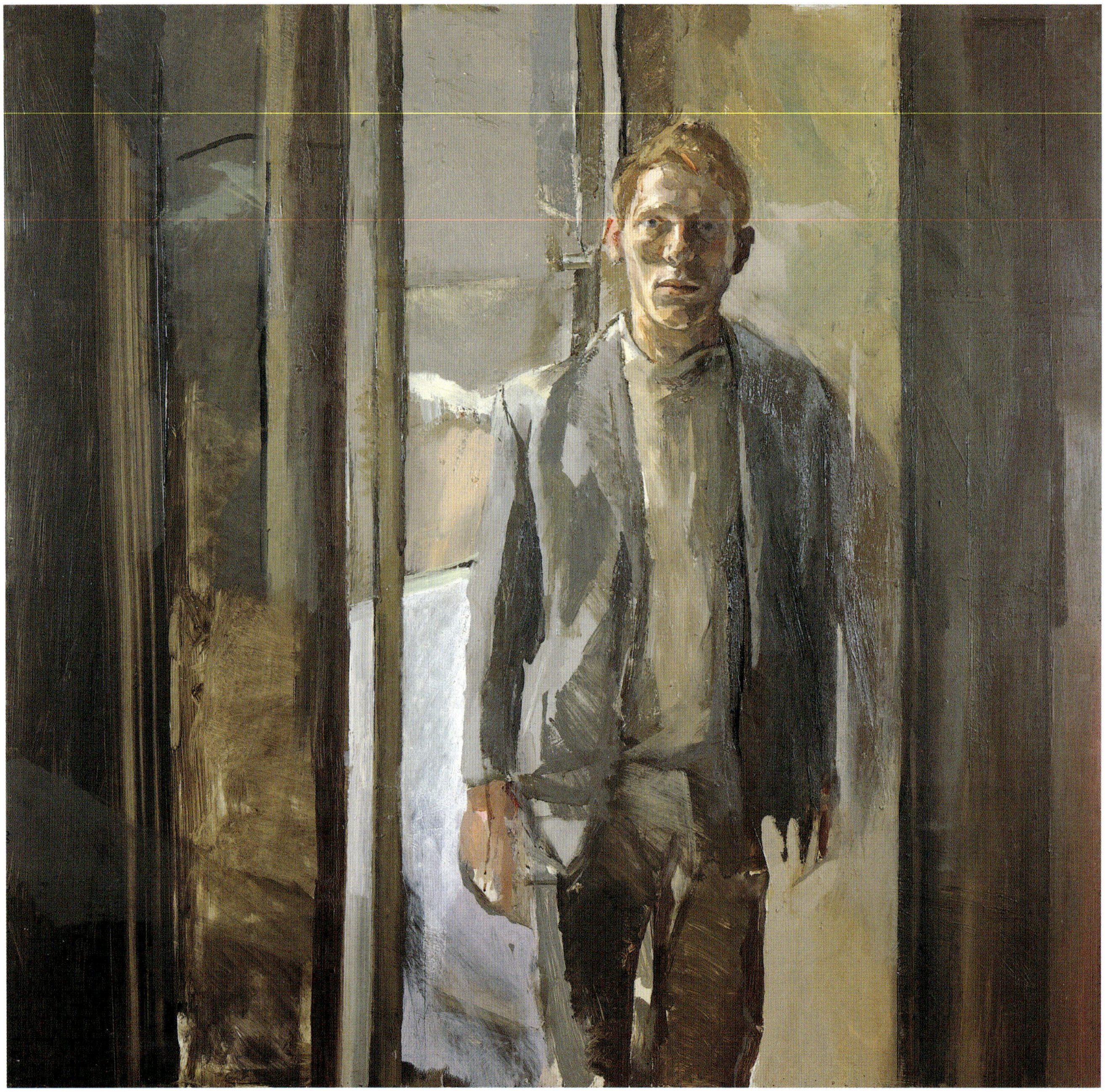

14
Portrait of Tim Behrens
1962
Oil on board
122 x 122

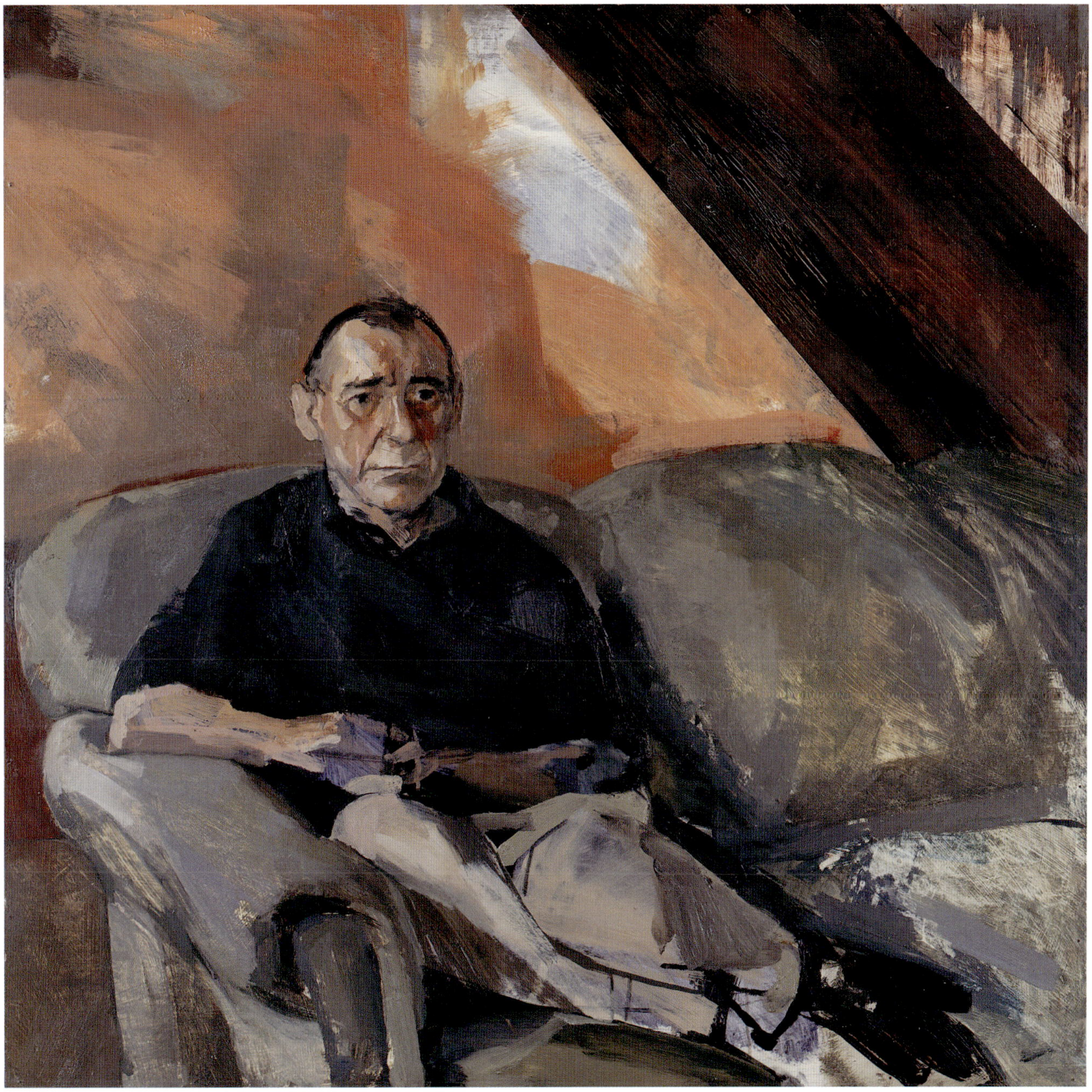

15
Portrait of John Deakin
1963
Oil on board
92 x 90

parties

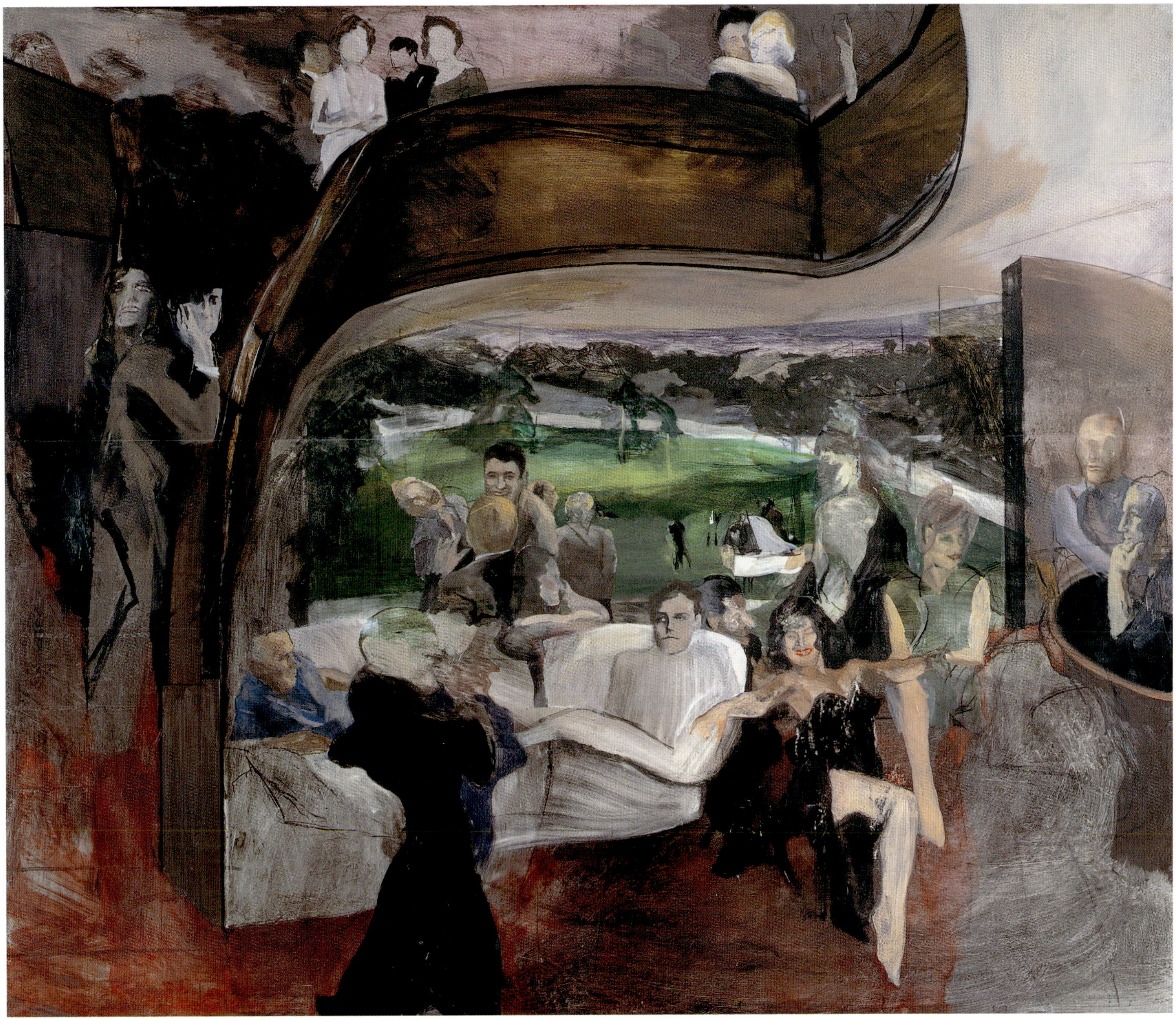

18
The Deer Park
1962
Oil on board
214 x 244.5

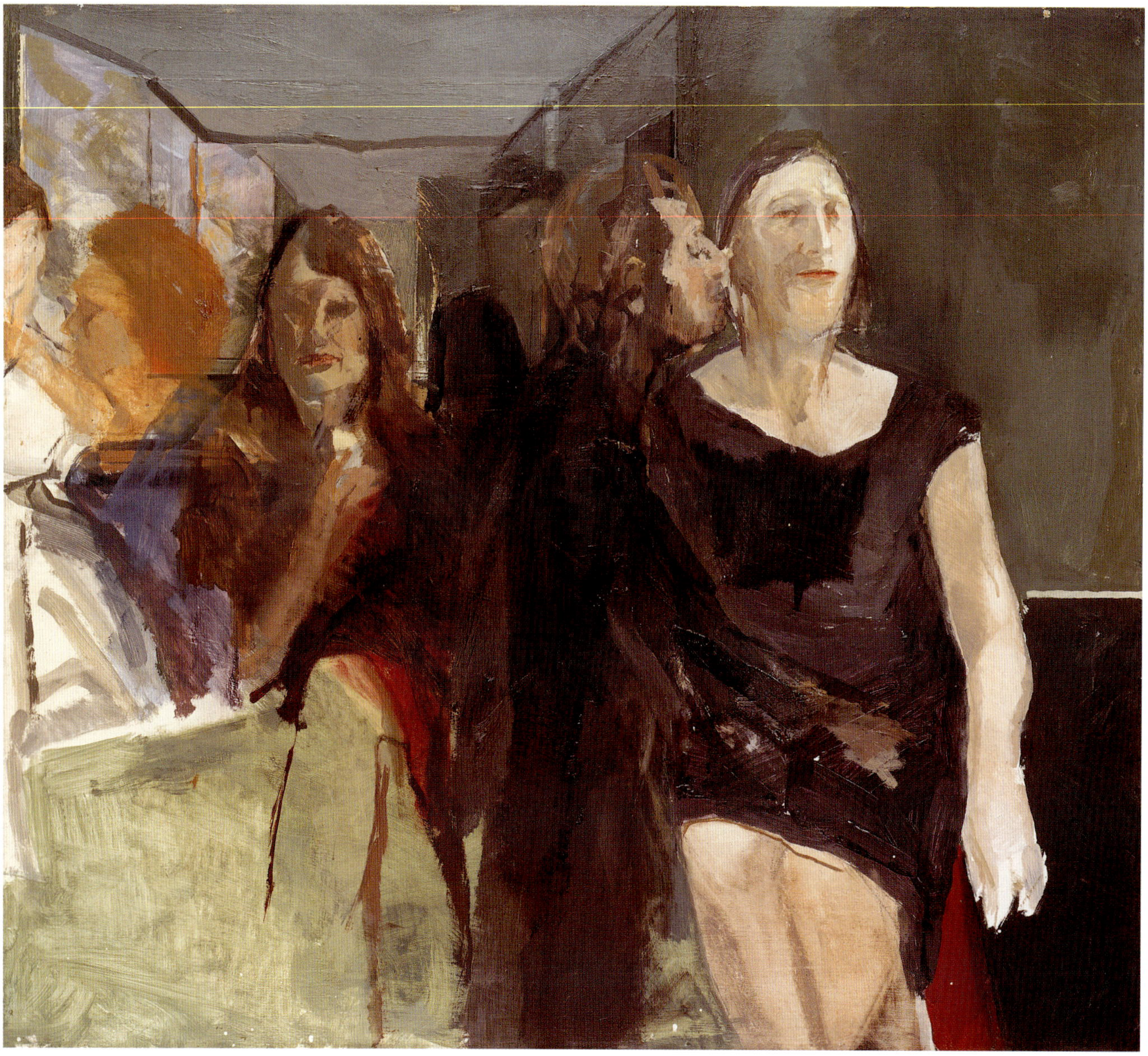

17
The Colony Room II
1962
Oil on hardboard
91.5 x 99

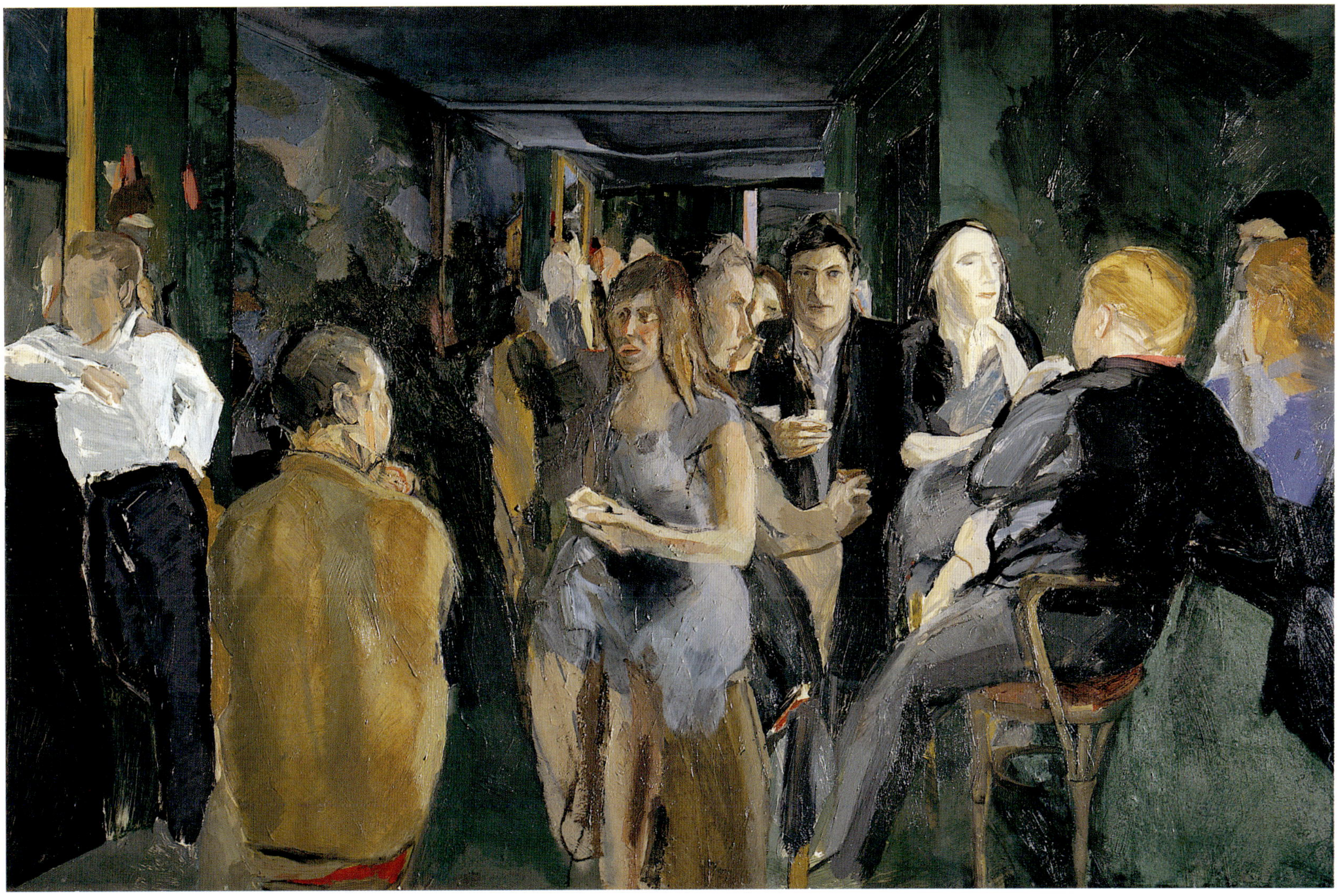

16
The Colony Room I
1962
Oil on hardboard
121.9 x 182.8

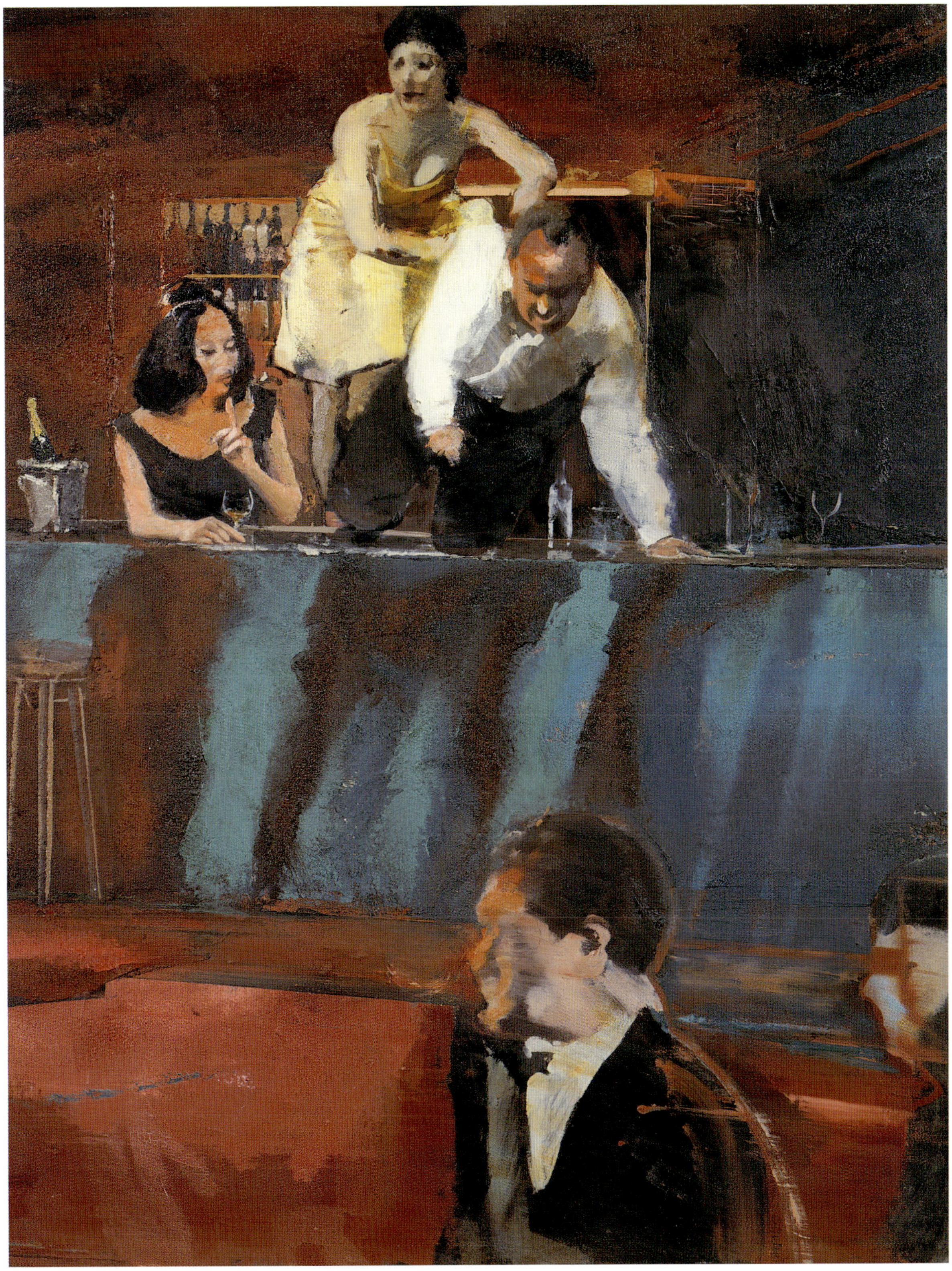

19
Study for 'All Night Long'
1963–4
Oil on canvas
100 x 74.5

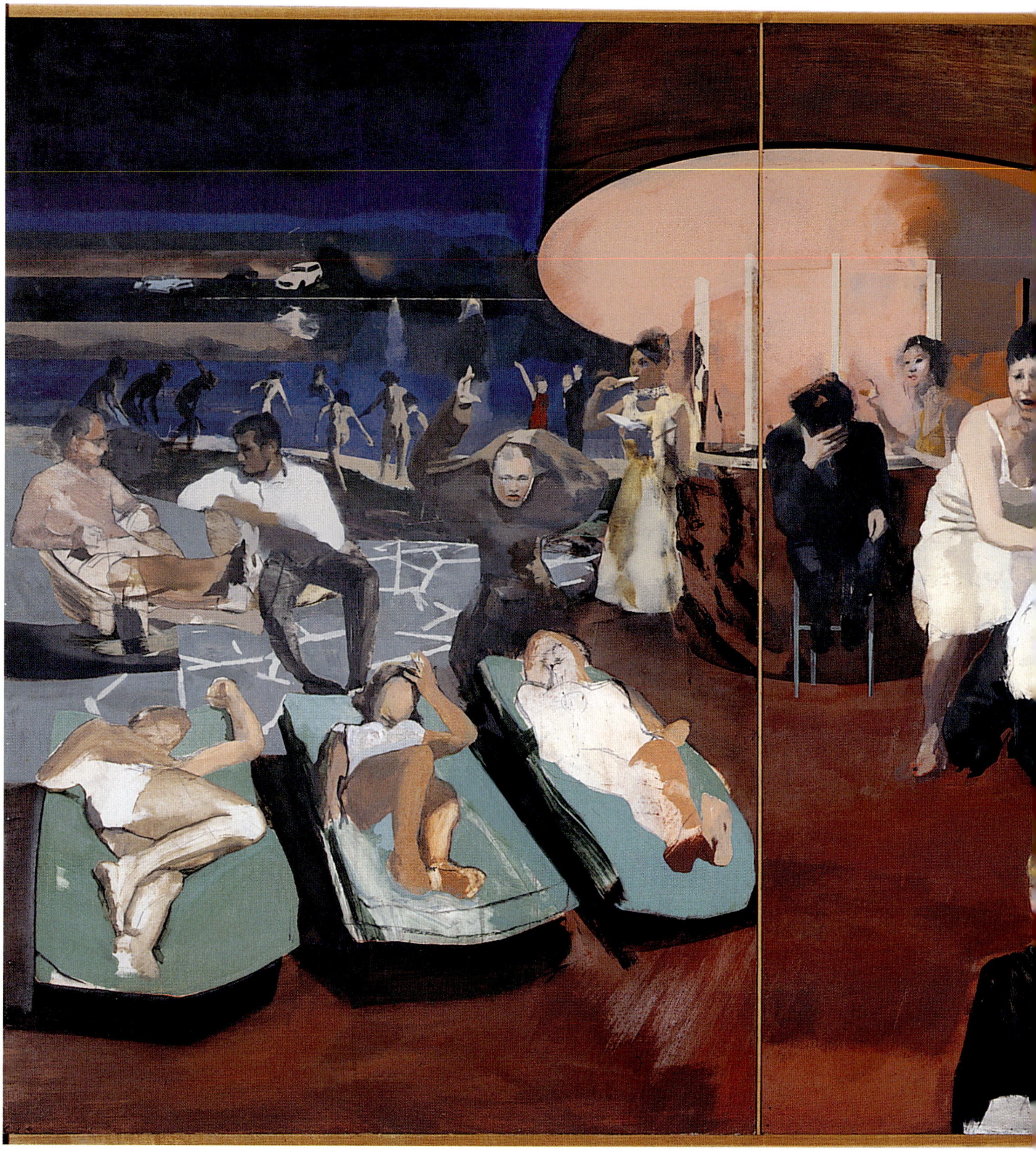

20
All Night Long
1963–4
Oil on composition board (3 panels)
183.5 x 368.3

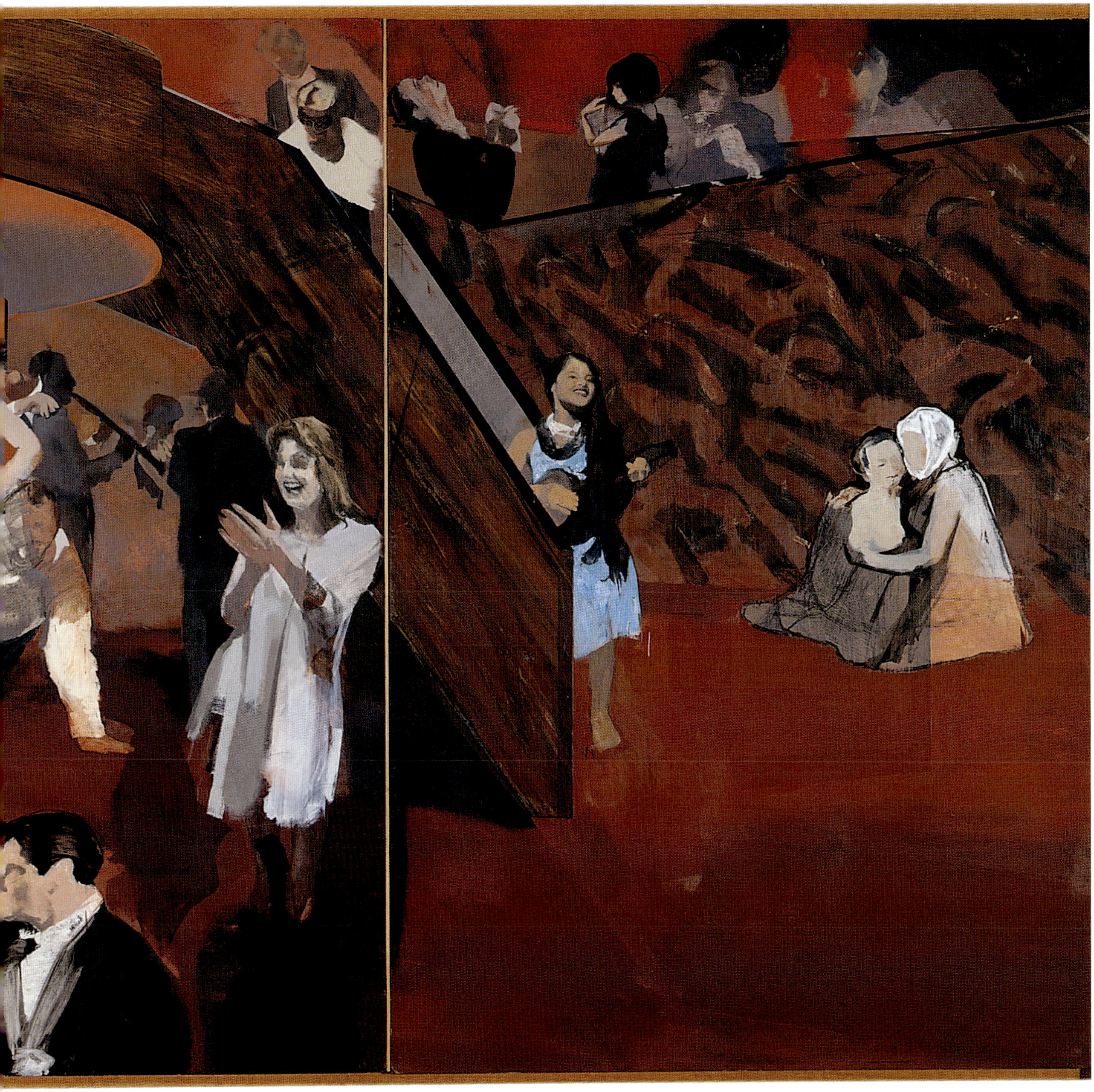

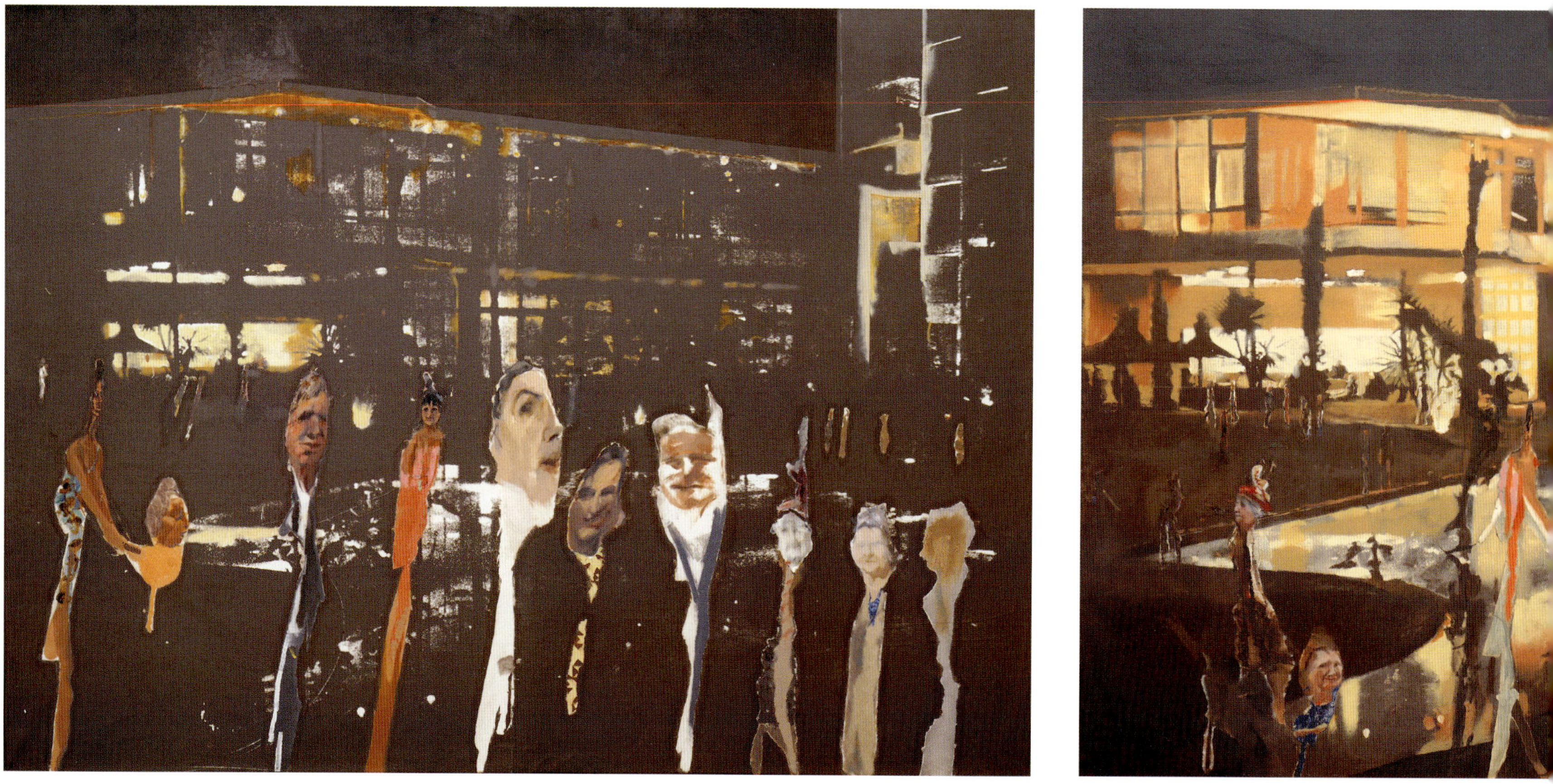

21
Good and Bad at Games
1964–8
Oil and silkscreen on canvas
(triptych)
152.4 x 203.4 (each canvas)

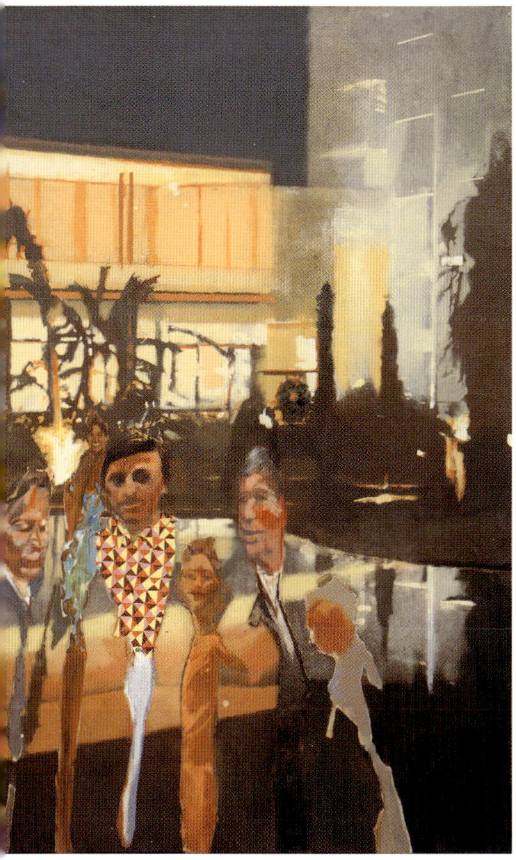

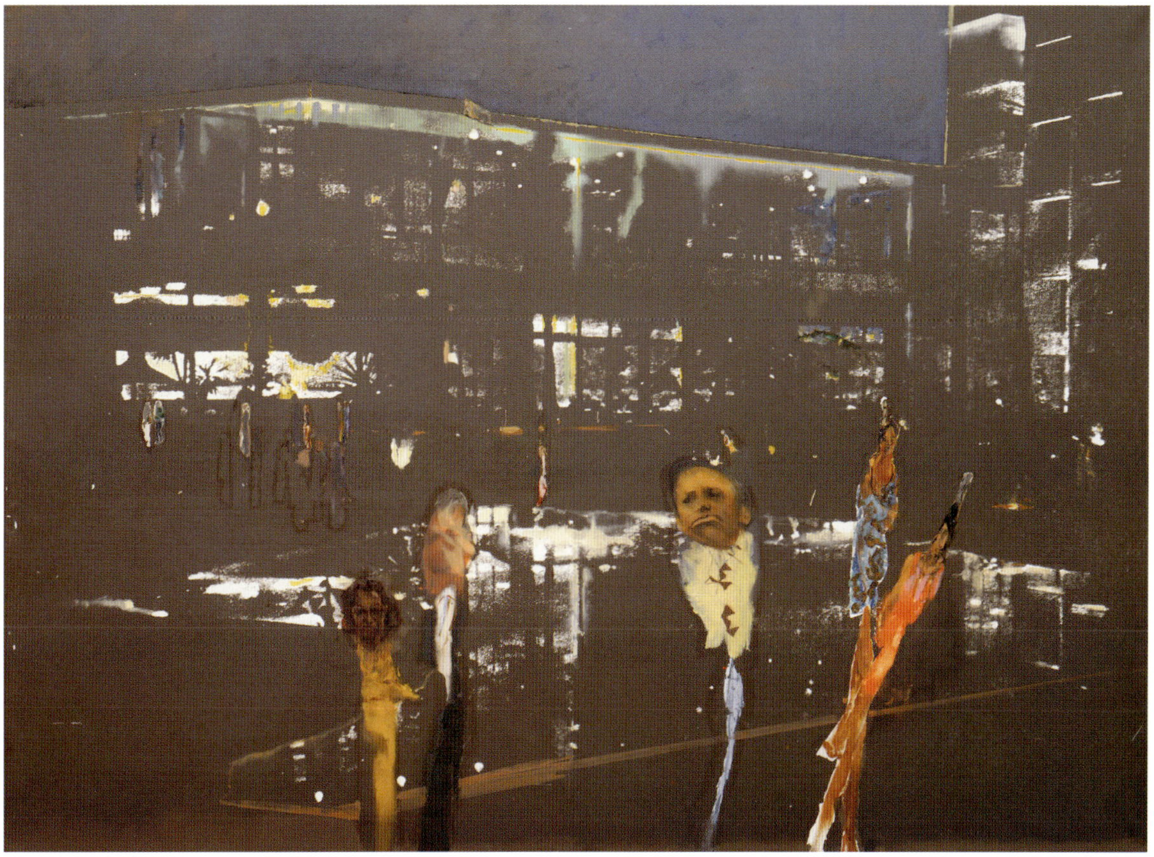

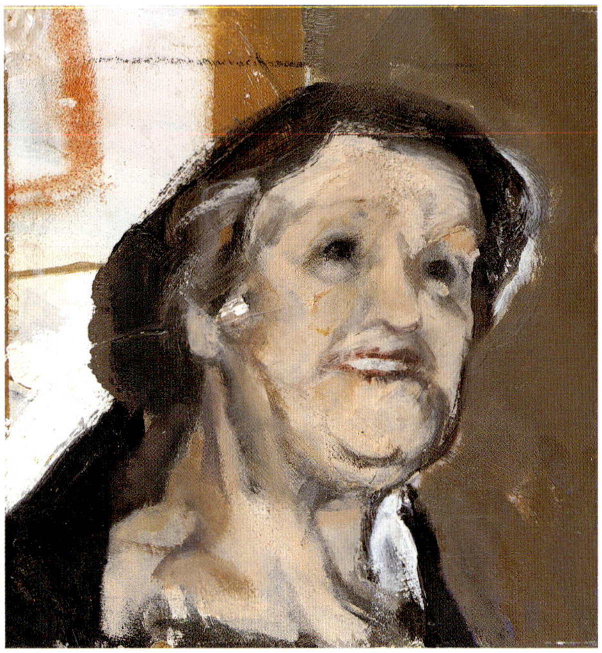

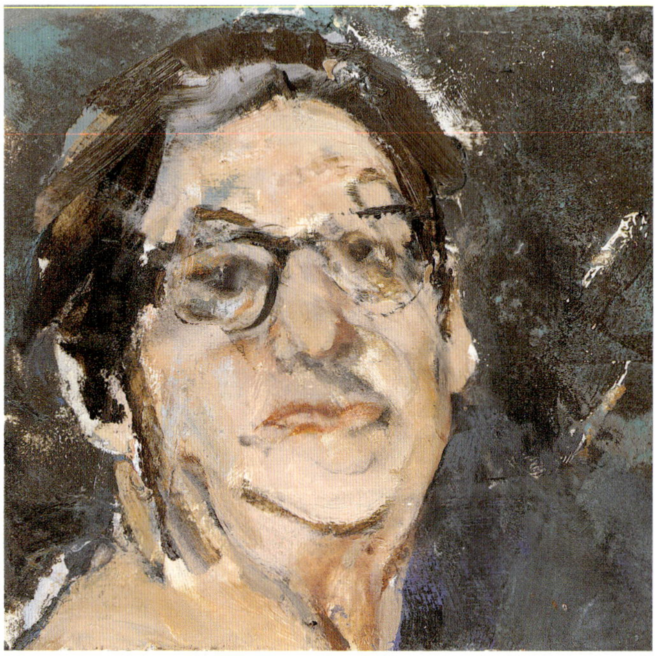

27
Study of a Head for a Group of Figures No 8
1967
Oil on board
22.2 x 22

24
Study of a Head for a Group of Figures No 4
1967
Oil on board
21 x 19.3

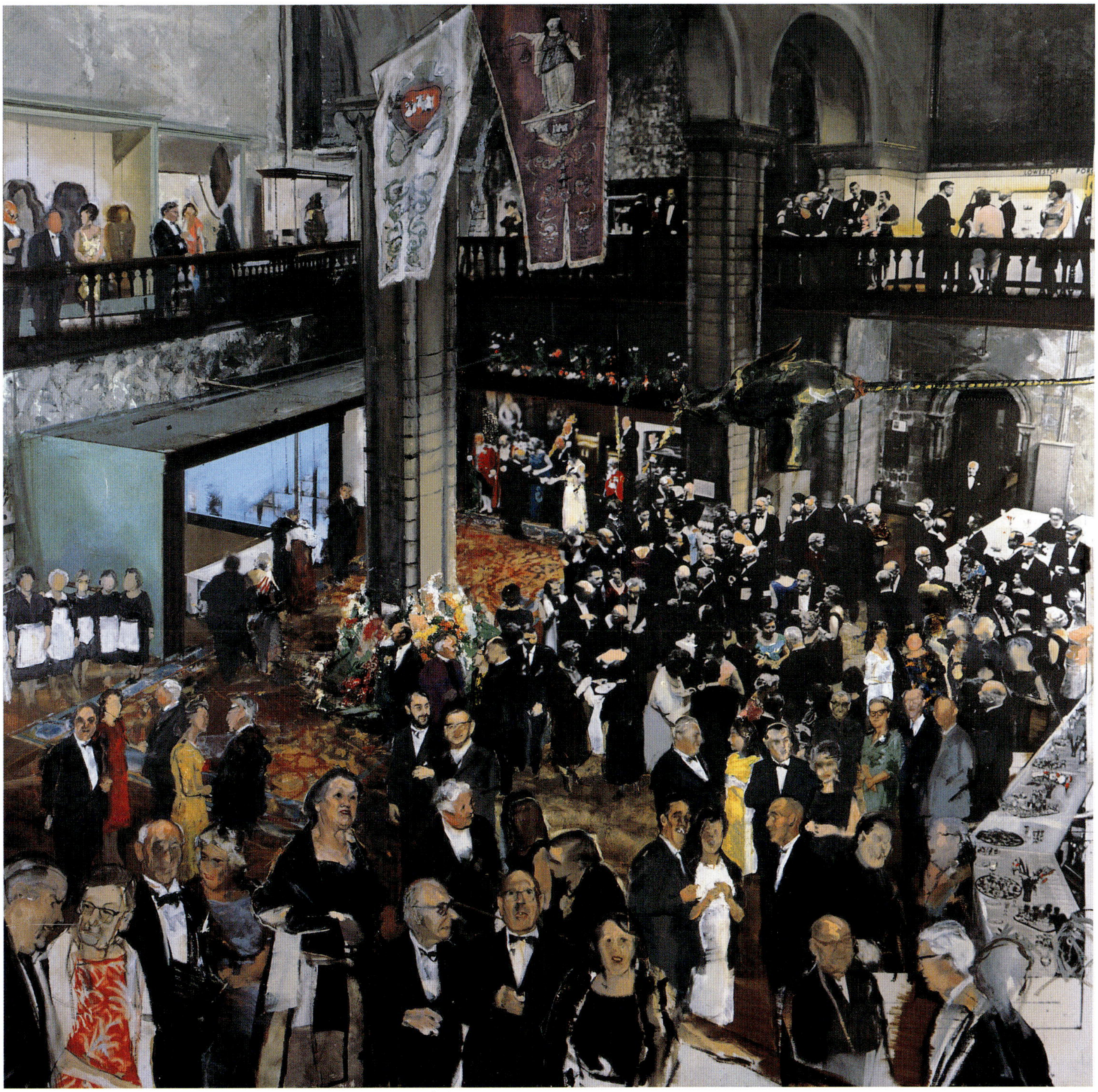

22
The Lord Mayor's Reception in Norwich Castle Keep on the eve of the installation of the first Chancellor of the University of East Anglia
1966–9
Oil and silkscreen on turaphot linen on canvas
213.3 x 213.3

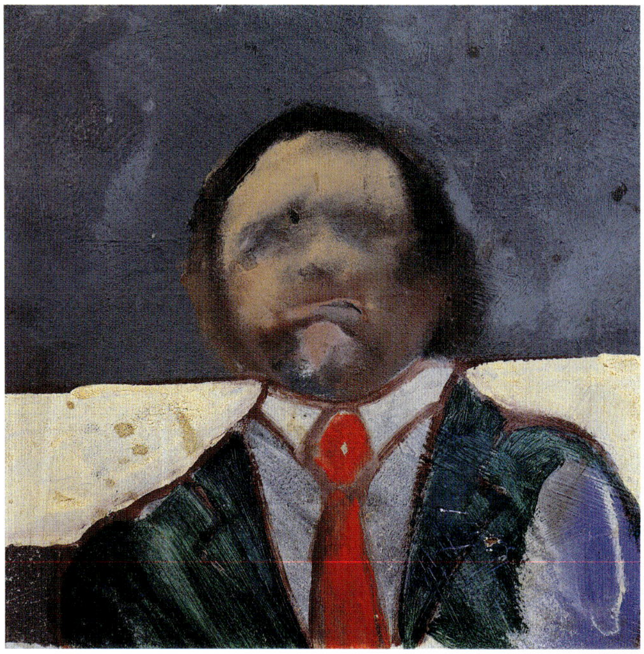

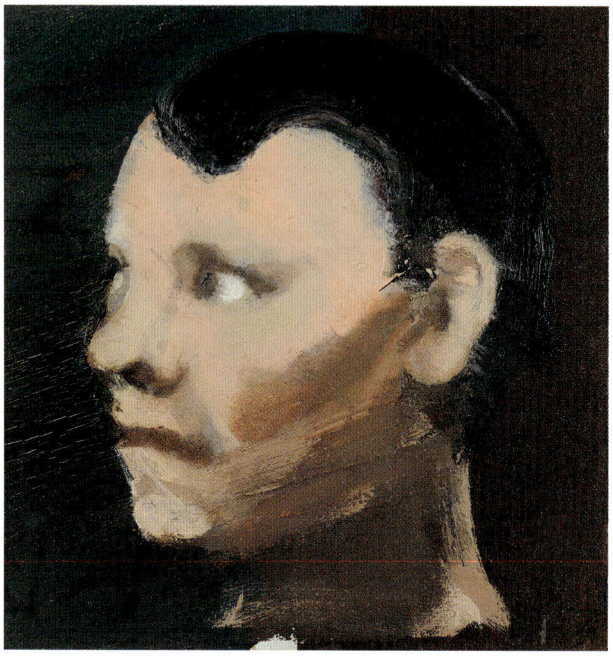

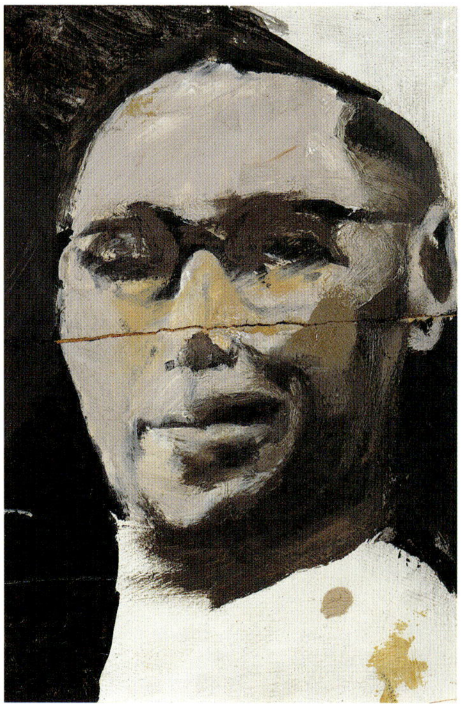

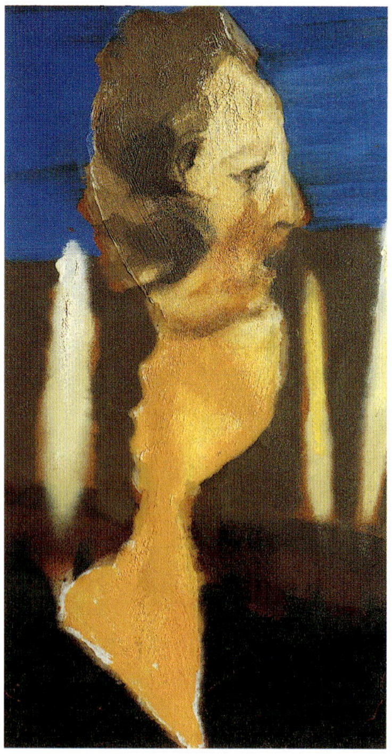

26
Study of a Head for a Group of Figures No 7
1967
Oil on board
23.7 x 23.7

23
Head of a Man
*c.*1967
Oil on board
19.5 x 21

25
Study of a Head for a Group of Figures No 6
1967
Oil on board
22 x 15

28
Study of a Head for a Group of Figures No 9
1967
Oil on board
22.5 x 21

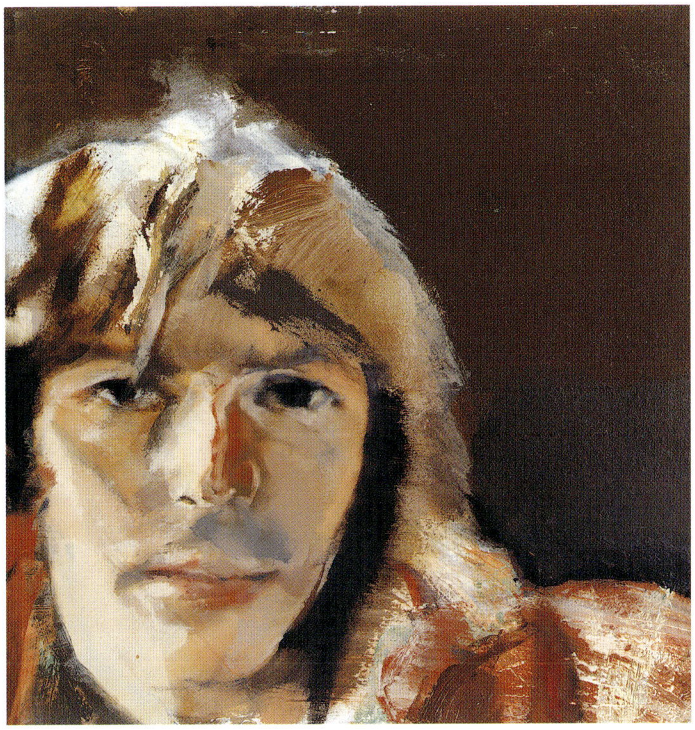

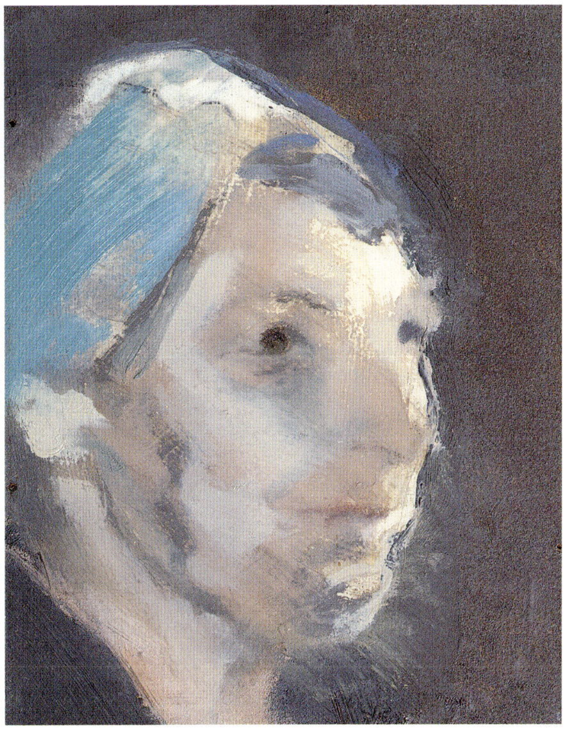

29
Study of a Head for a Group of Figures No 10
1967
Oil on board
31.6 x 16.5

30
Study of a Head with Green Turban
1967
Oil on board
21.5 x 16.5

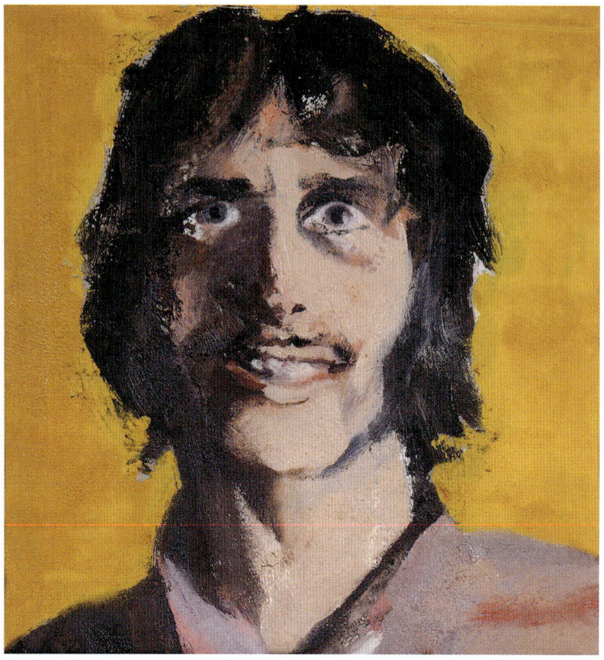

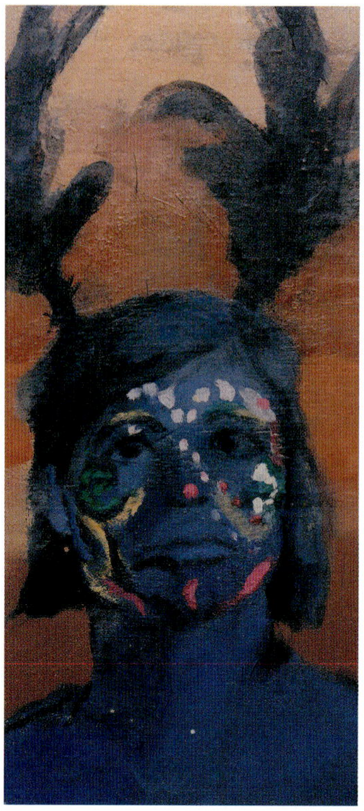

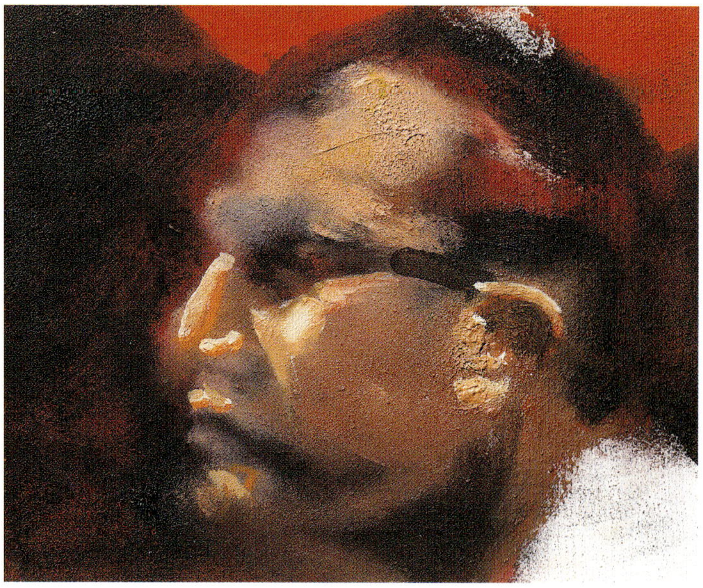

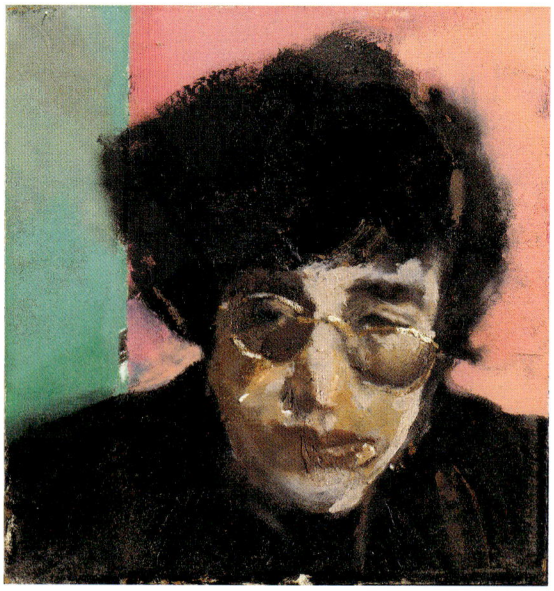

34
Study of a Head for 'Lights' No 5
1968
Oil on board
21 x 19.4

31
Study of a Head of Arthur Brown (for 'Lights')
1968
Oil on board
20 x 17.7

32
Study of a Head for 'Lights' No 1
1968
Oil on board
34.2 x 15.2

33
Study of a Head for 'Lights' No 2
1968
Oil on board
15 x 17.5

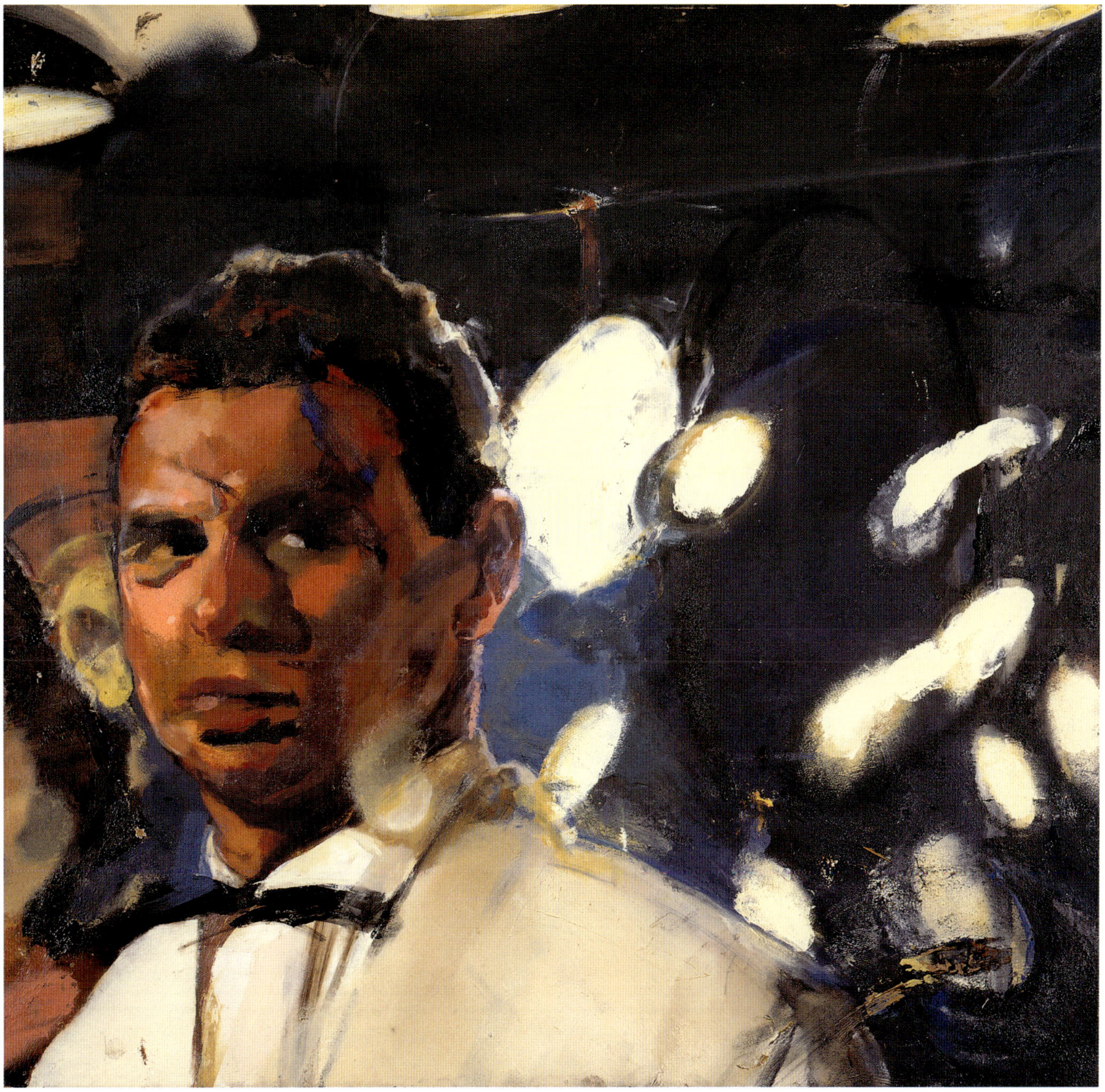

35
The Blue and Yellow of the Yacht Club
1969
Oil on hardboard
61 x 61

lights

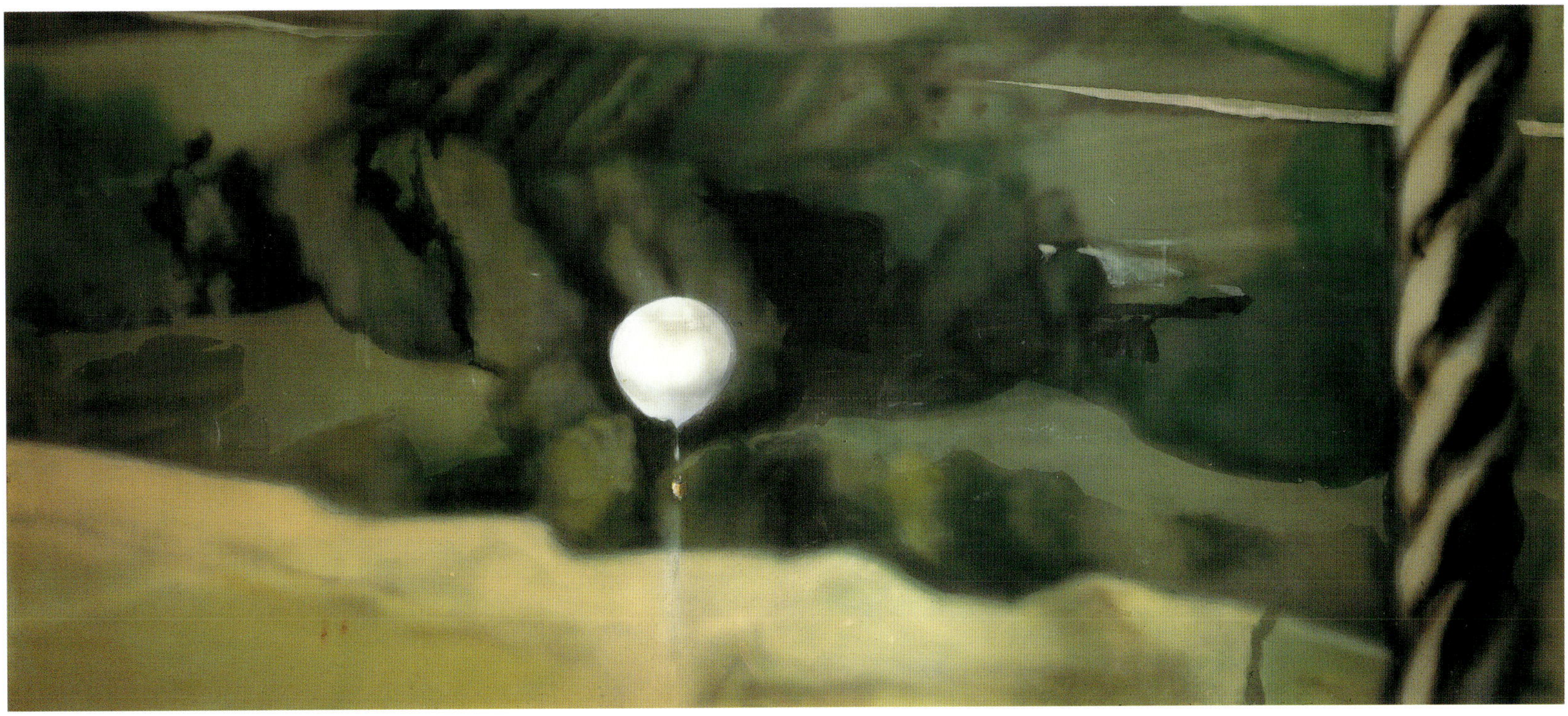

36
Lights I: Out-of-Doors
1970
Acrylic on canvas
142.3 x 312

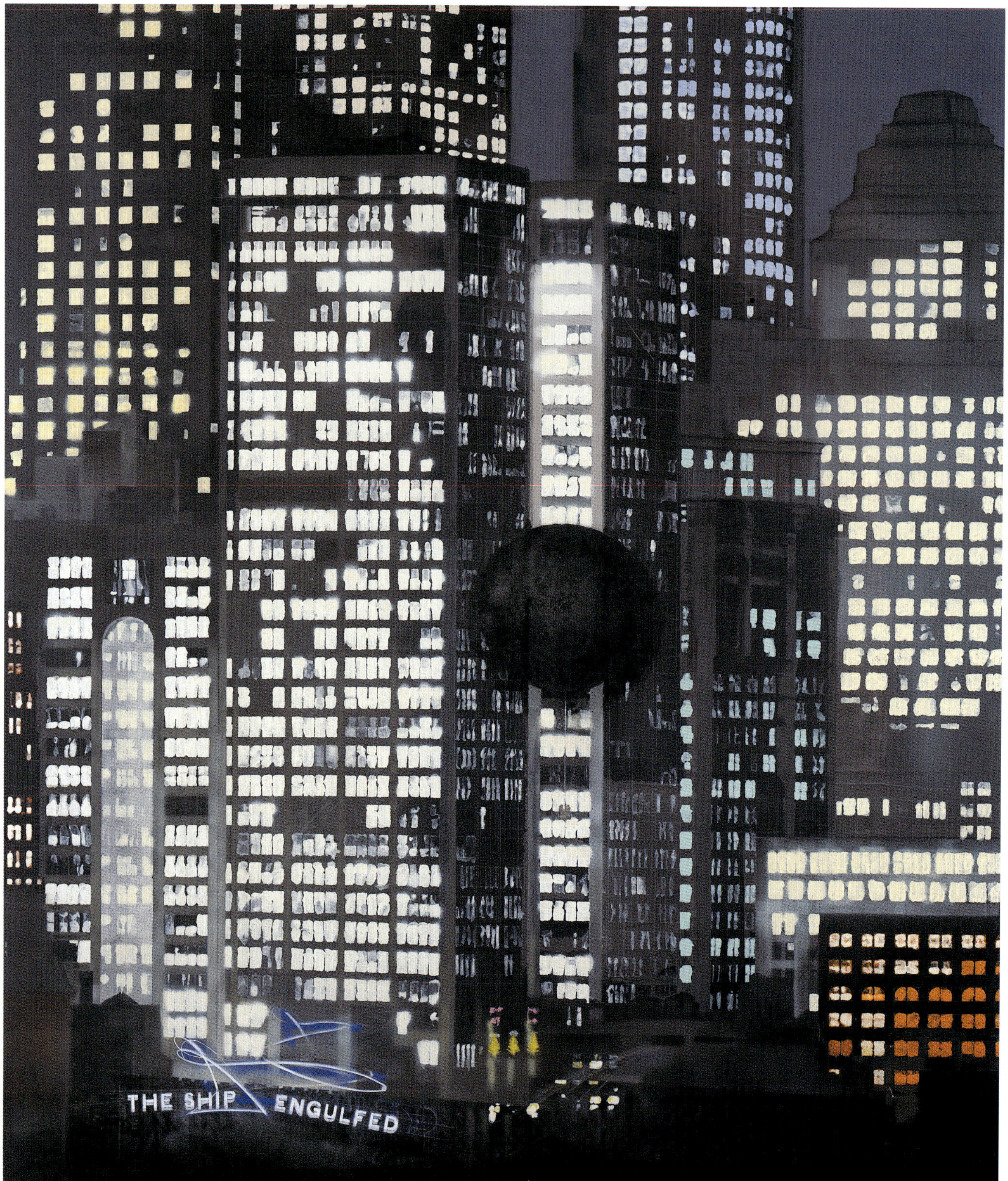

38
Lights II: The Ship Engulfed
1972
Acrylic on canvas
183 x 153.5

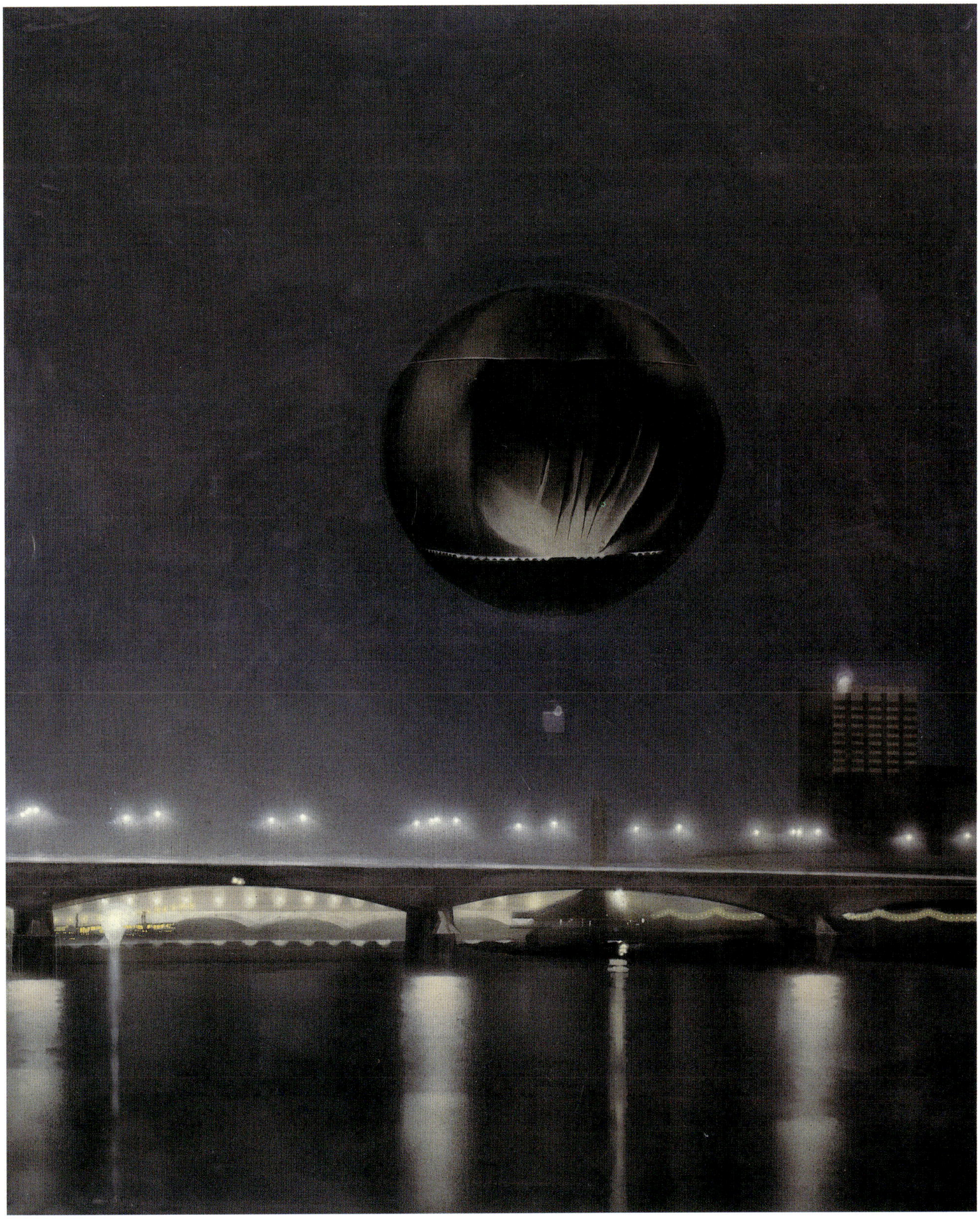

39
Lights III: The Black Balloon
1973
Acrylic on canvas
160 x 129.5

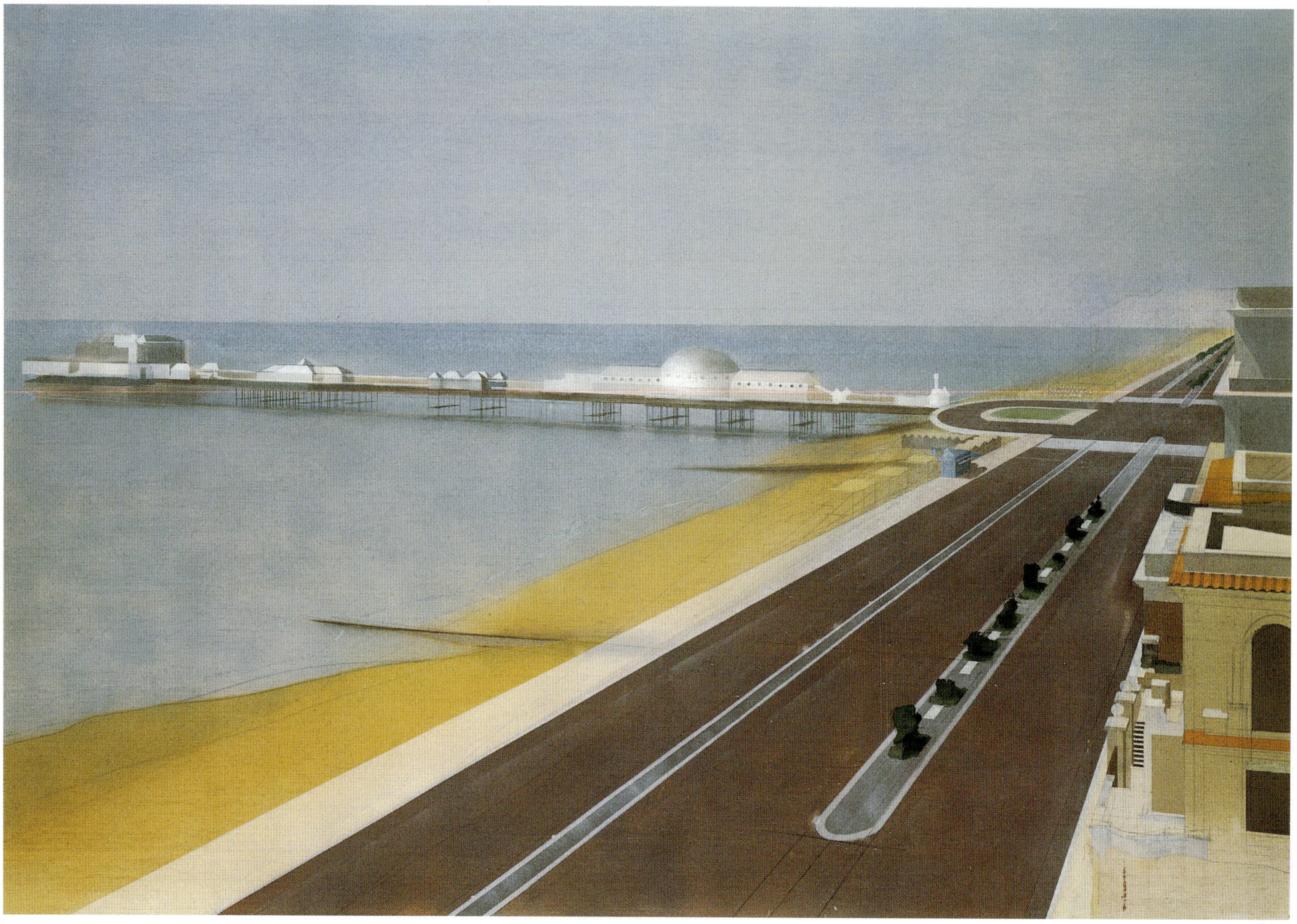

40
Lights IV: The Pier and the Road
1973
Acrylic on canvas
152.4 x 213.4

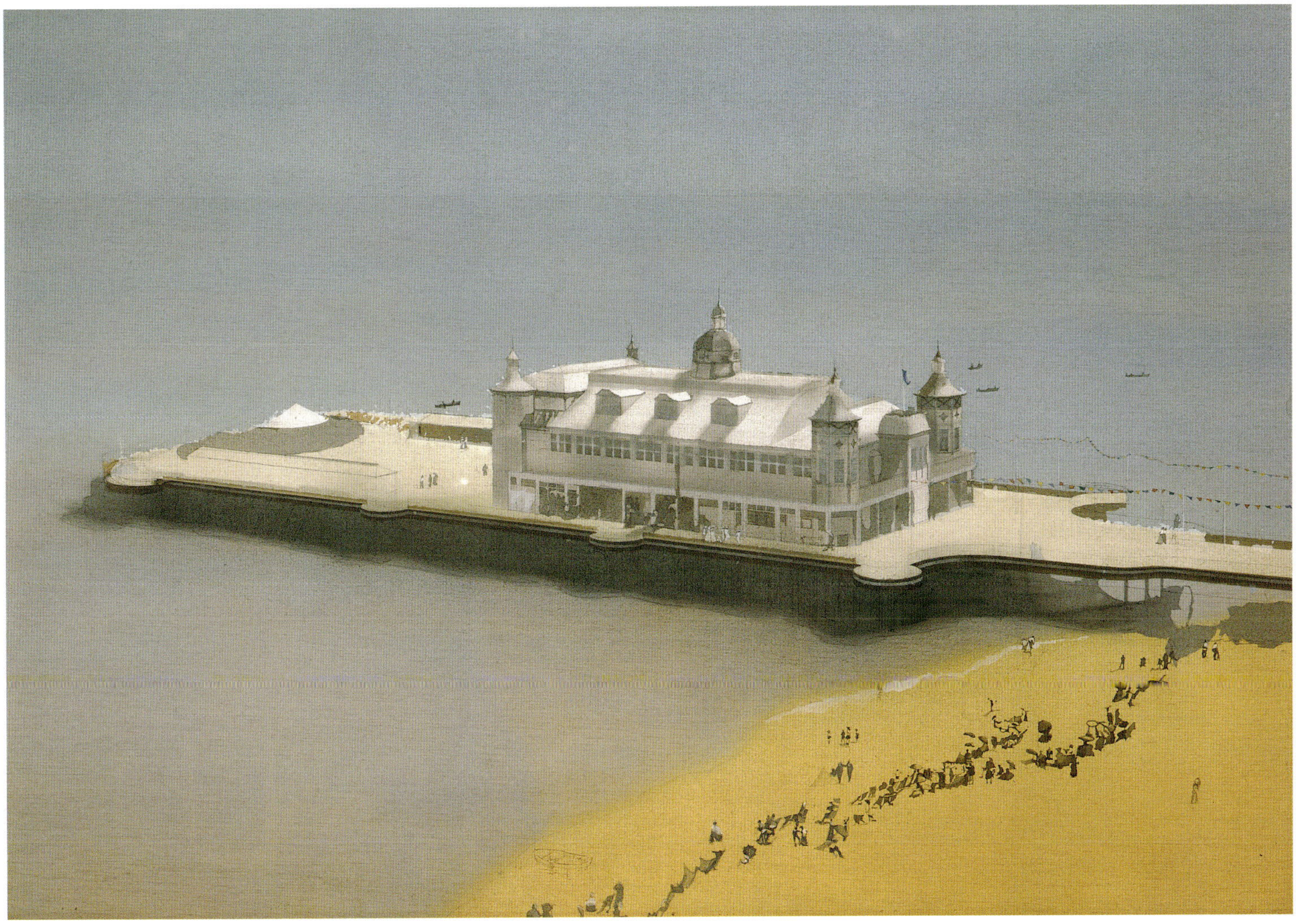

41
Lights V: The Pier Pavilion
1973
Acrylic on canvas
152.4 x 213.3

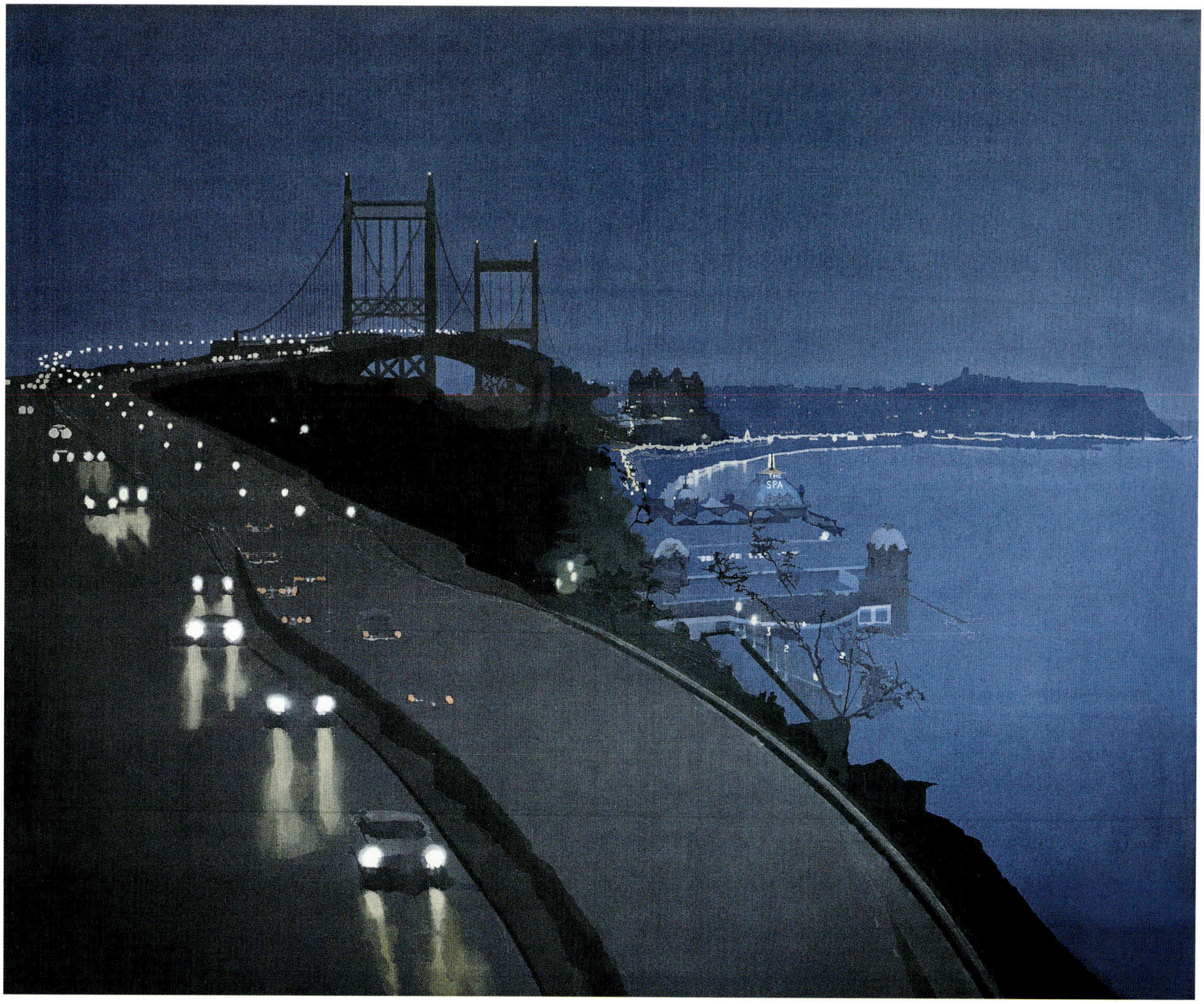

42
Lights VI: The Spa
1974
Acrylic on canvas
152 x 182

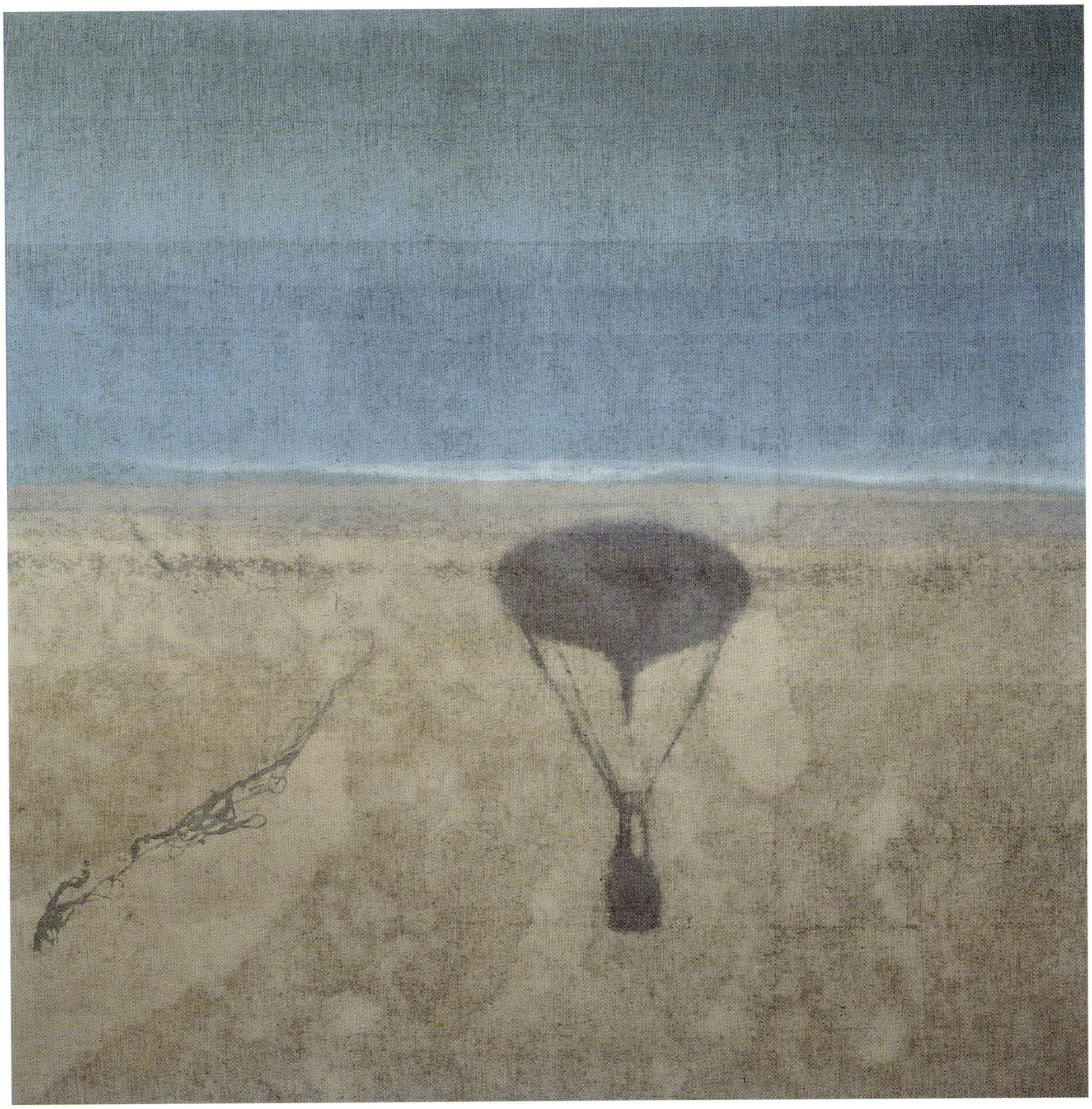

43
Lights VII: A Shadow
1974
Acrylic on canvas
182.9 x 182.9

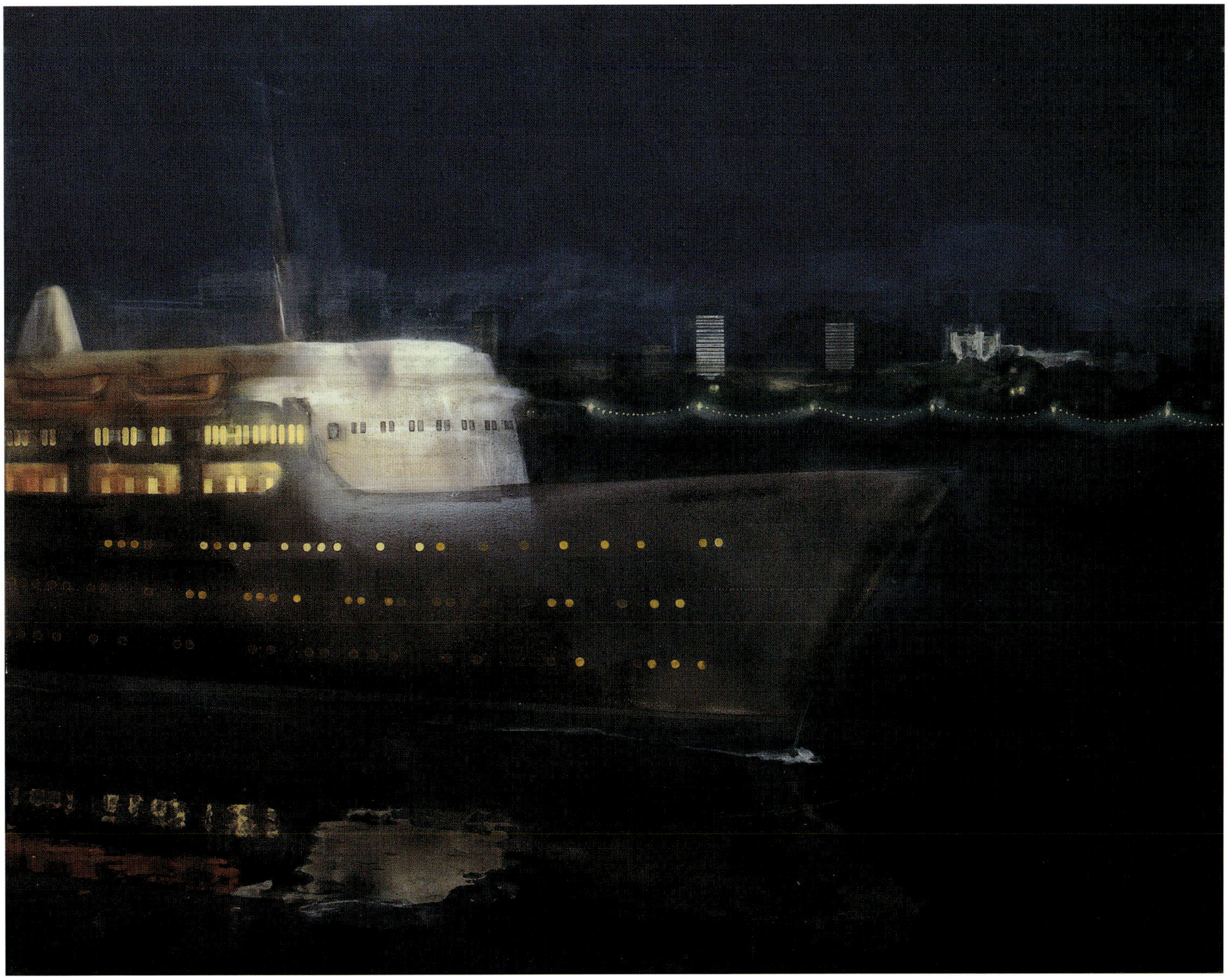

37
Liner
1971–2
Acrylic on canvas
152.5 x 183

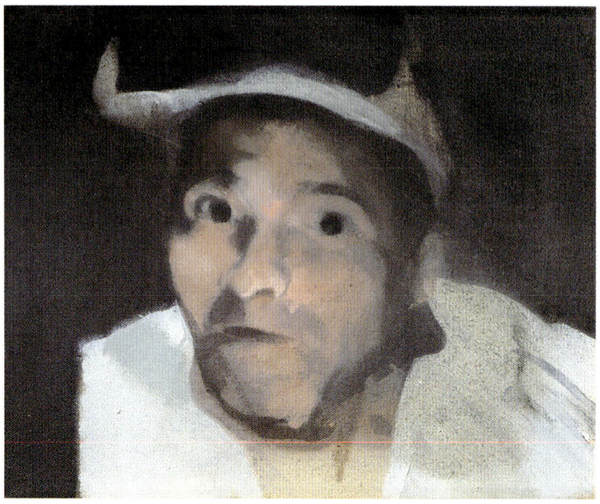

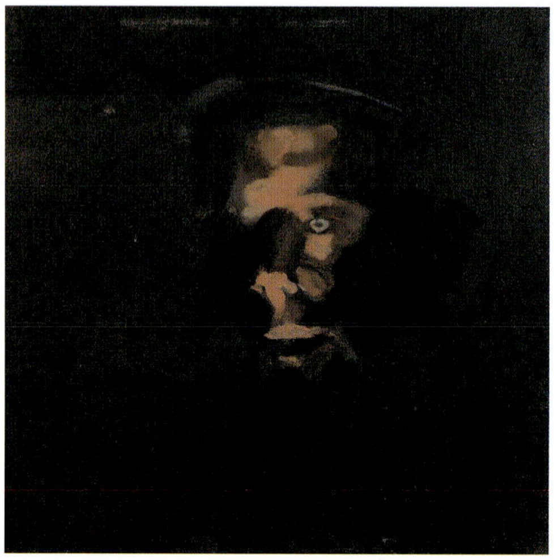

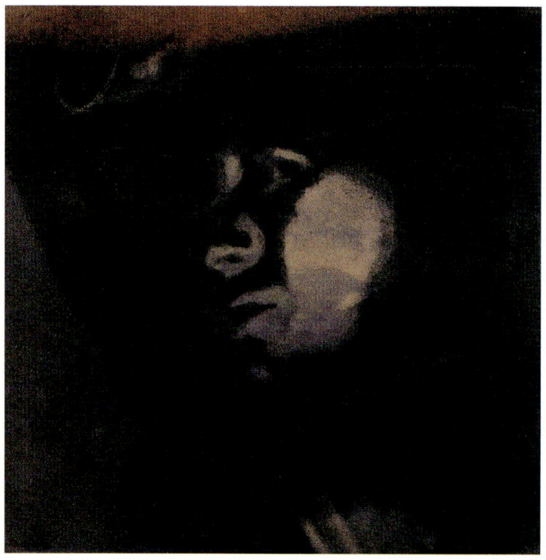

44
Cabin: Sketch I
1975
Acrylic on canvas
24.7 x 29.8

45
Cabin: Sketch II
1975
Acrylic on canvas
30.4 x 30.4

46
Cabin: Sketch III
1975
Acrylic on canvas
38 x 38

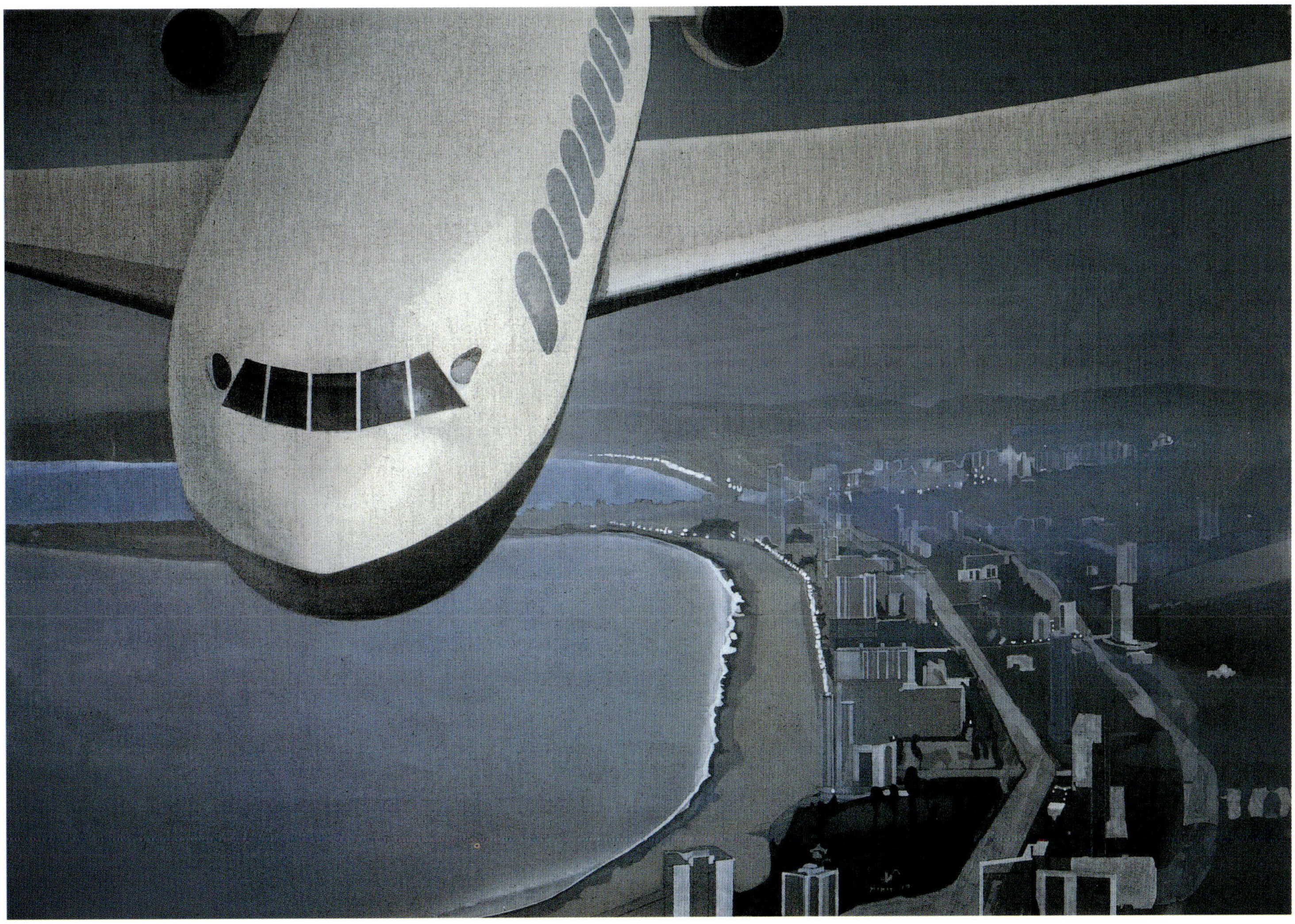

47
Cabin
1975
Acrylic on canvas
152.4 x 213

school

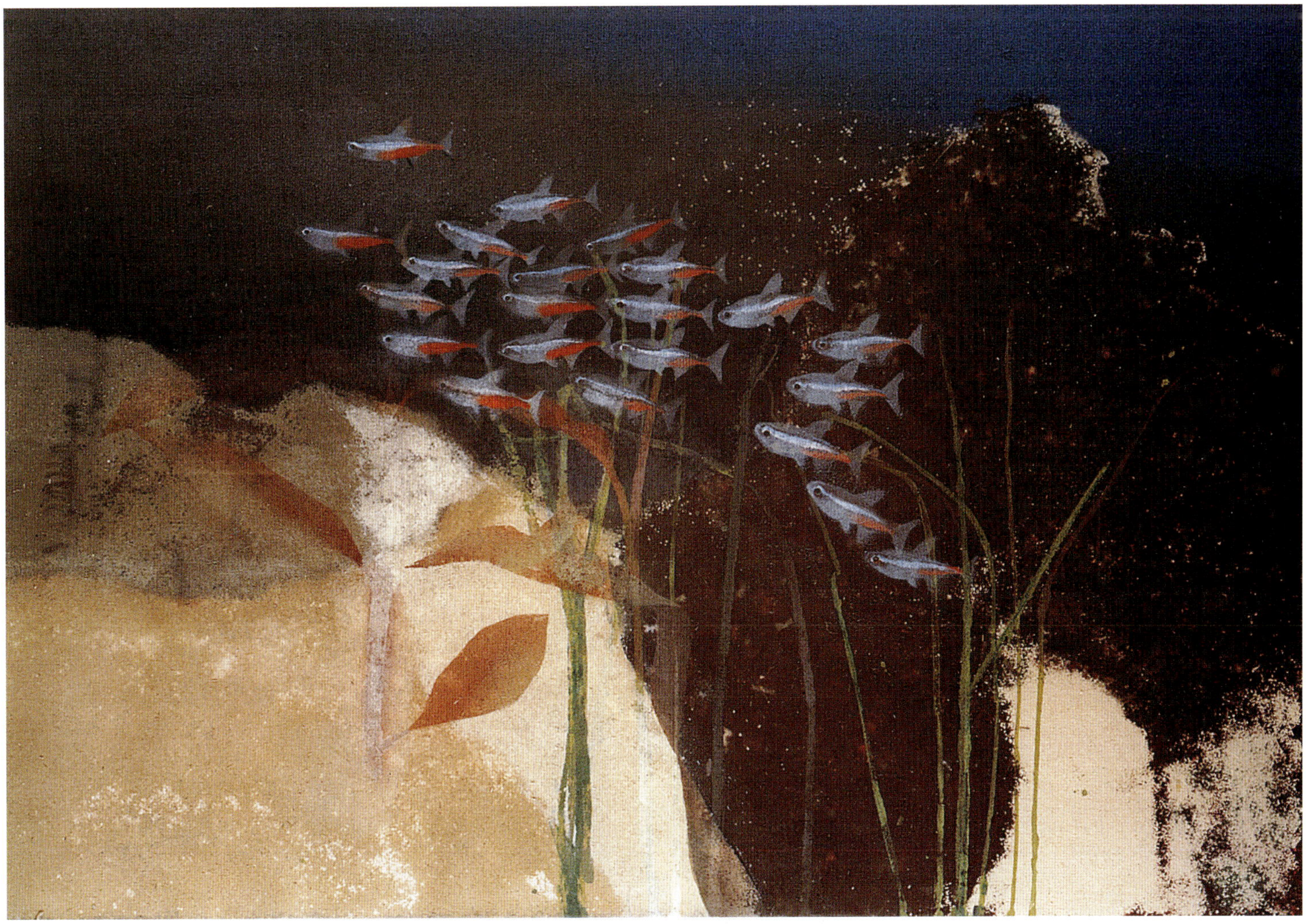

48
School I
1977
Acrylic on canvas
152.5 x 213

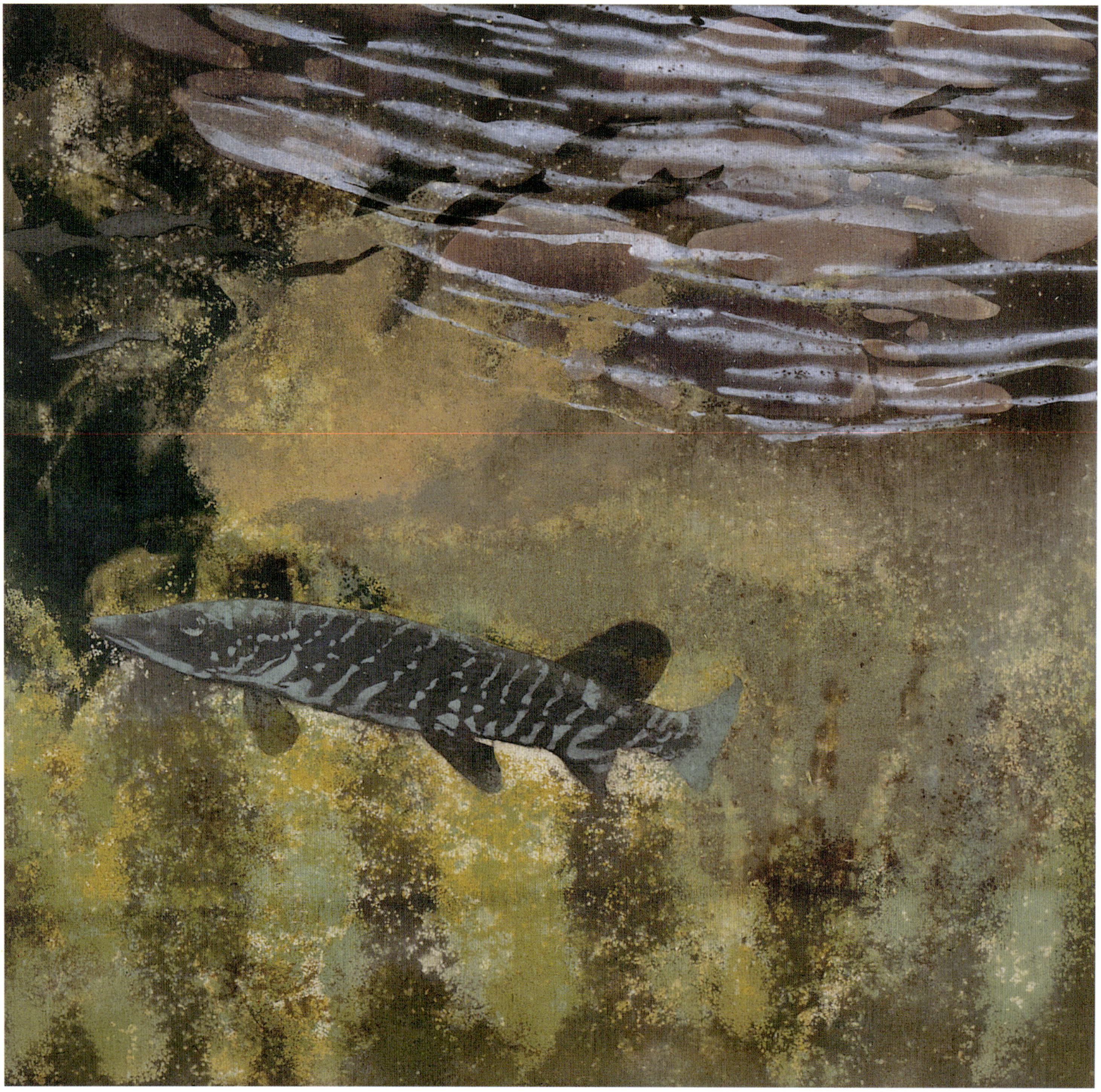

51
School II: Pike and Roach
1977
Acrylic on canvas
122 x 122

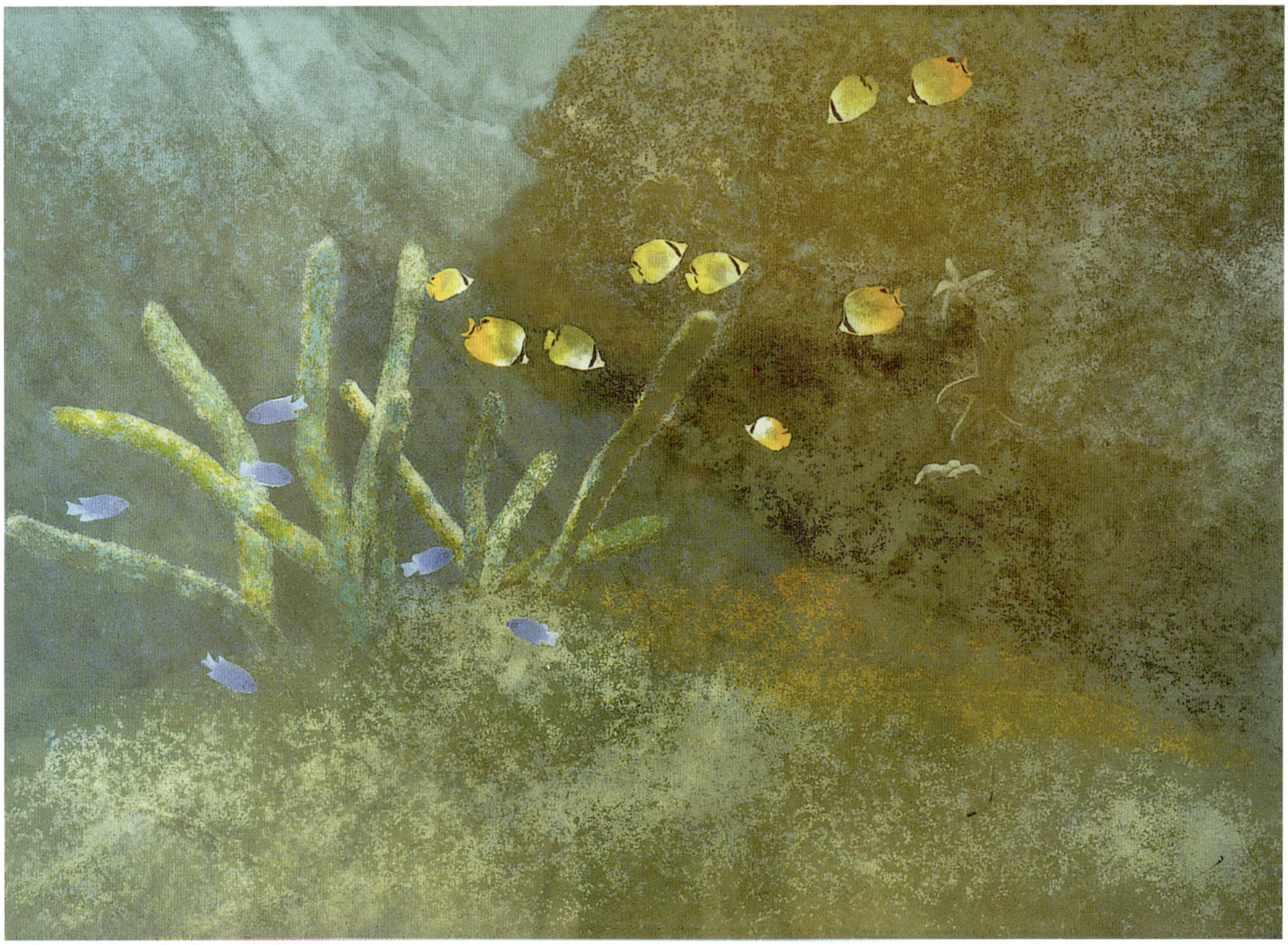

57
School III: Butterfly Fish and Damsel Fish
1978
Acrylic on canvas
152.4 x 213.3

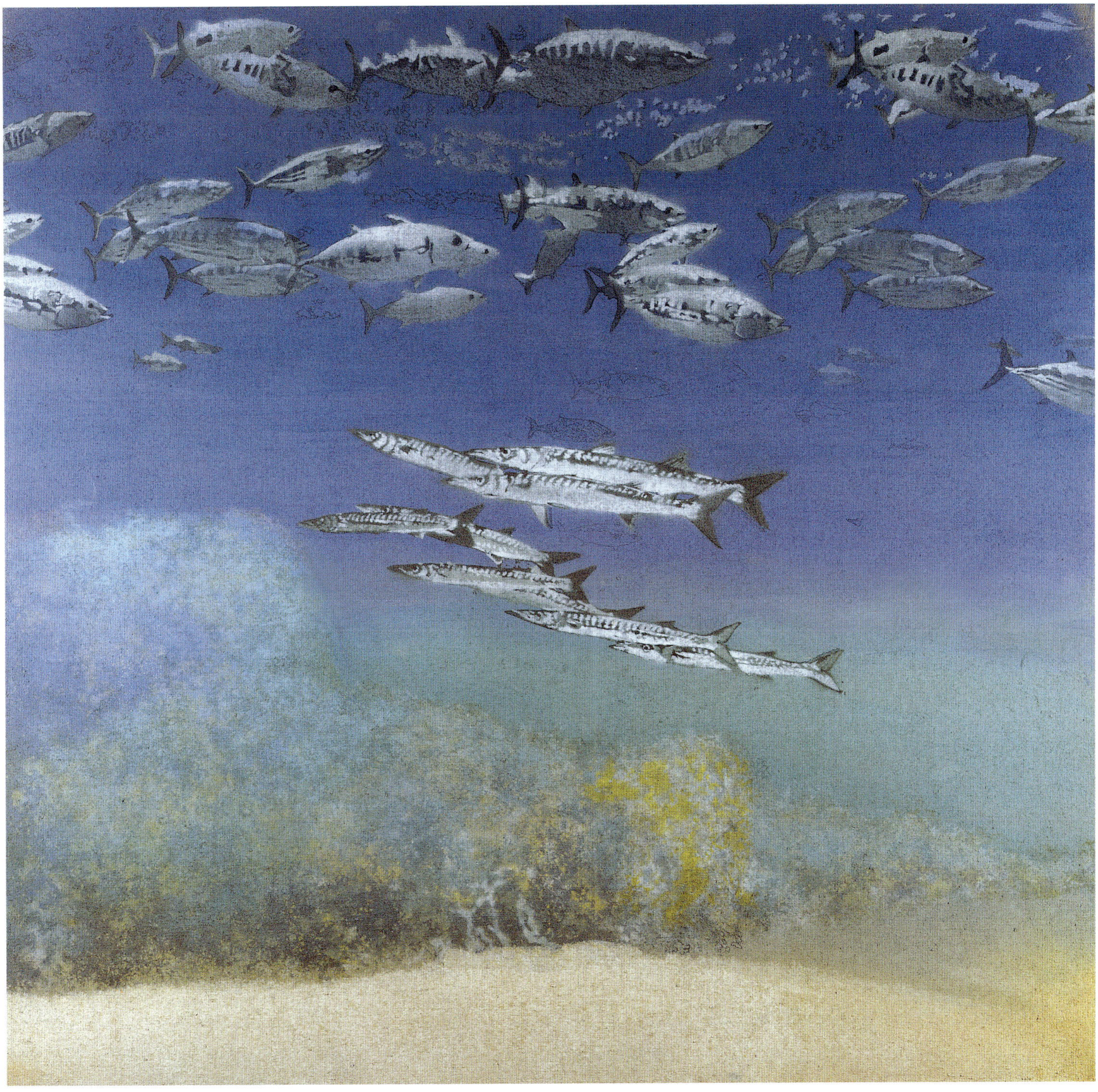

58
School IV: Barracuda under Skipjack Tuna
1978
Acrylic on canvas
175.2 x 175.2

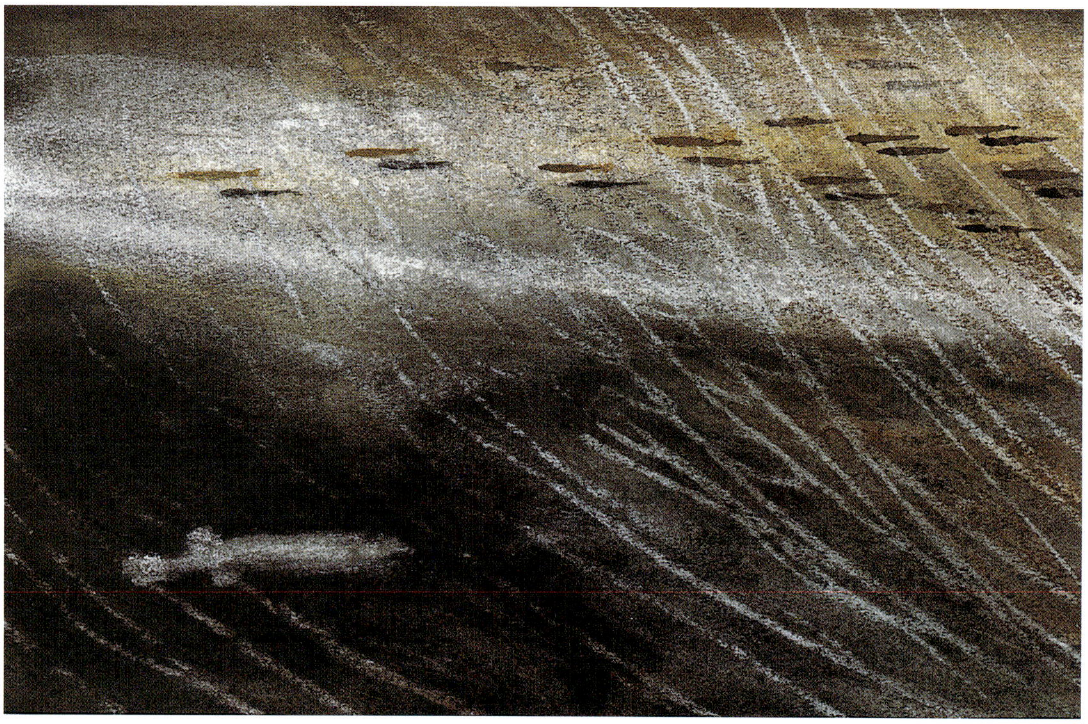

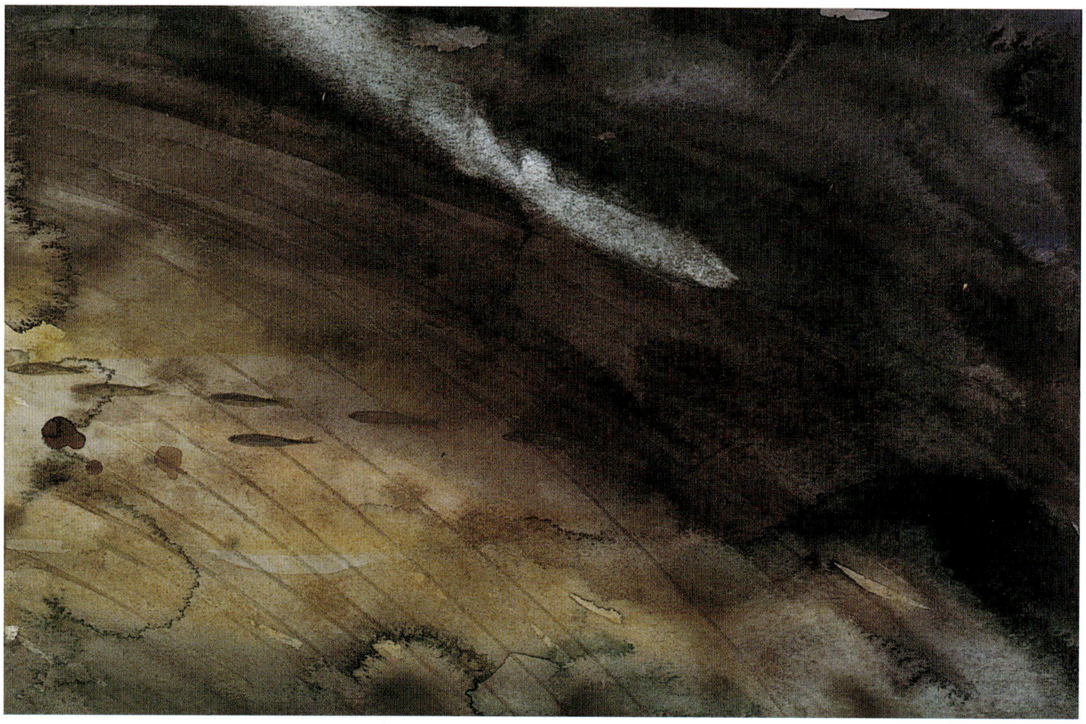

49
Pike and Roach: Study for 'School II'
1977
Watercolour
15.8 x 23.5

50
Pike and Roach III: Study for 'School II'
1977
Watercolour
15 x 22.5

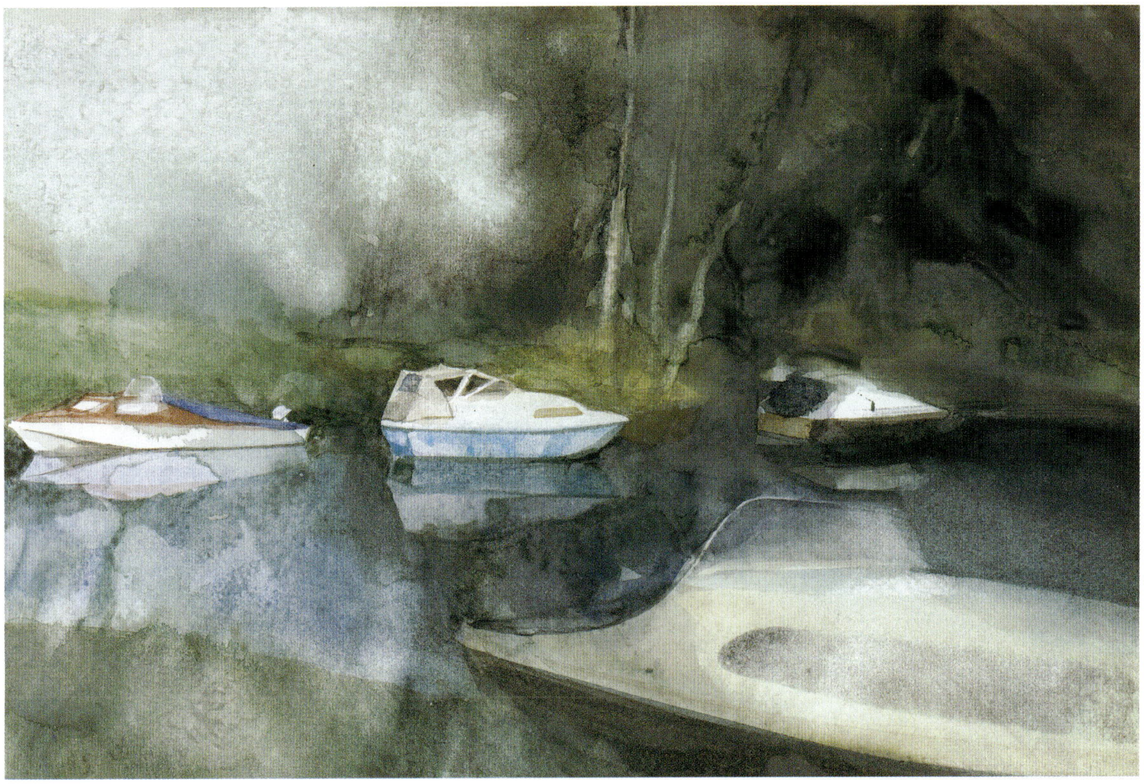

61
First Sketch for Sundance, Escargot, Lady Ottoline and Lynda
1981
Watercolour and acrylic

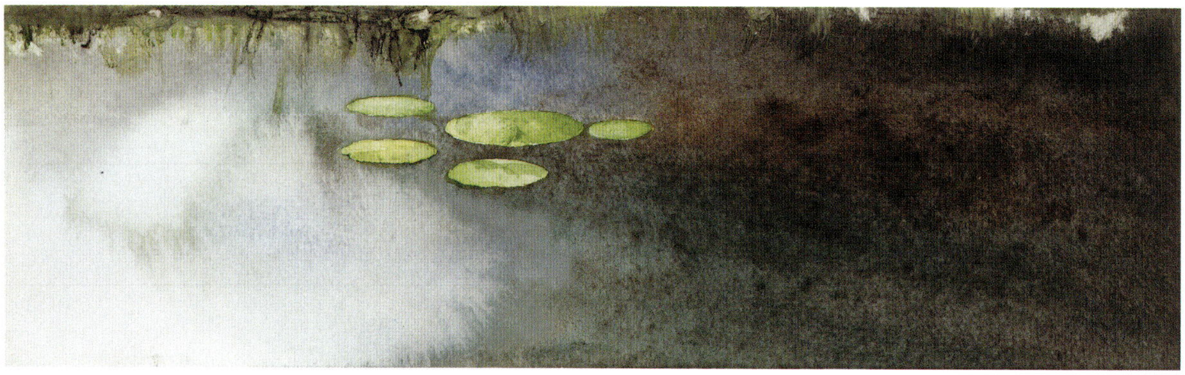

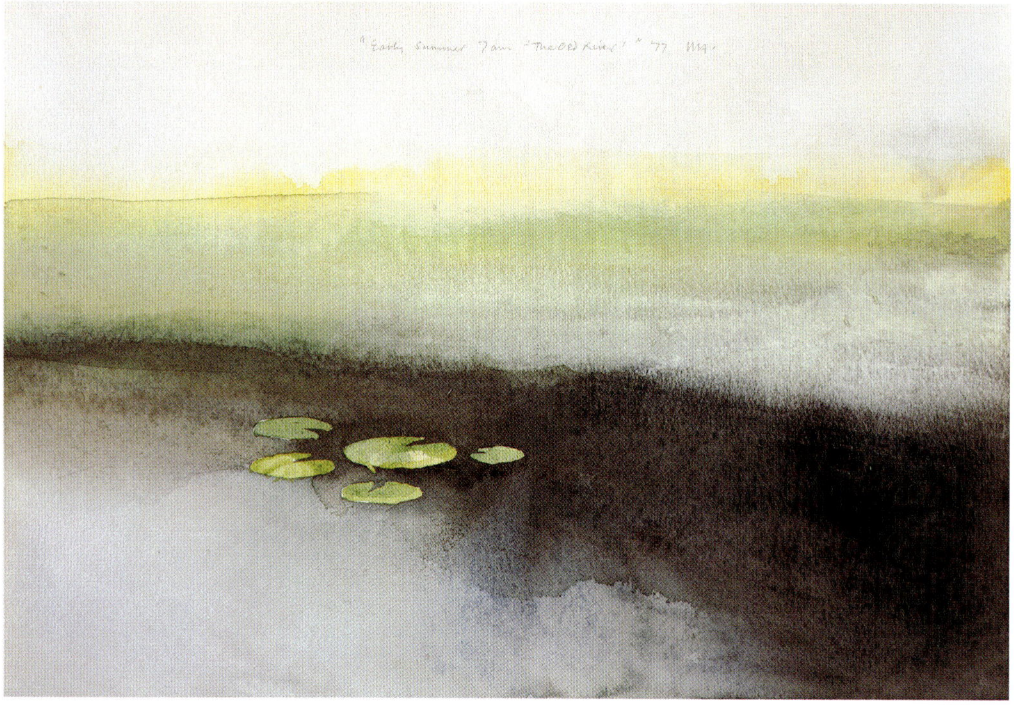

54
Early Summer, 7am, 'The Old River'
1977
Watercolour
22.6 x 32.4

56
Early Summer: Stretch of Water: 'The Old River'
1977
Watercolour
10.2 x 32.4

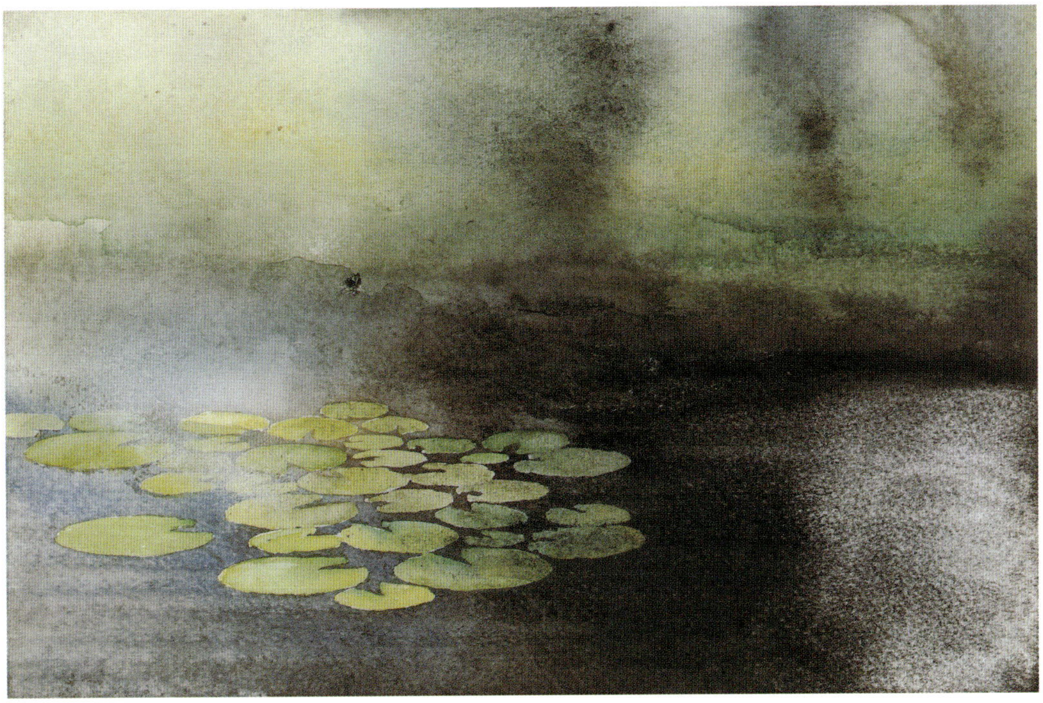

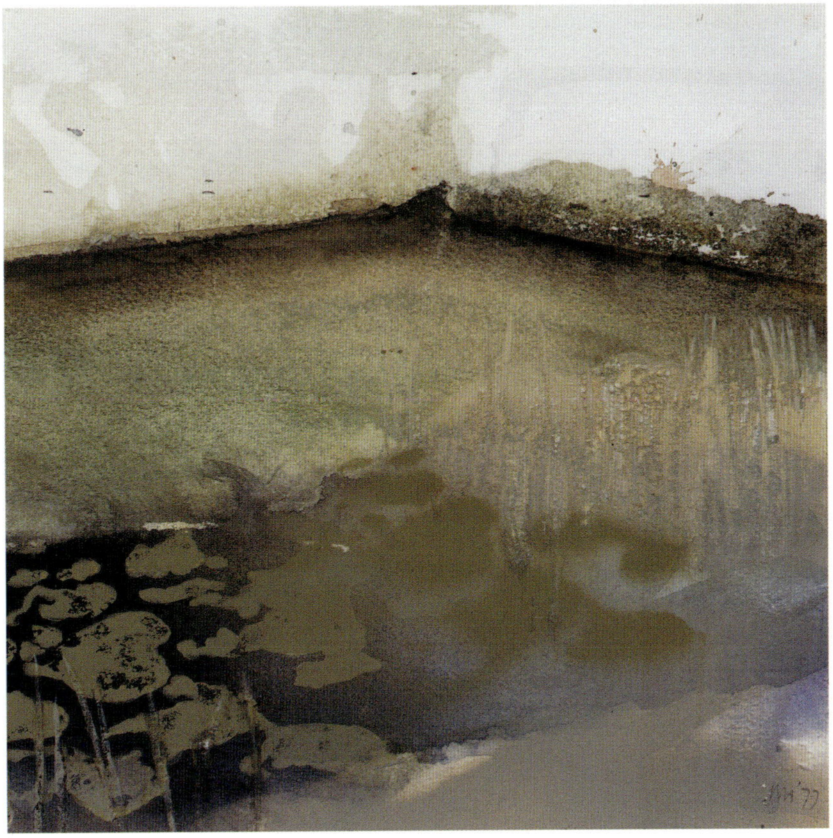

55
Early Summer: 'The Old River'
1977
Watercolour
15.2 x 22.6

53
A Pond: Spring
1977
Acrylic and watercolour on paper
22 x 22

52
The Sun Reflected in the River
1977
Acrylic on paper
32 x 22.9

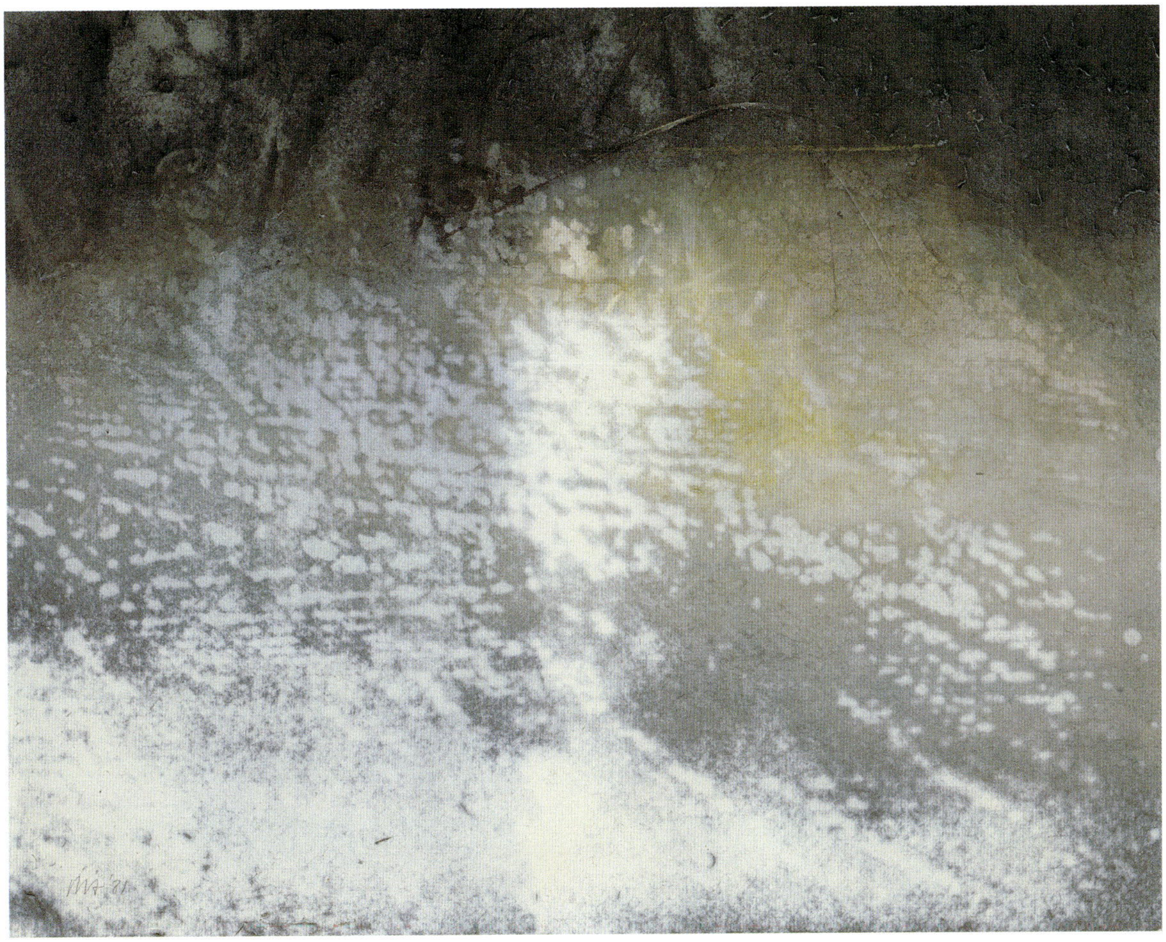

60
Angler: Geldeston, The Glittering River 2
1981
Watercolour
27.5 x 34

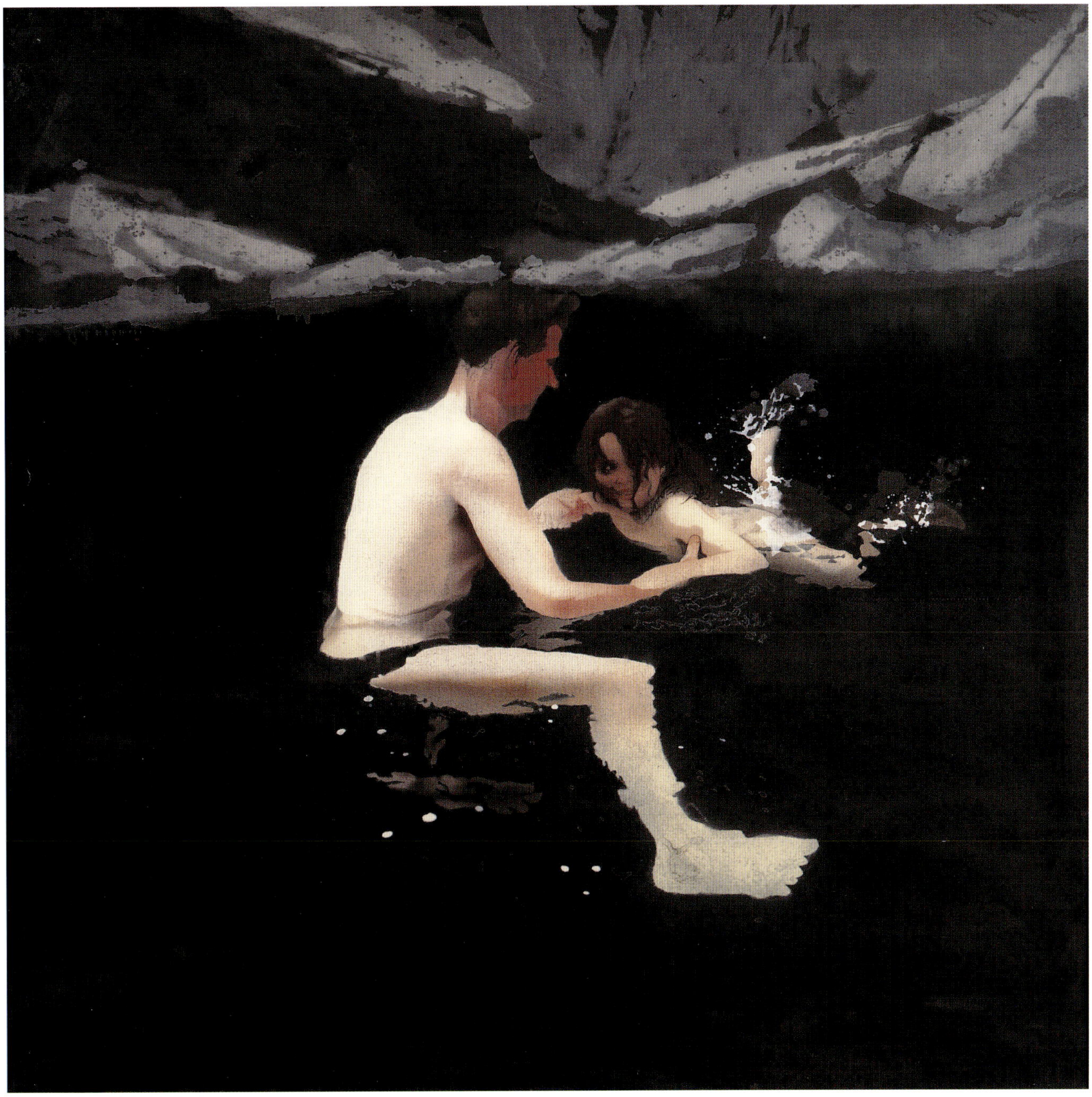

59
Melanie and Me Swimming
1978–9
Oil on canvas
182.9 x 182.9

holiday

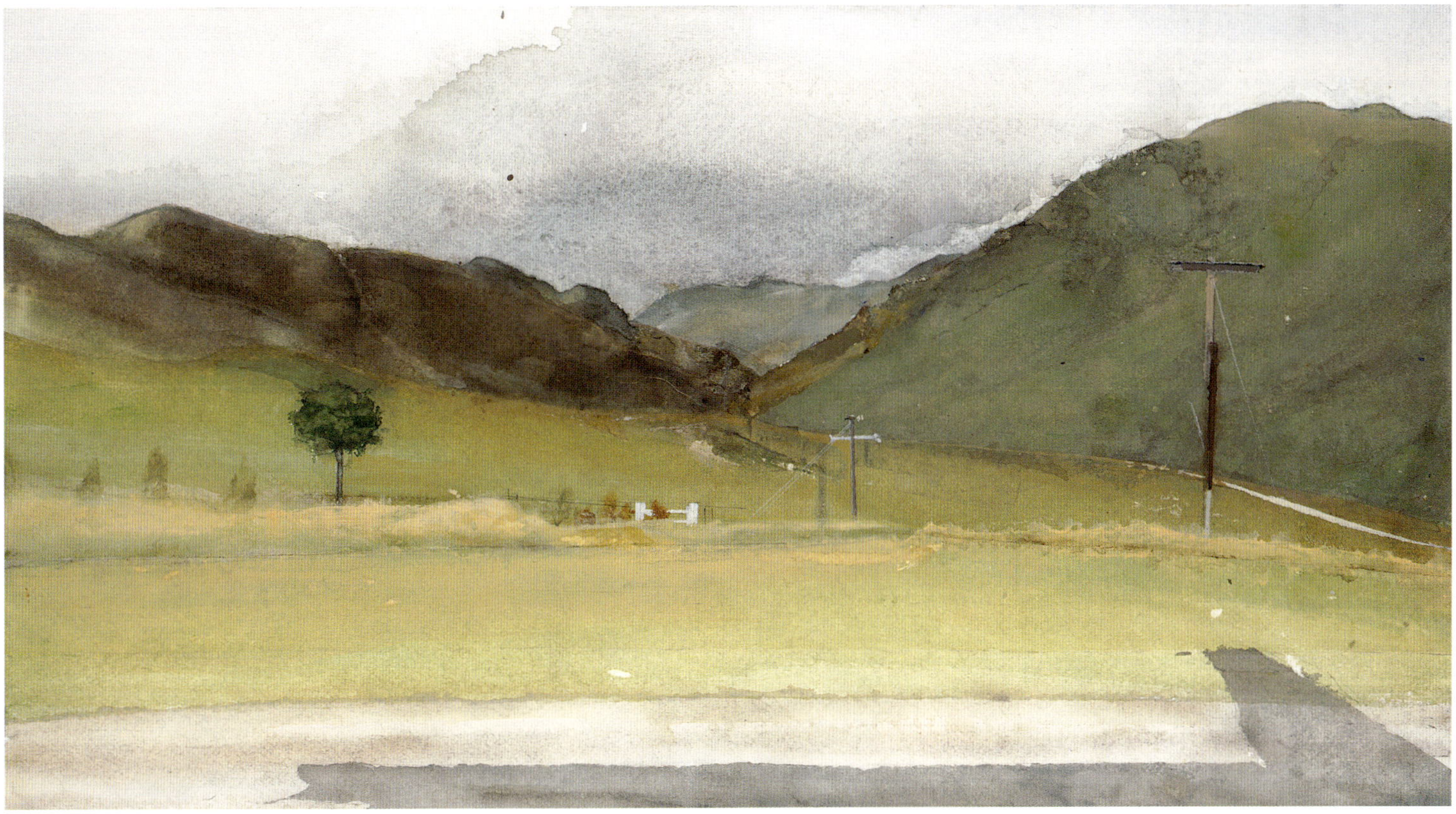

62
Glenartney: Sketch from the Harness Room
1975–6
Acrylic and pencil on paper
27.5 x 49

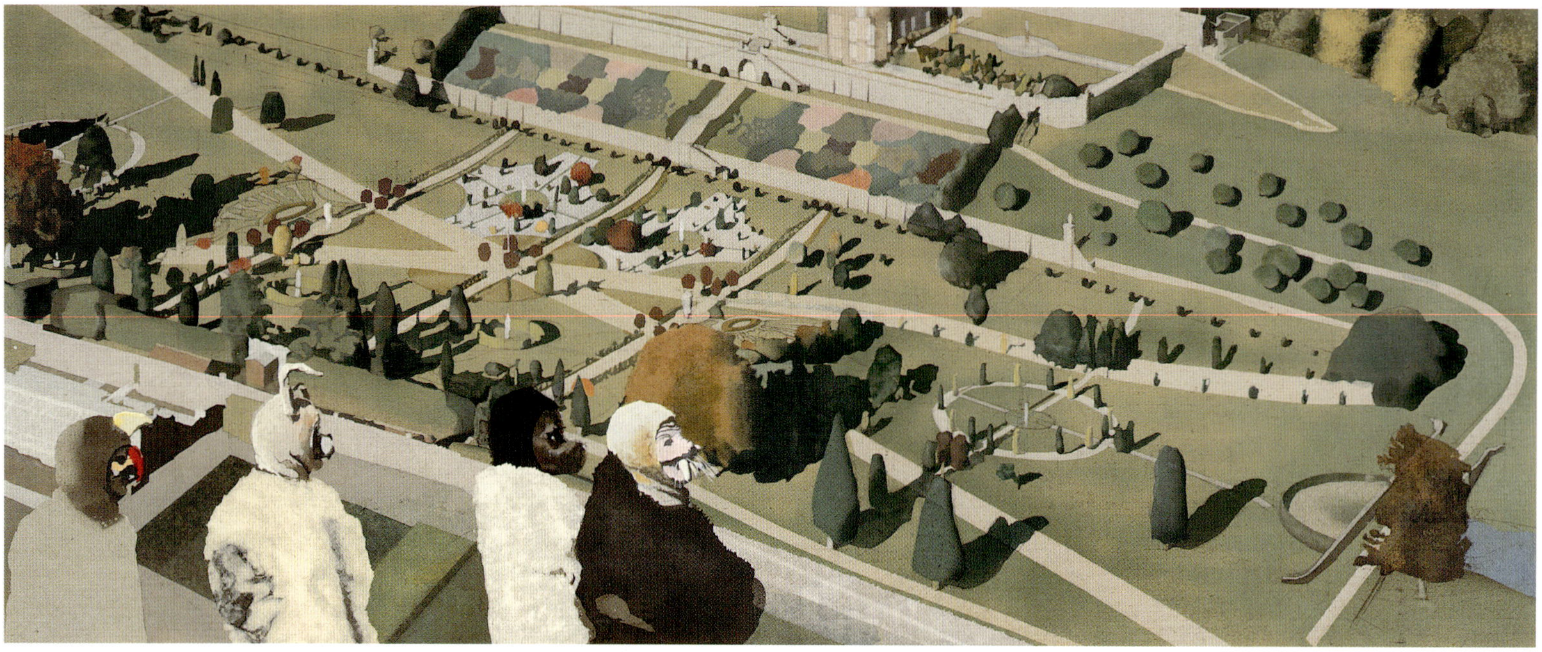

63
A Design: The Garden at Drummond from Higher Ground
1976
Oil and acrylic on canvas
132 x 313.6

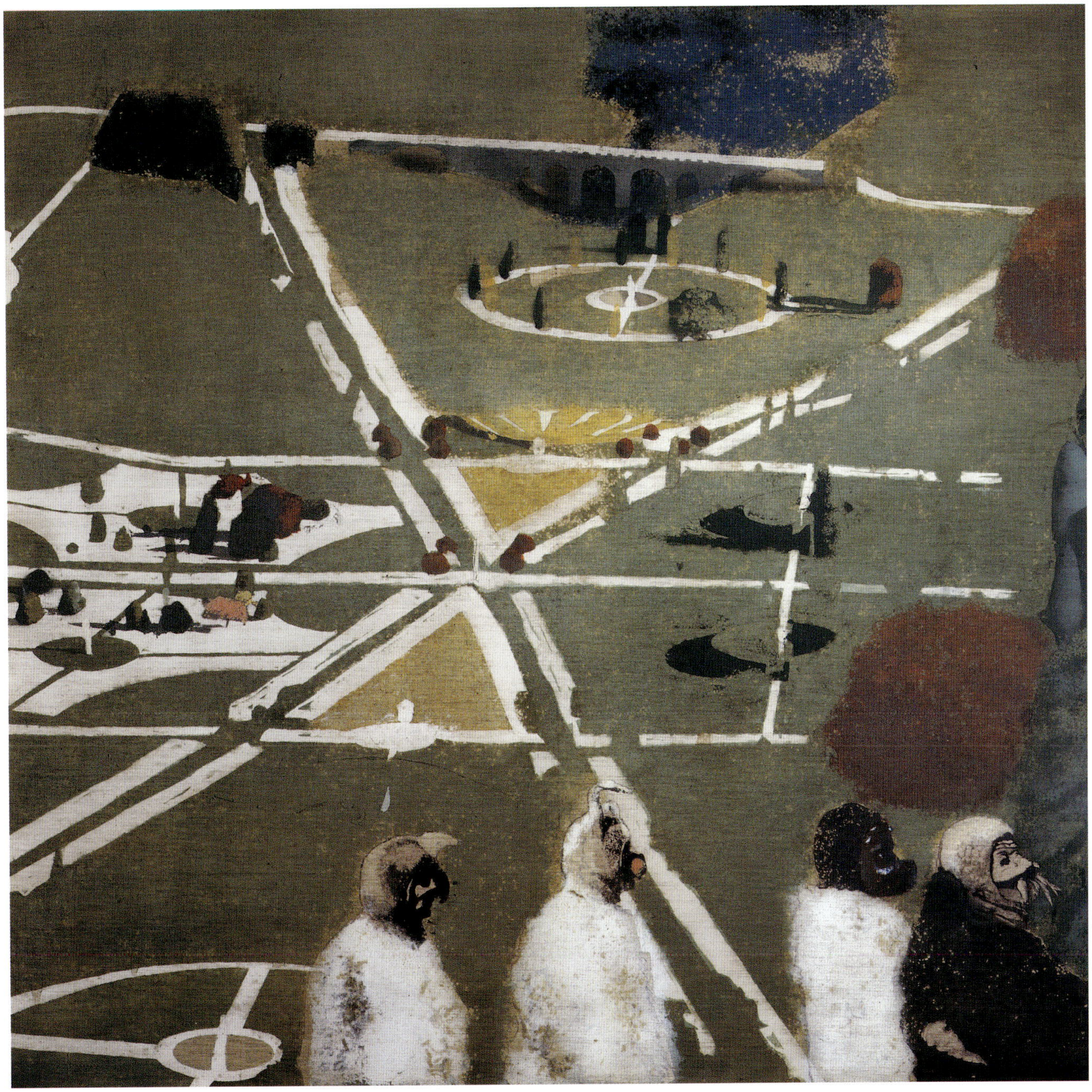

66
Drummond: the Multi-coloured Parterre; Fractions of the Grand Design
1977
Acrylic on canvas
183 x 183

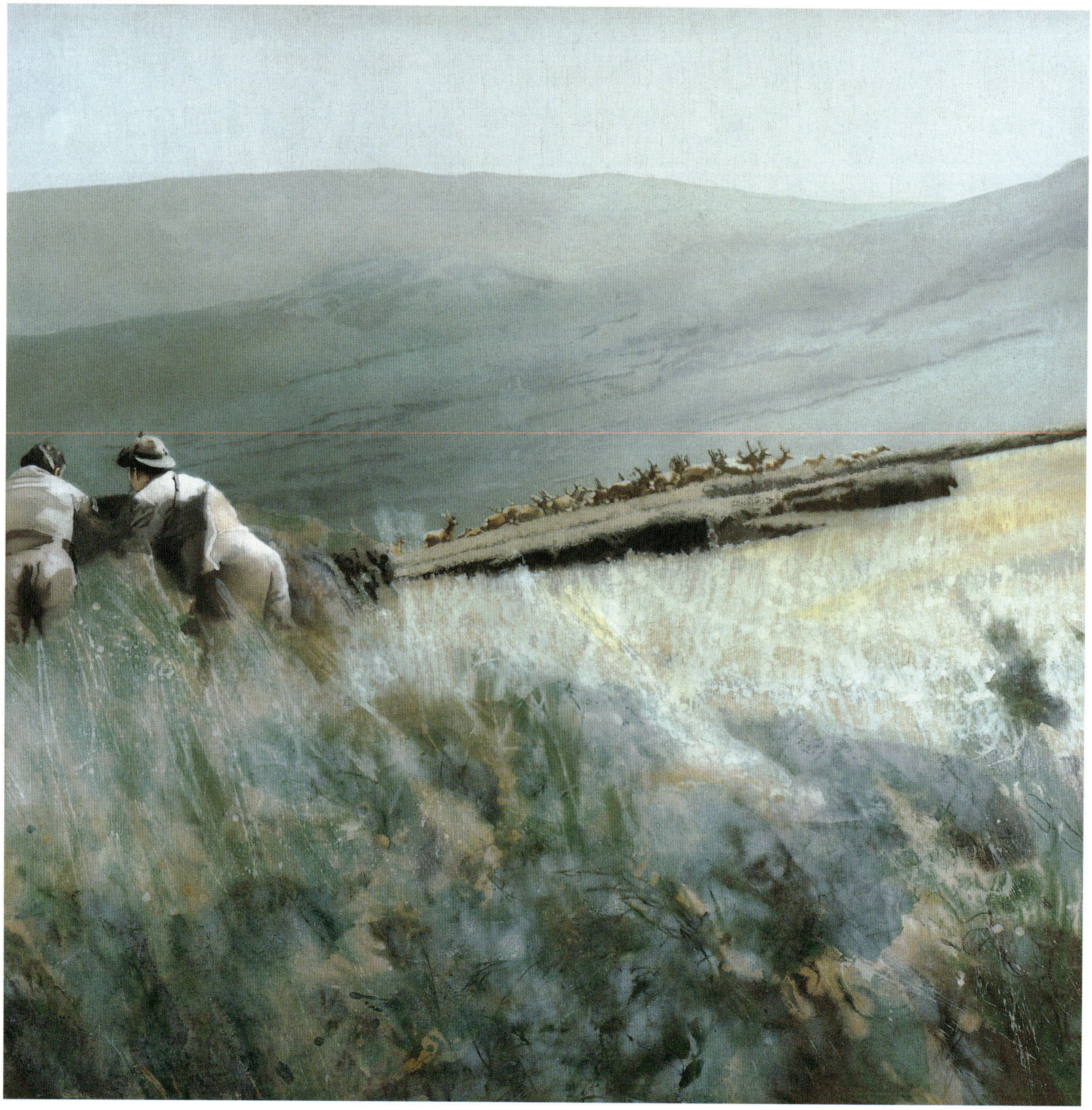

67
Peter's Day: 3rd Stalk
1979
Acrylic on canvas
183 x 183

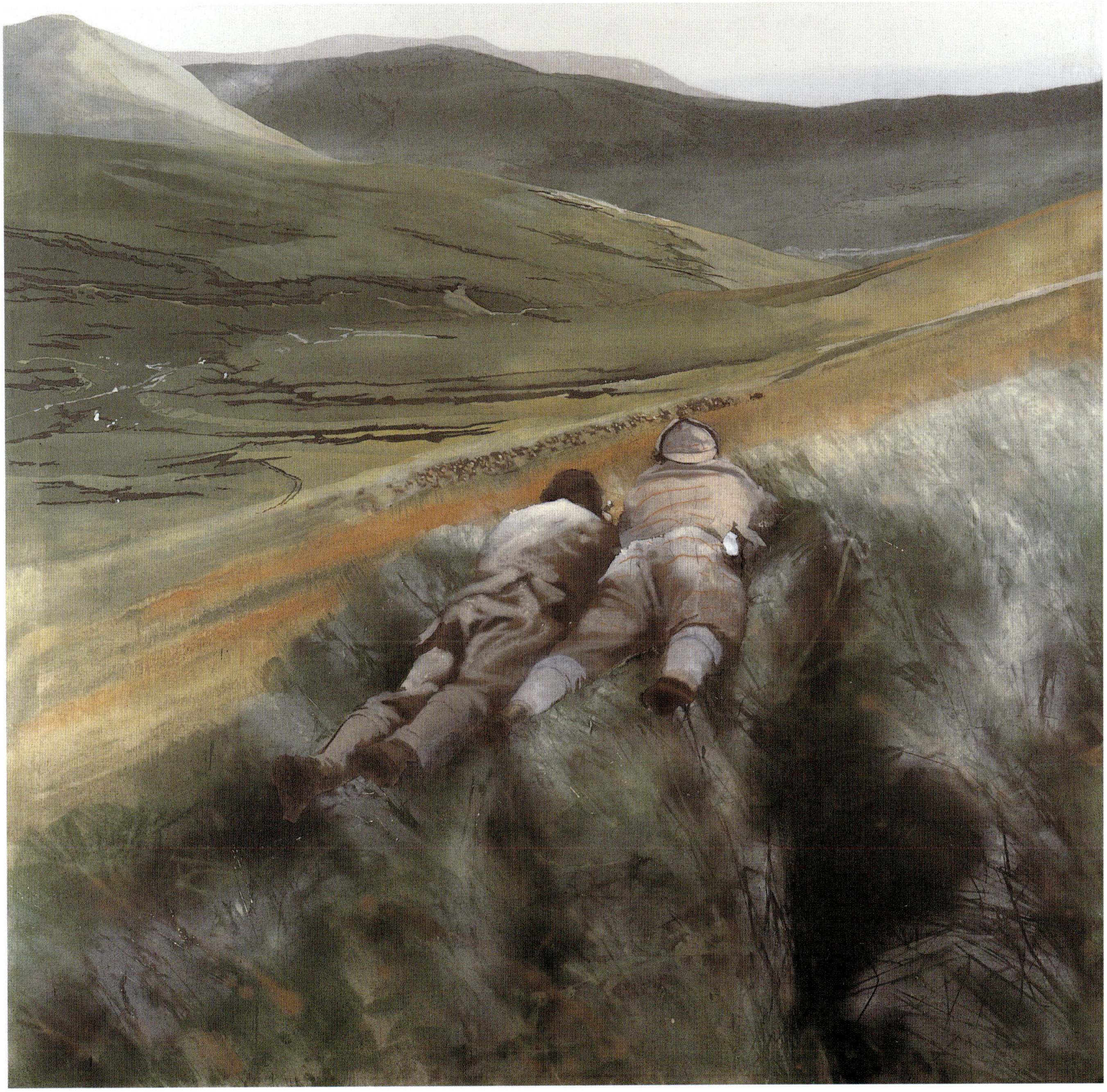

68
Alistair's Day: 2nd Stalk
1980
Acrylic on canvas
183 x 183

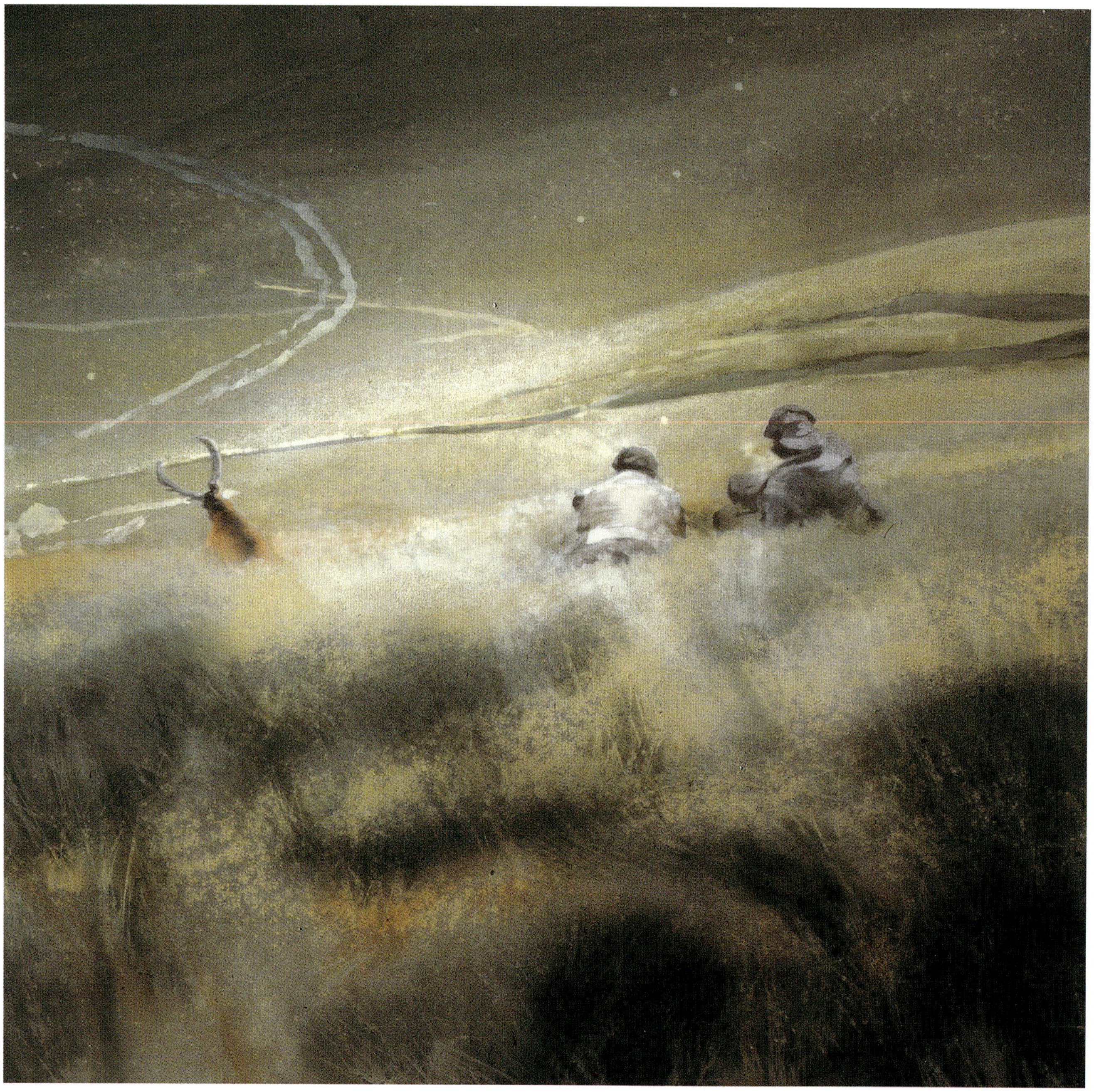

69
Alistair's Day: 2nd Shot
1980
Acrylic on canvas
127 x 127

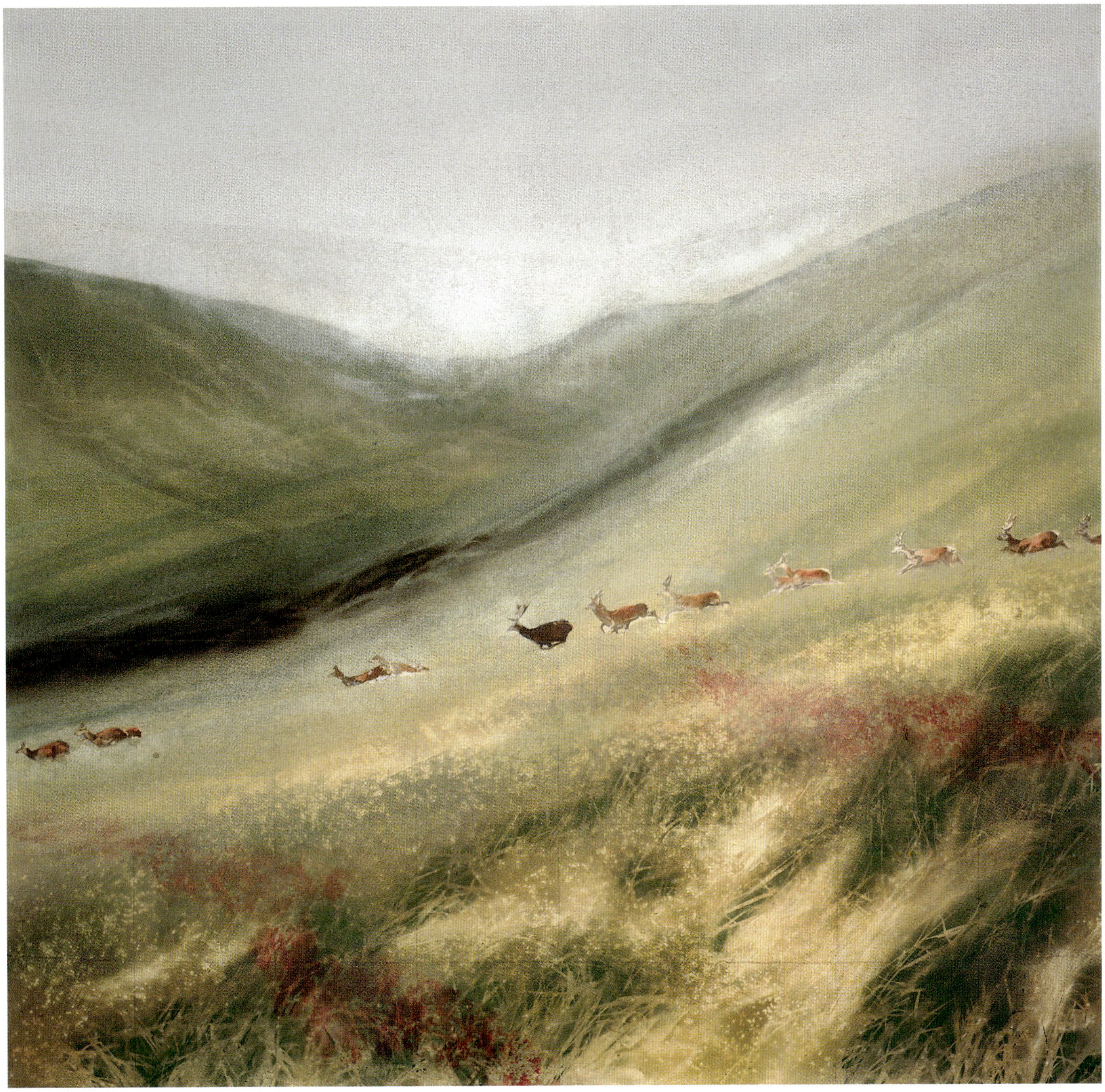

70
Running with the Deer
1980
Acrylic on canvas
127 x 127

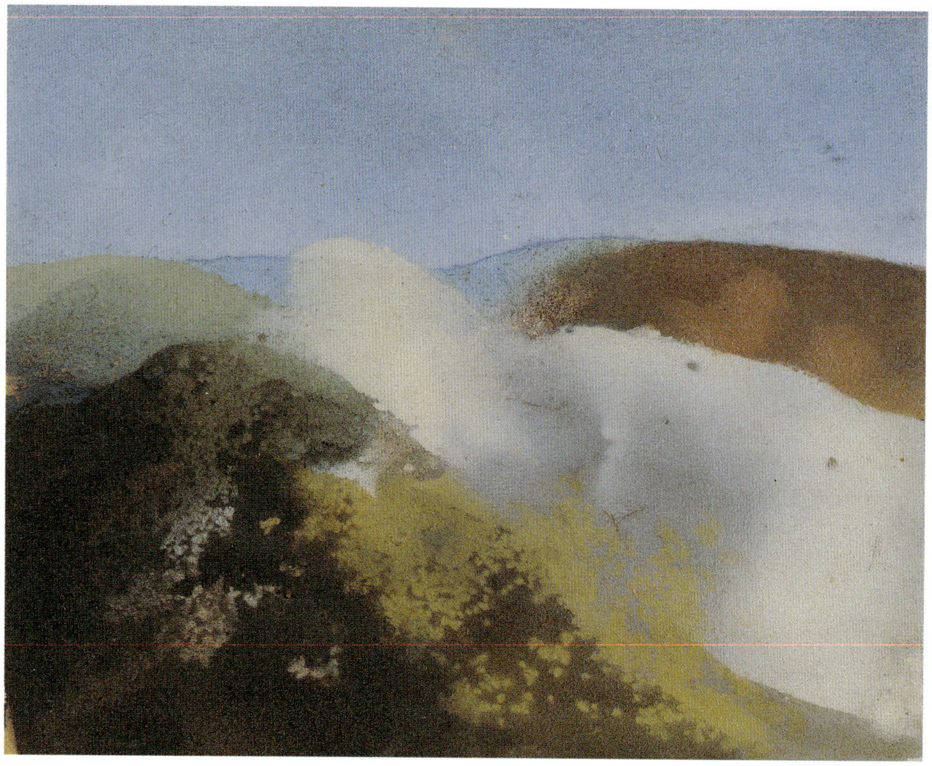

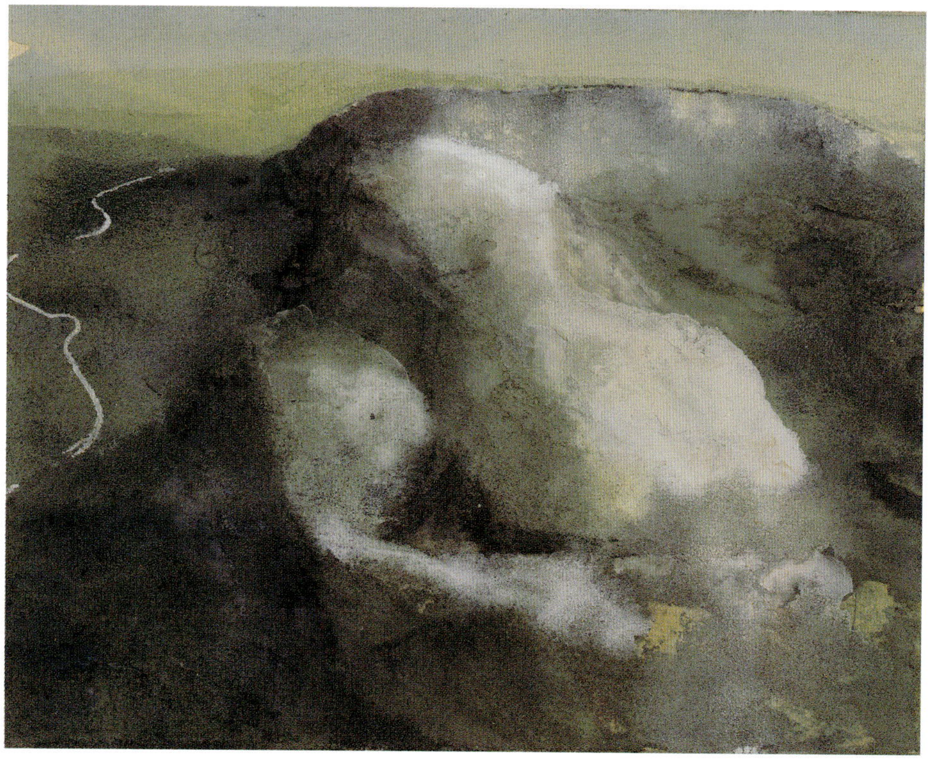

64
Glenartney: August 1976, about 6pm, Coire Fearna Beat, Straith a 'Ghlinne
1976
Acrylic on sandpaper
20 x 26

65
Early Morning in Hot Weather: Glenartney
1976–7
Acrylic on sandpaper
22.8 x 27.3

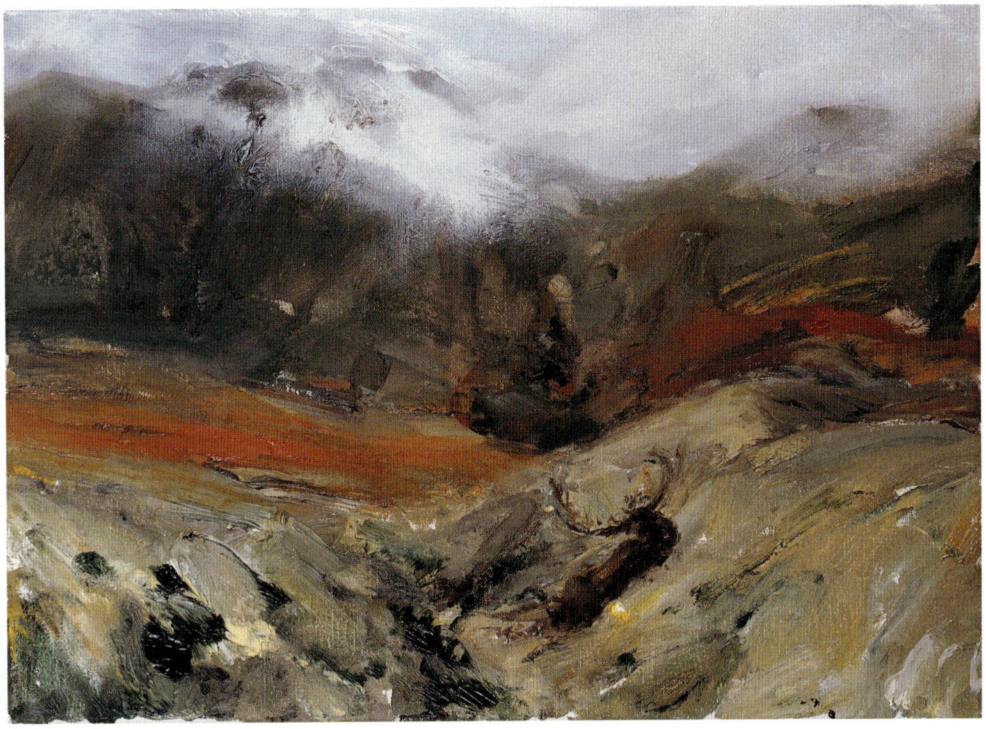

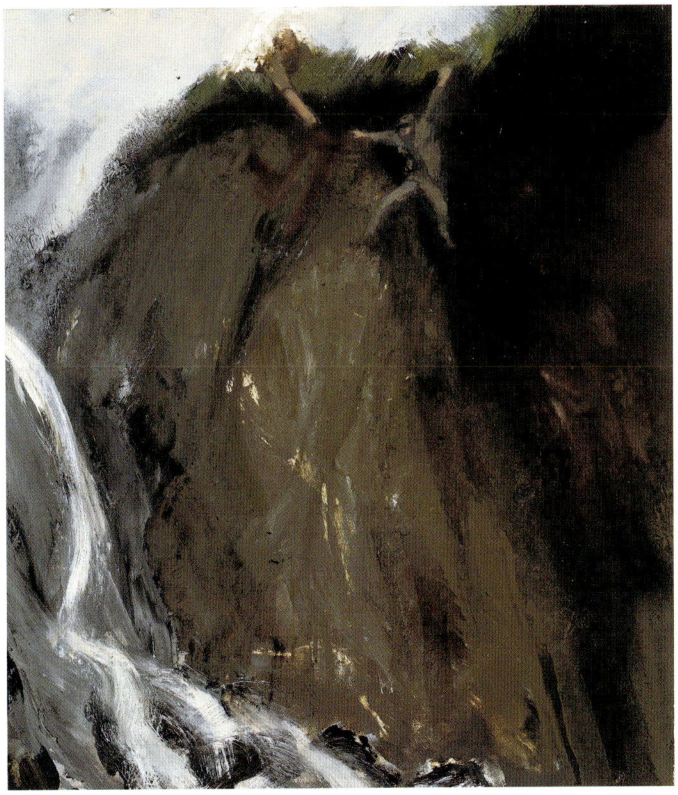

71
Glenartney, 19 October '89.
The Imperial
1989
Oil on canvas
30.5 x 40.6

76
Recollection of a Moment in October 1989 –
The Tobasnich Burn: Glenartney
1992
Oil on board
30.5 x 25.5

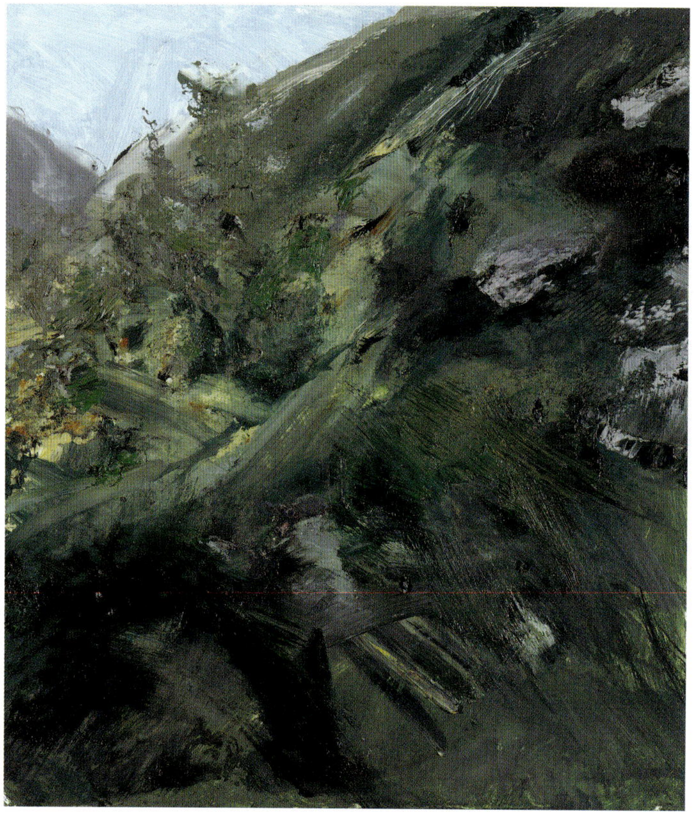

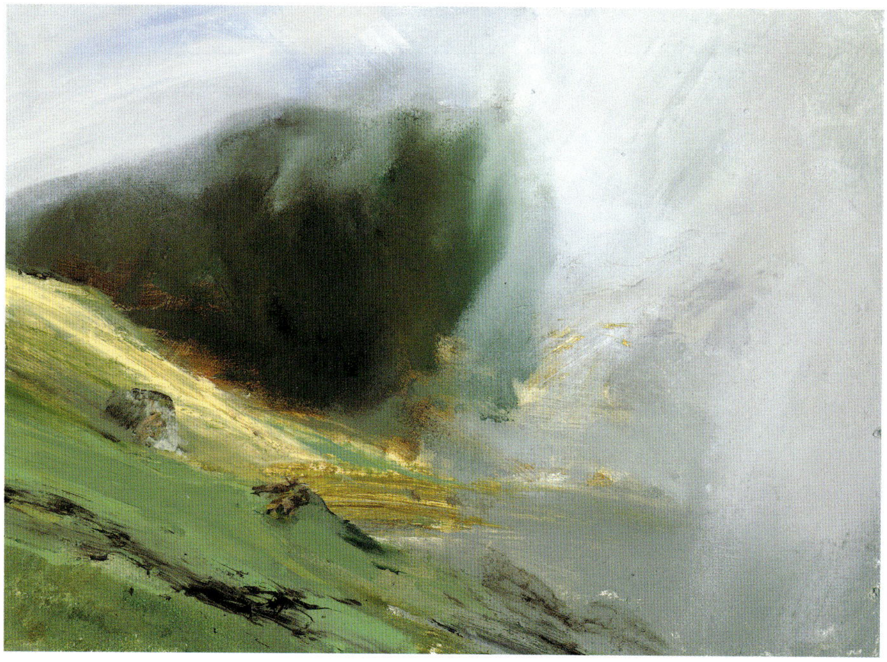

72
October '90, with Jock on Dundurn
1991
Oil on board
30.5 x 25.4

73
Mist Clearing, Glenartney
1991
Oil on board
26.7 x 35.5

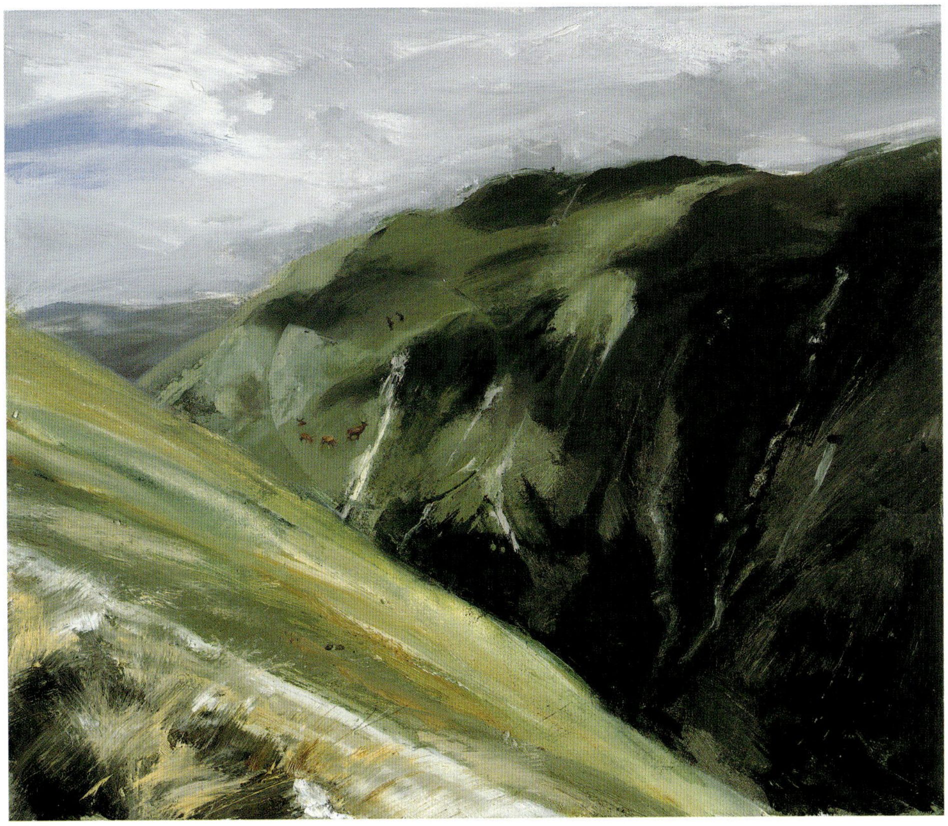

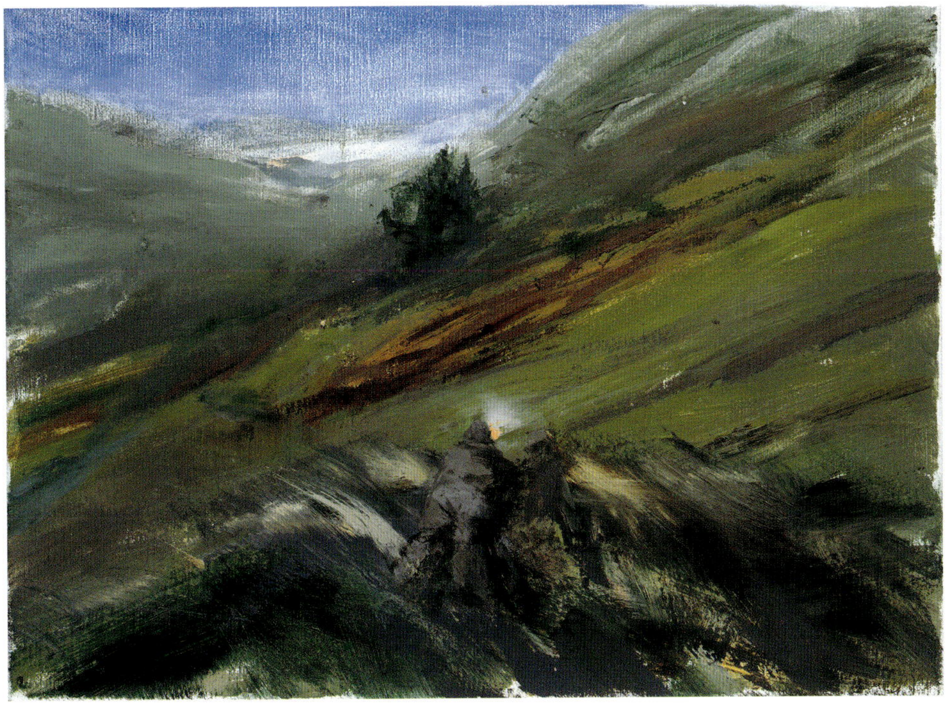

74
The Forest Beat through a Telescope
1991
Oil on canvas
35.5 x 40.6

75
'Give me the Rifle...!' 6.30pm, 17th October, Glenartney
1991
Oil on canvas
30.5 x 40.6

rock of ages cleft for me

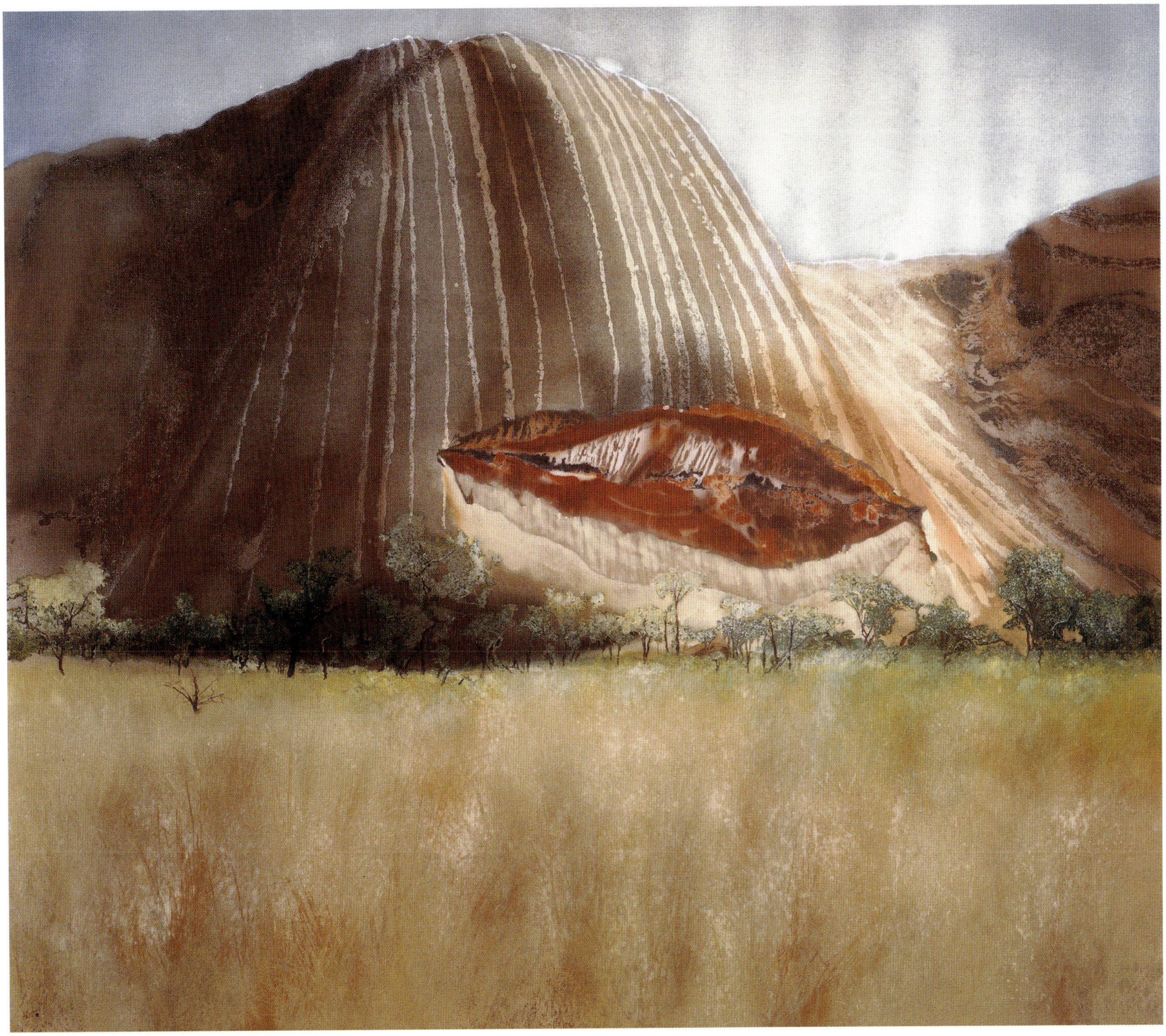

77
Laughter Uluru (Ayers Rock)/ The Cathedral I
1985
Acrylic on canvas
228.6 x 274.3

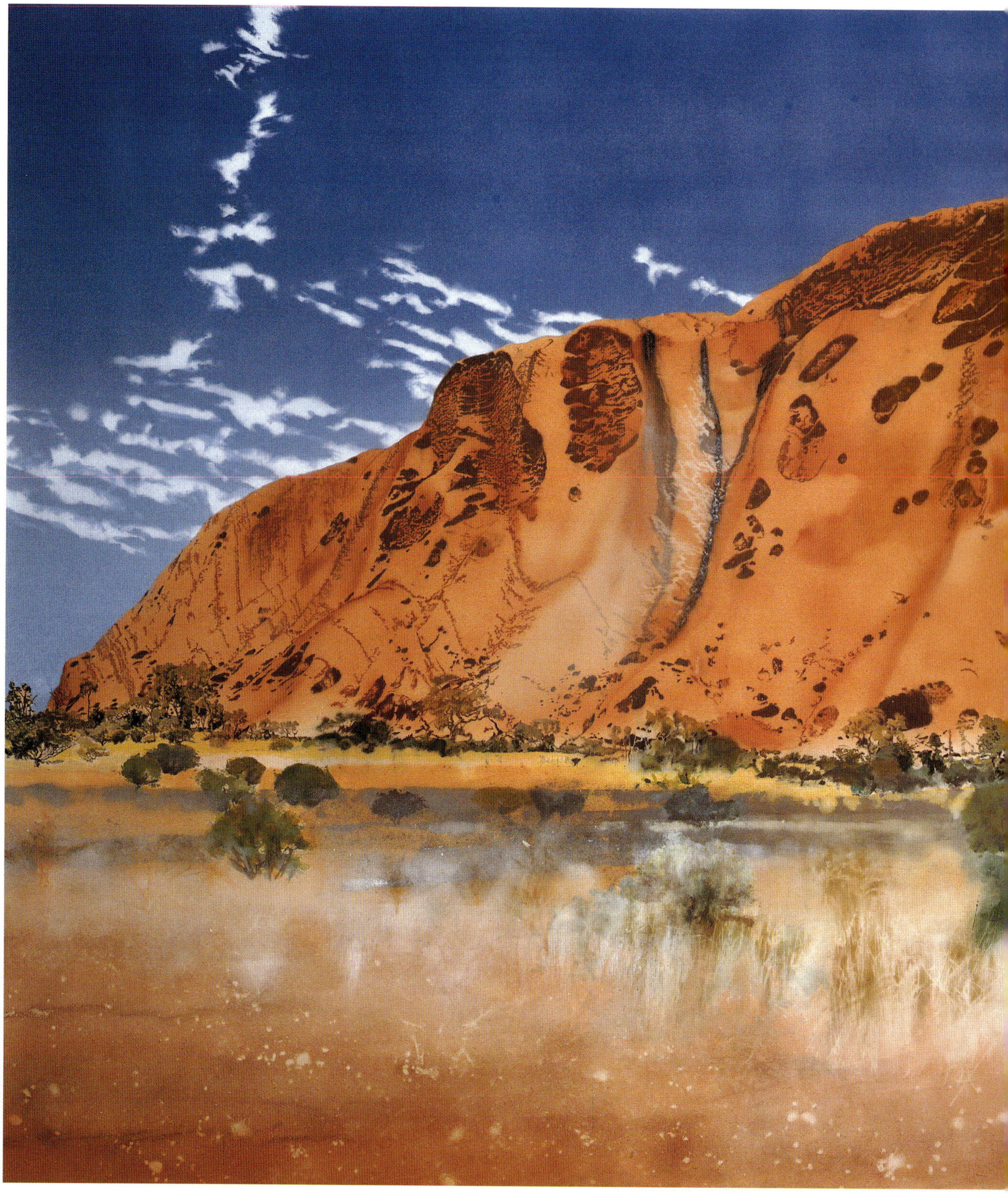

78
The Cathedral, The North East Face/Uluru (Ayers Rock)
1985
Acrylic on canvas
243.8 x 426.7

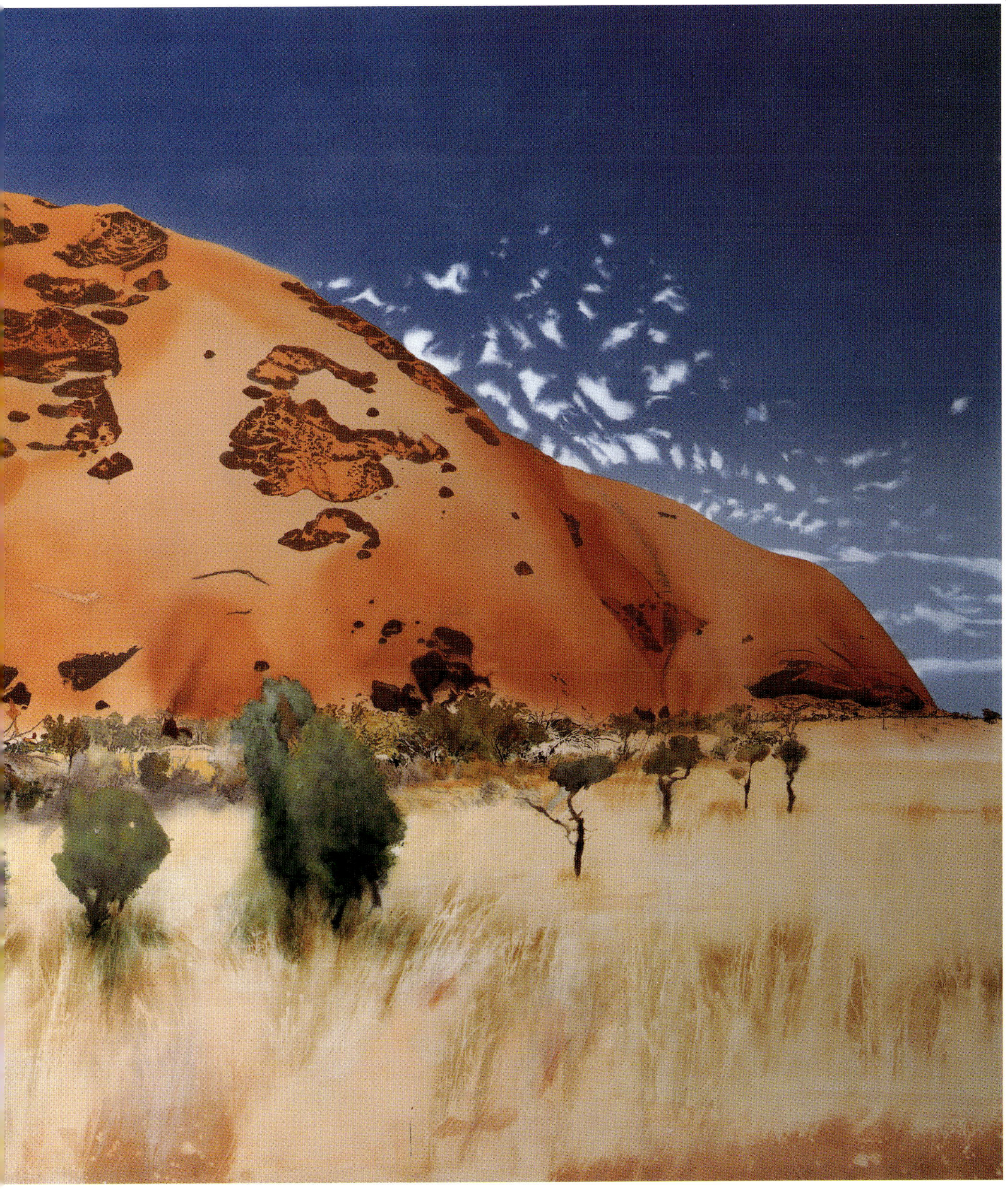

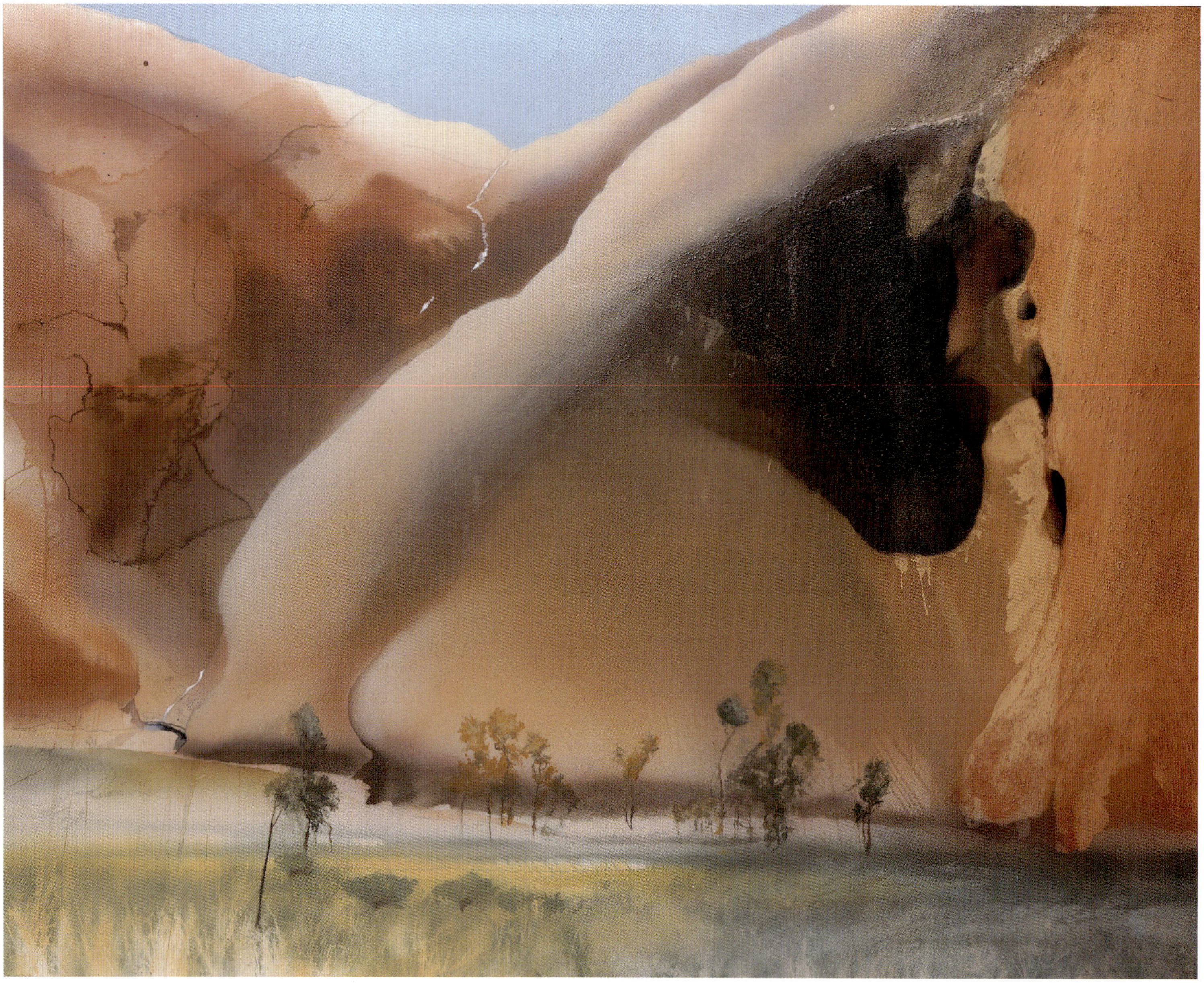

79
Permanent Water Mutidjula, by the Kunia massif (Maggie Springs, Ayers Rock)
1985–6
Acrylic on canvas
213.4 x 259.1

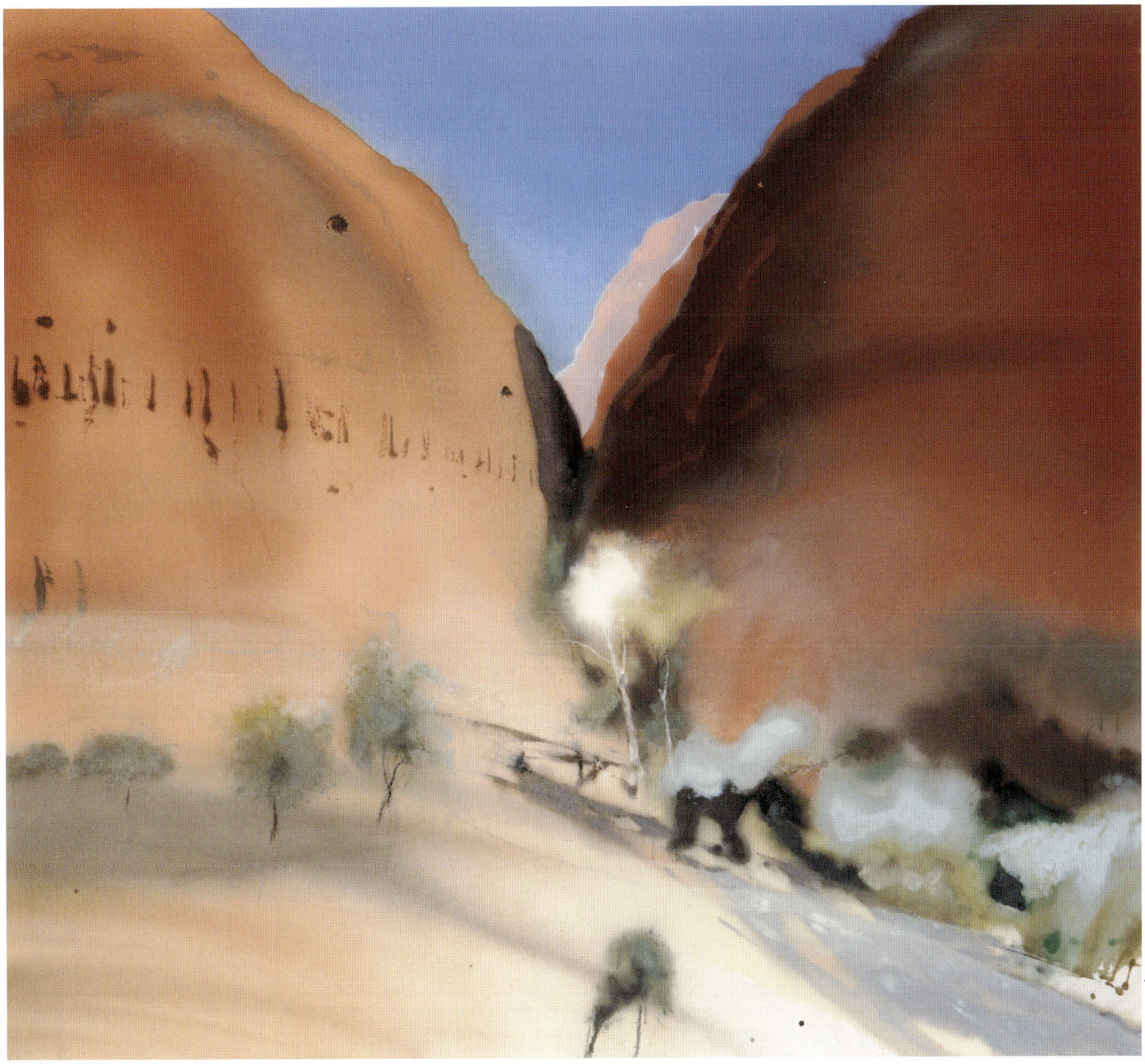

81
In Shade, Foot of Olga Gorge, Katatjuta (The Olgas)
1987
Acrylic on canvas
213.4 x 228.6

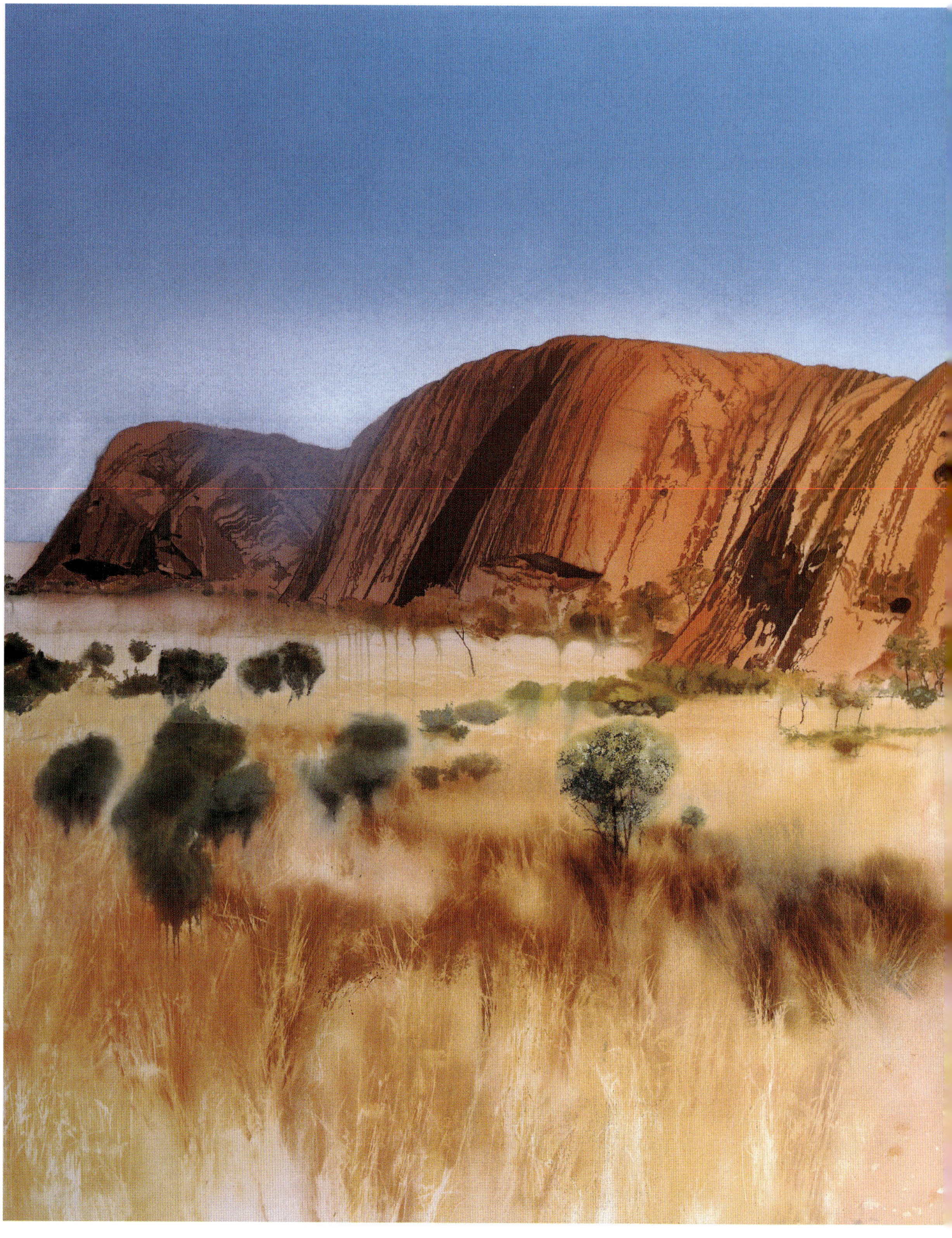

82
The Cathedral, The Southern Faces/Uluru (Ayers Rock)
1987
Acrylic on canvas
243.8 x 388.6

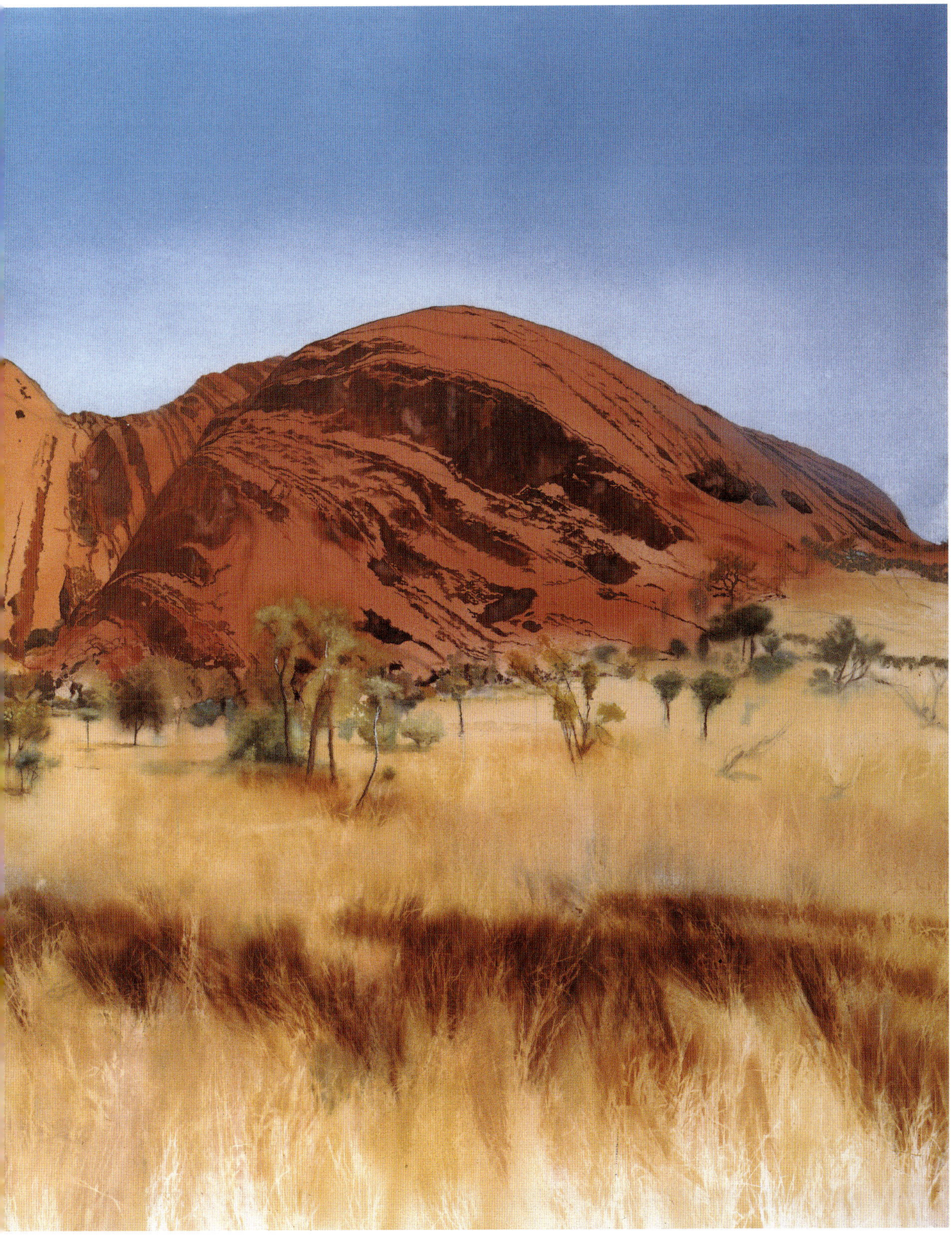

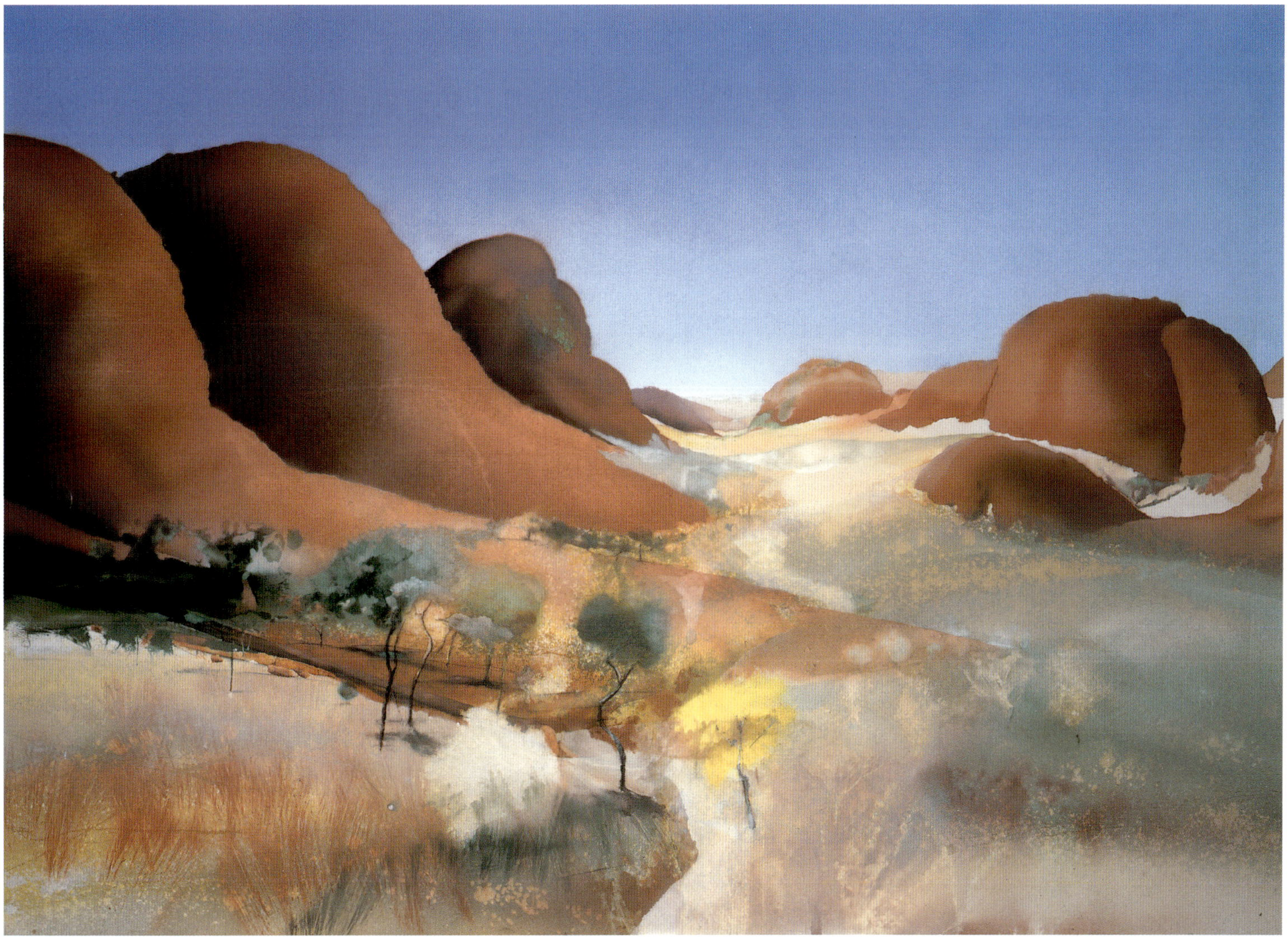

80
Valley of the Winds Katatjuta (The Olgas)
1985–6
Acrylic on canvas
213.4 x 289.6

british landscape

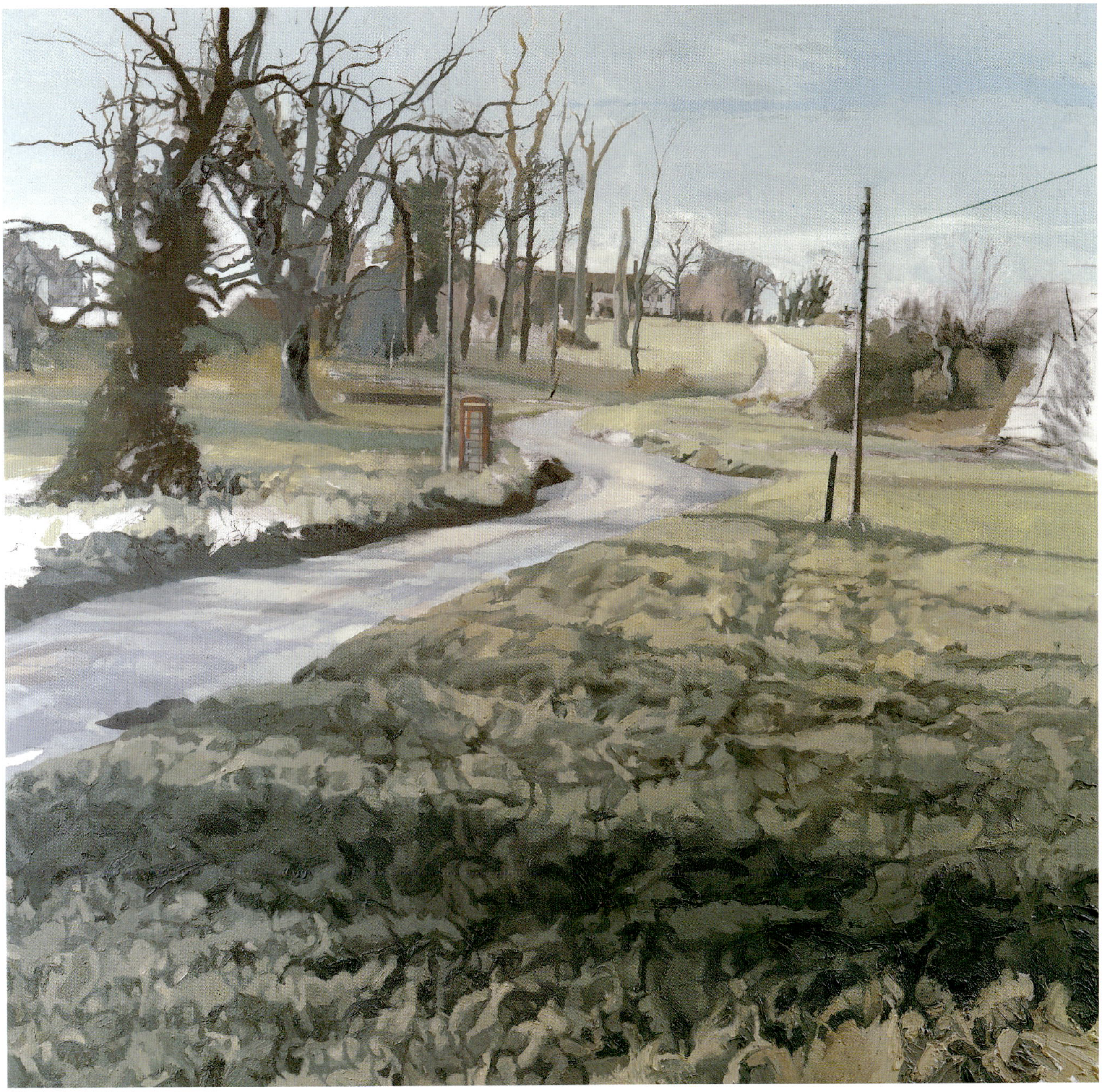

83
SAX A.D. 832 – Second Painting
1982
Oil and acrylic on canvas
152.4 x 152.4

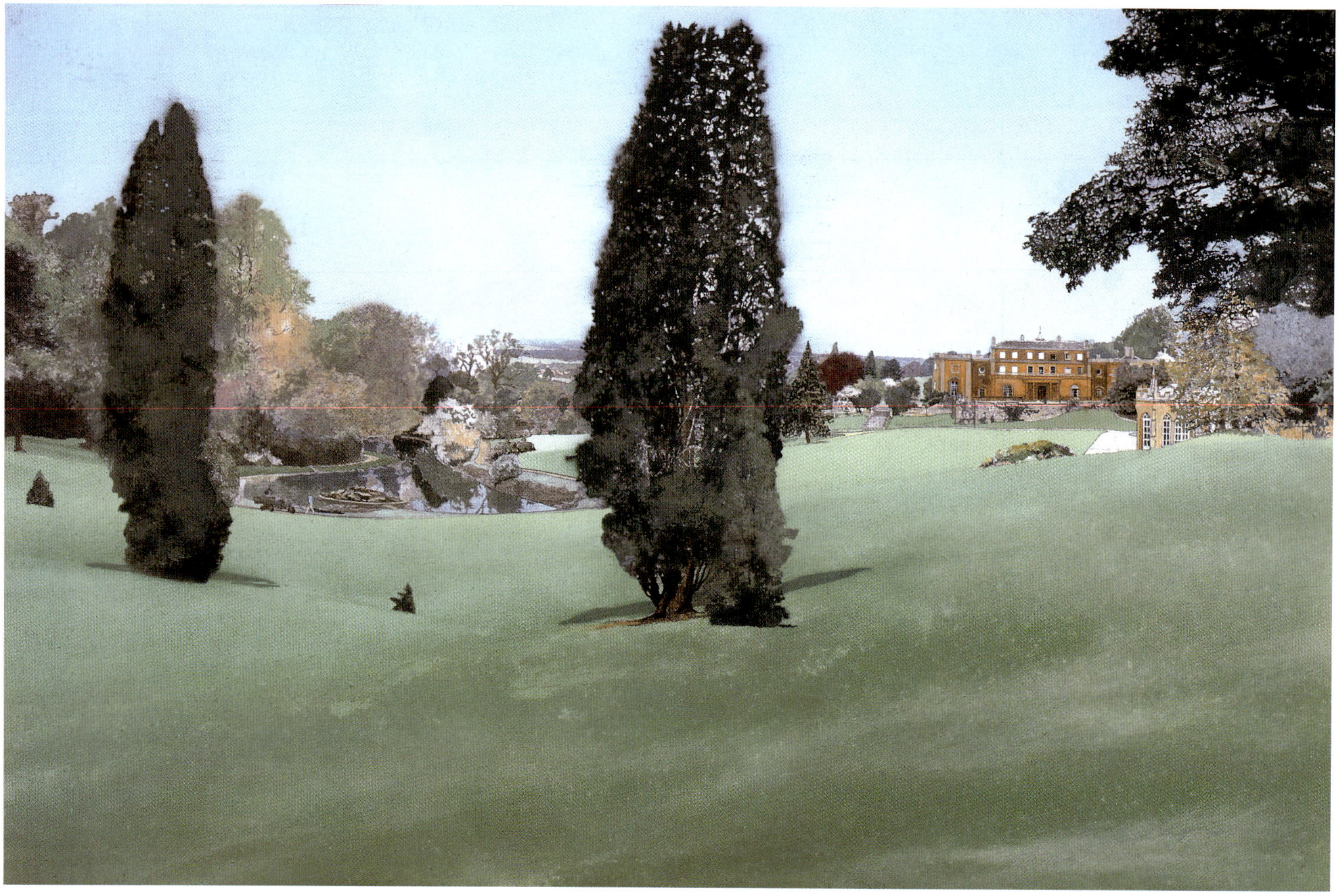

84
Daylesford
1983–4
Oil on canvas
122 x 183

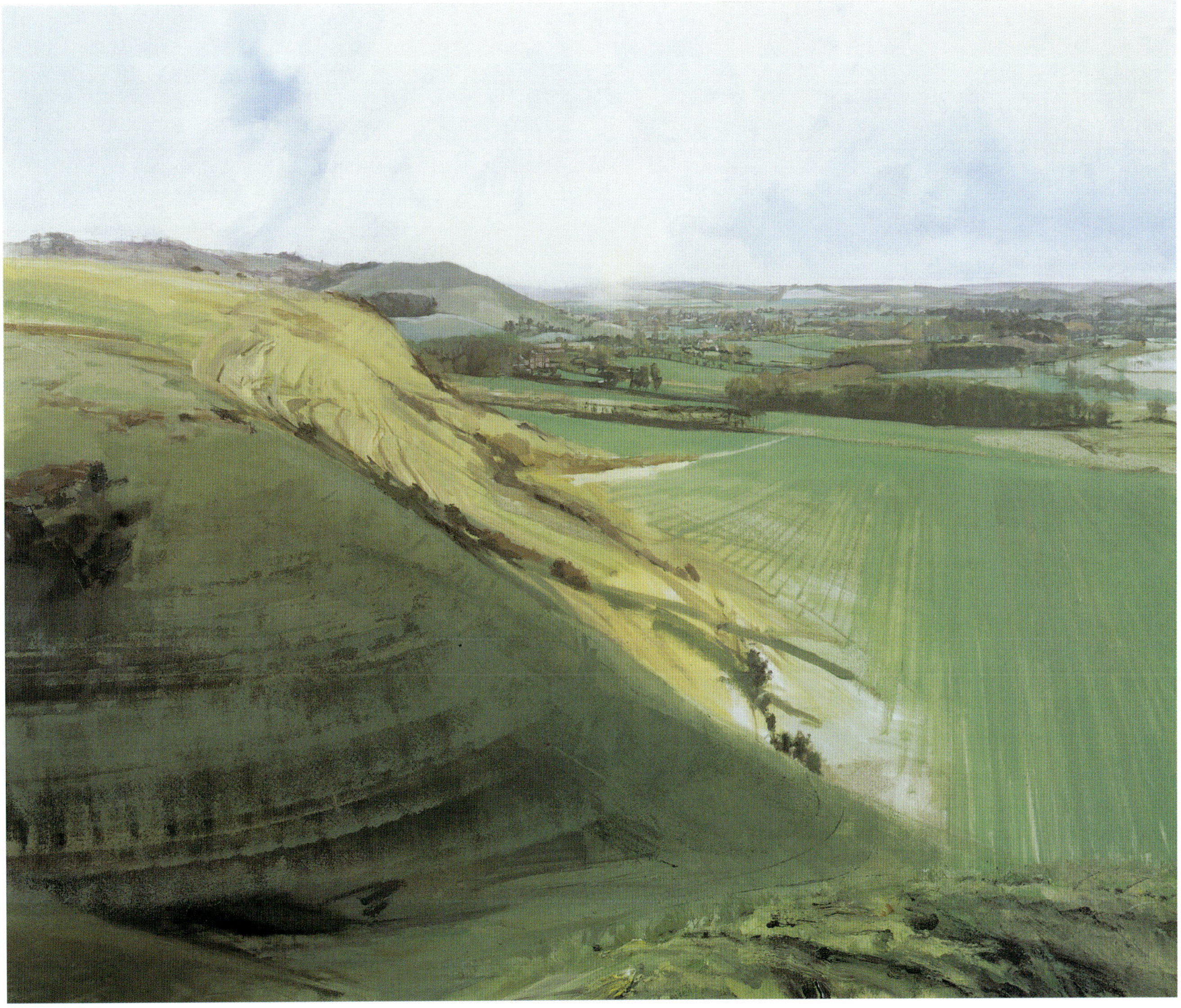

85
Oare, the Vale of Pewsey
1989–91
Oil on canvas
182.9 x 212.1

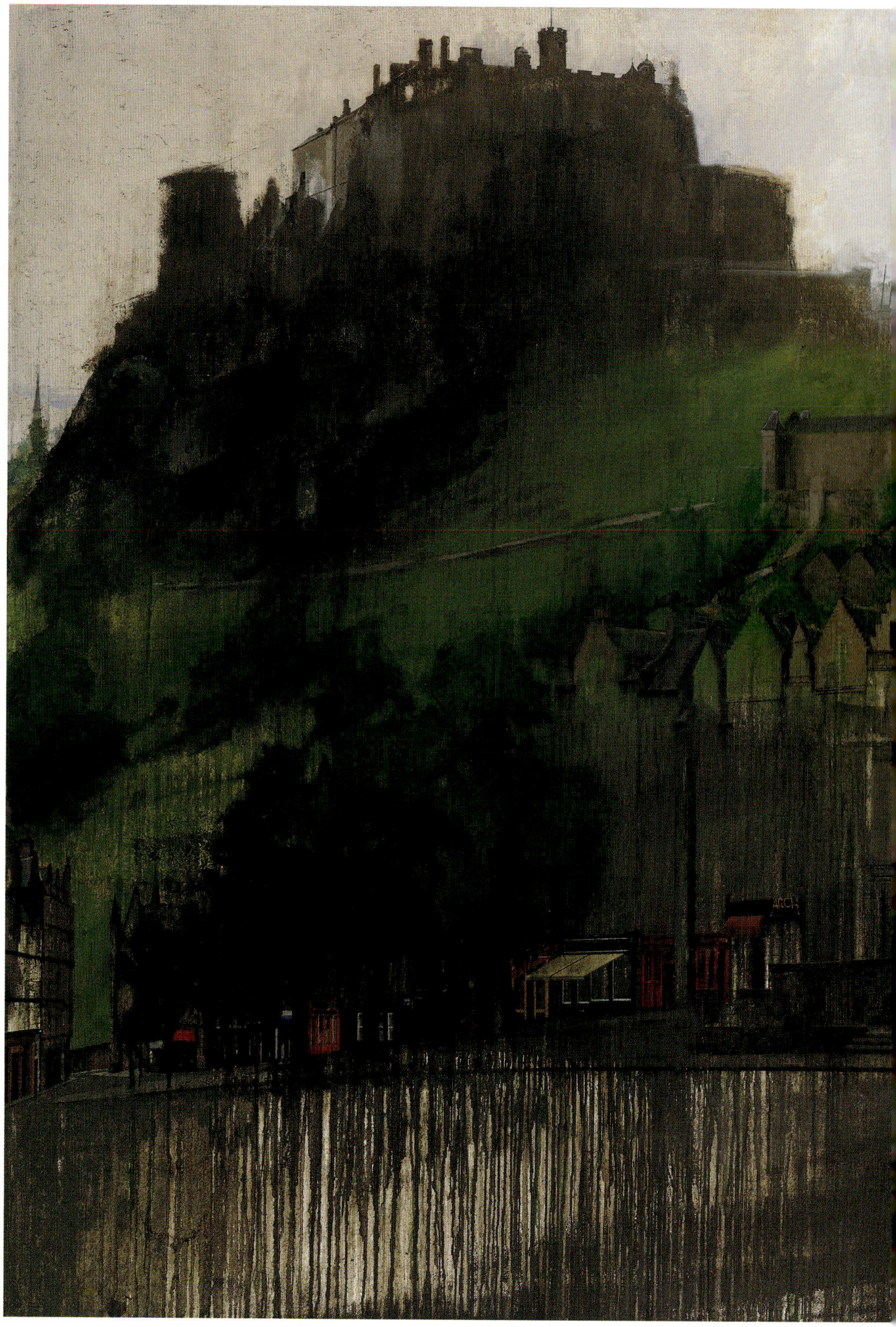

87
Edinburgh (Old Town)
1990–3
Oil on canvas
183 x 274.3

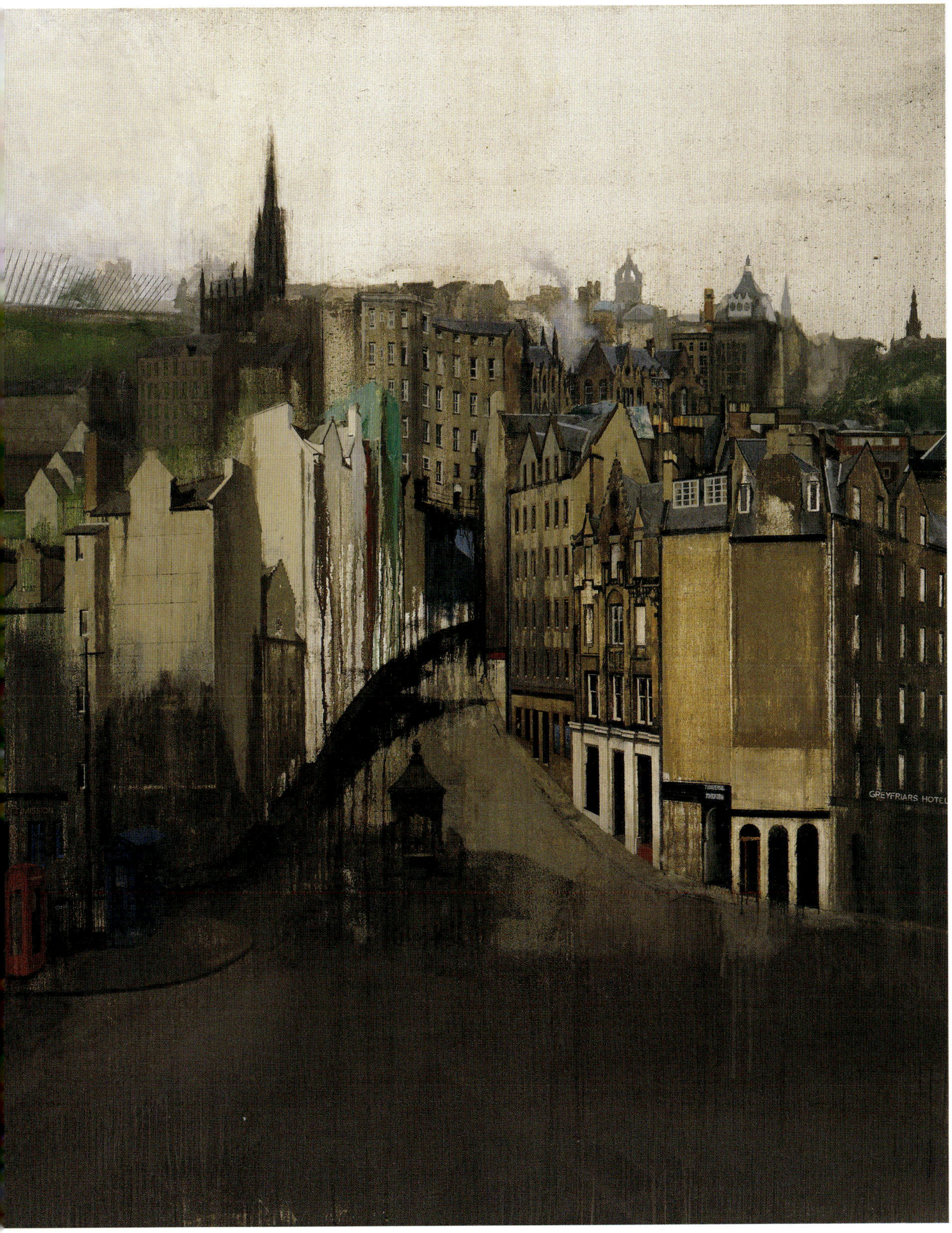
GREYFRIARS HOTEL

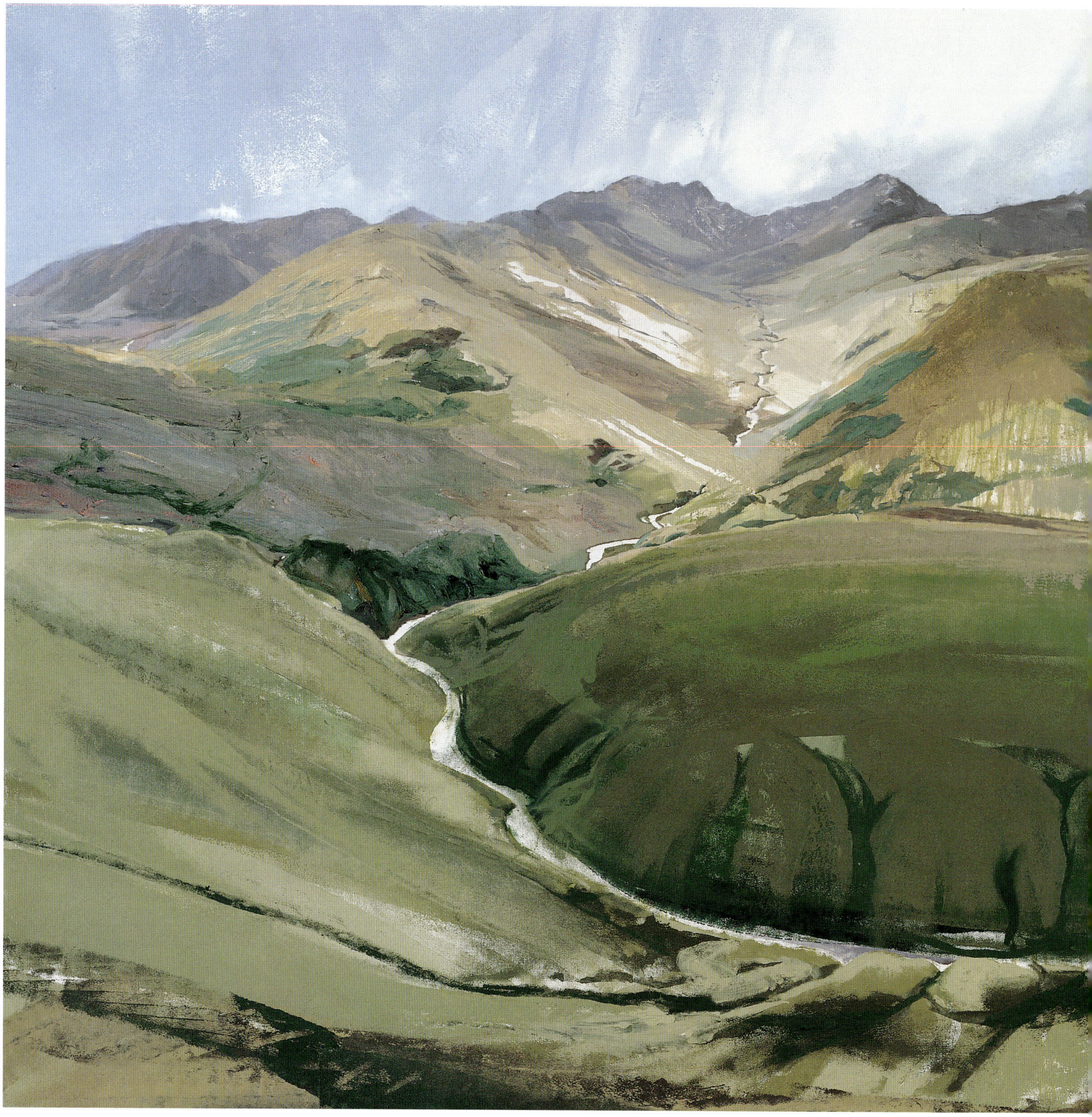

86
A View from Uamh Mhor
1990–1
Oil on canvas
177.8 x 355.6

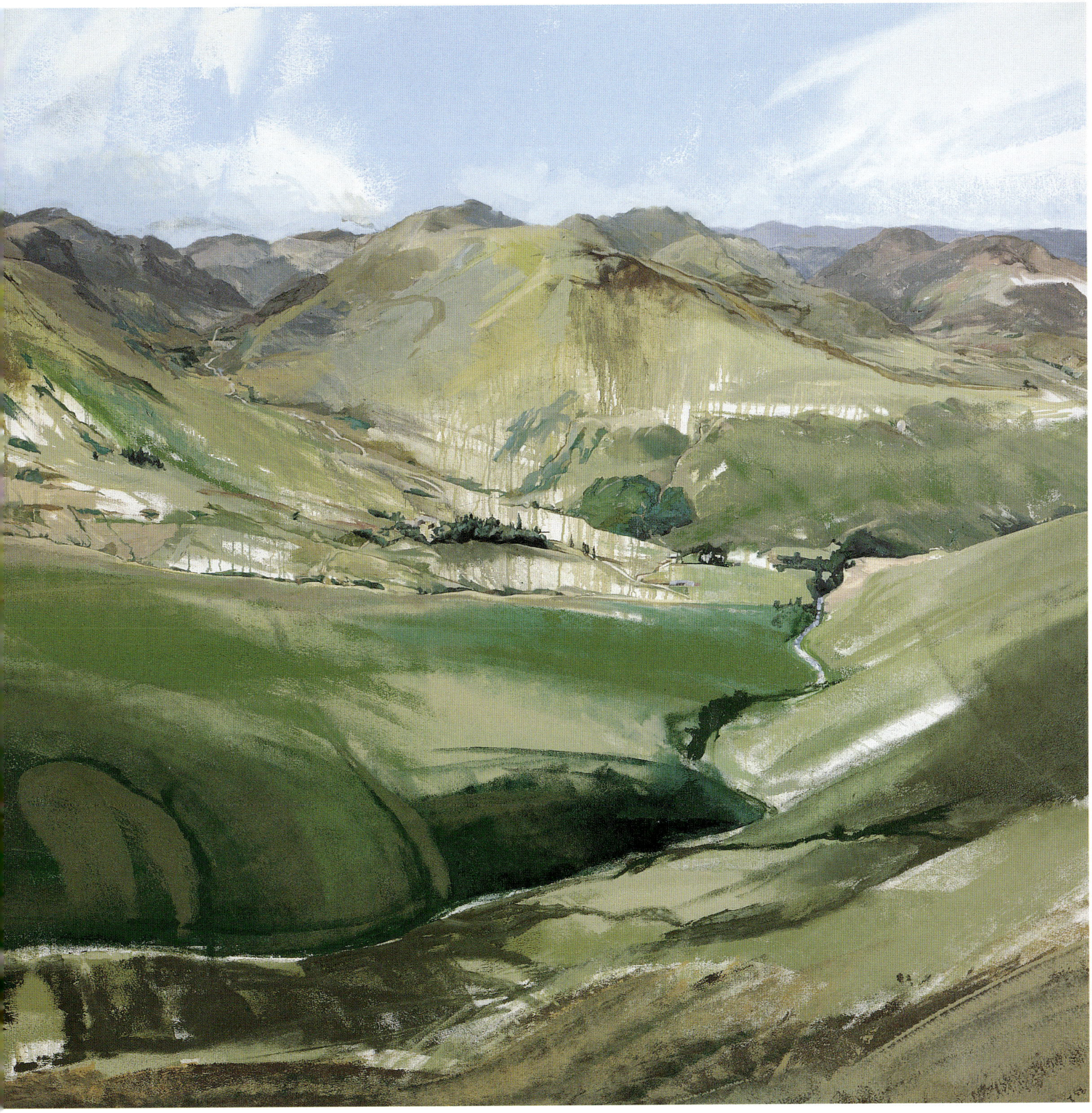

late works

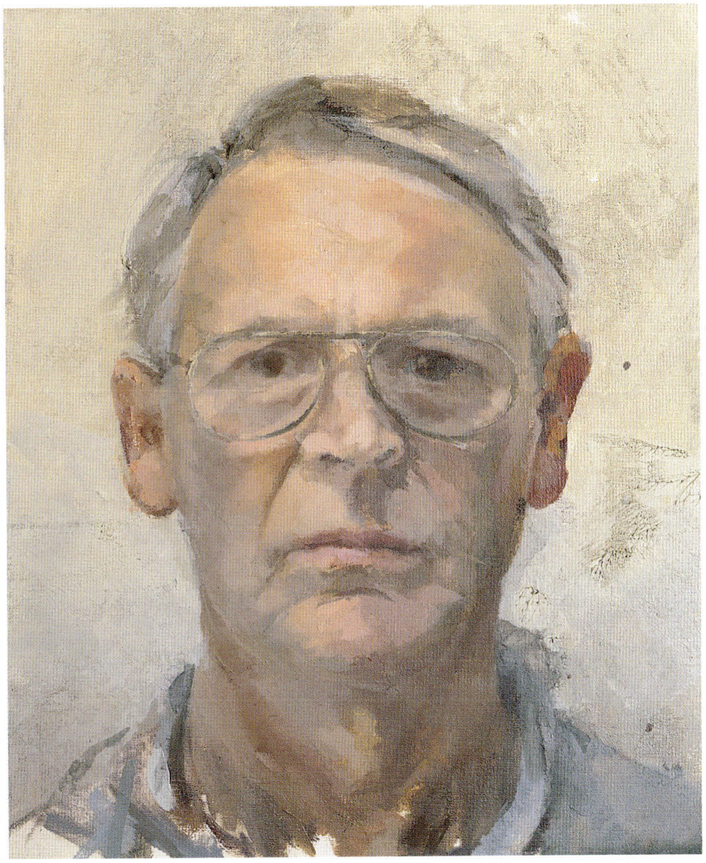

88
Self-Portrait
1988
Oil on board
25 x 20.3

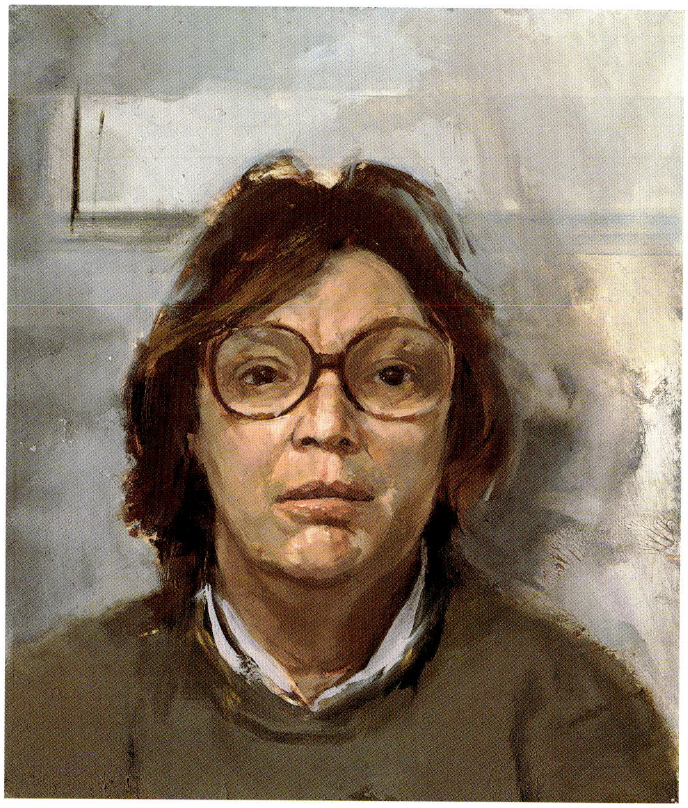

89
Portrait of June
1992
Oil on board
30.5 x 25.5

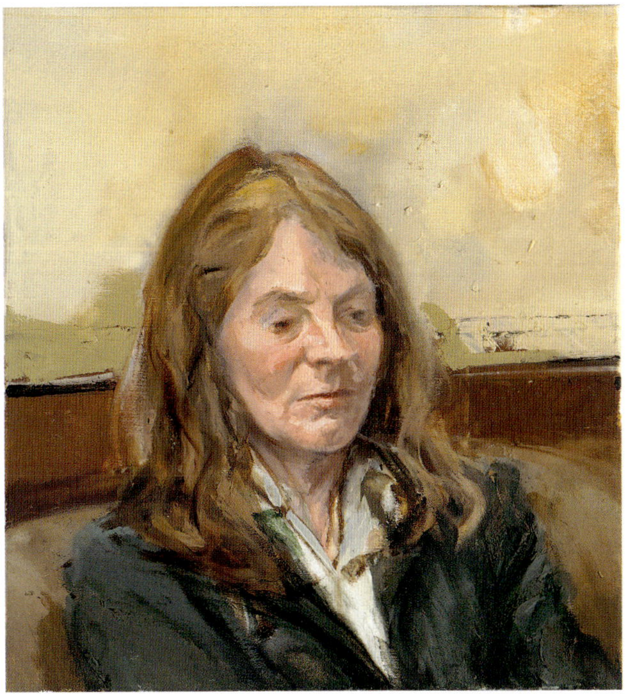

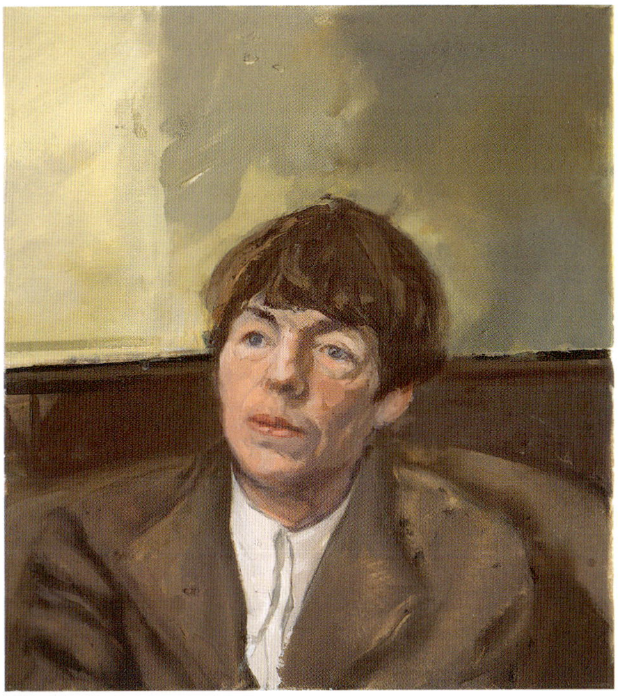

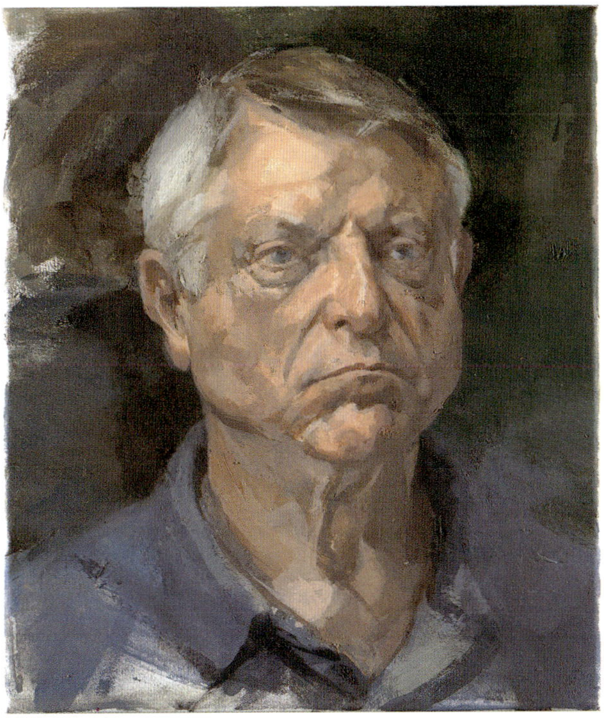

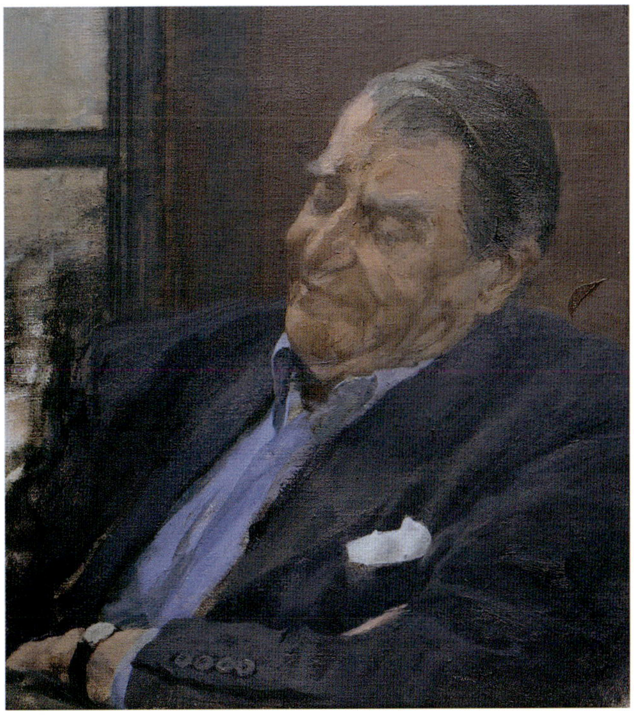

90
Portrait of Jane Willoughby
1989–91
Oil on canvas, 40.7 x 35.6

91
Portrait of Serena
1989–91
Oil on canvas, 40.7 x 35.6

93
Portrait of Colin St John Wilson
1993–5
Oil on canvas, 30.5 x 25.5

92
Portrait of David Astor
1993
Oil on canvas, 52 x 47

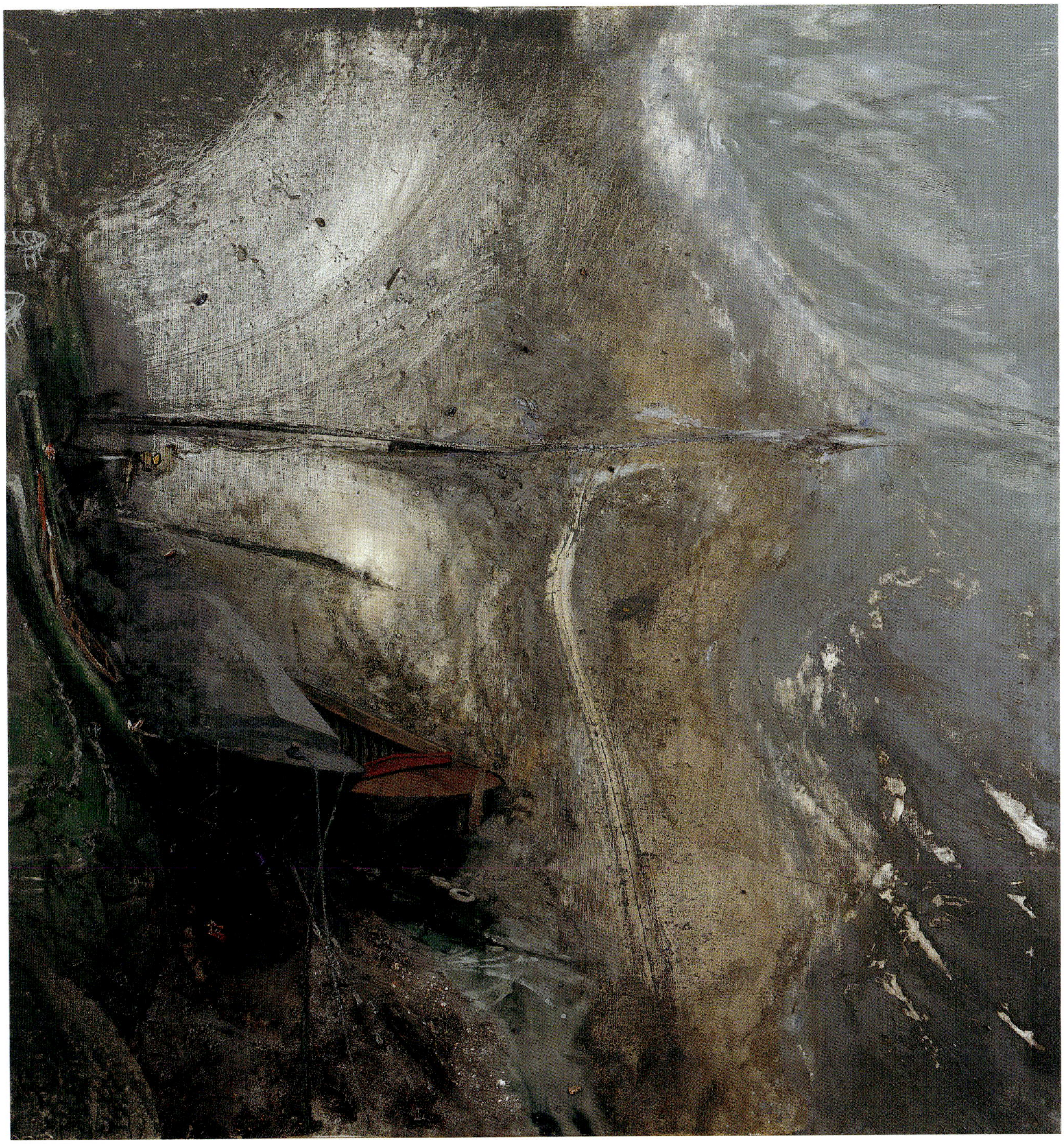

94
The Thames at Low Tide
1994–5
Oil on canvas
182.9 x 167.6

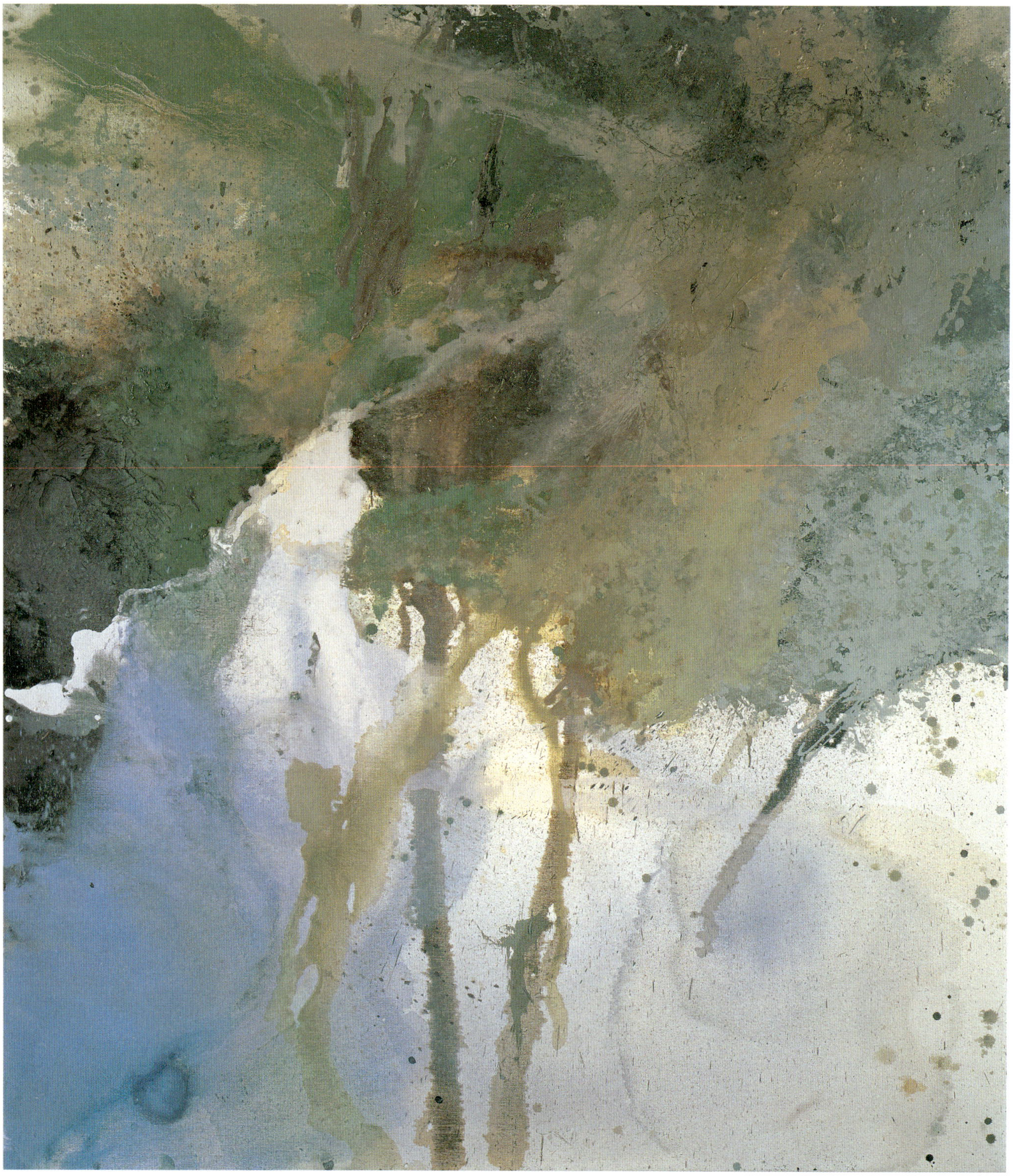

96
Source of the Thames
1994–5
Oil on canvas
183 x 213.5

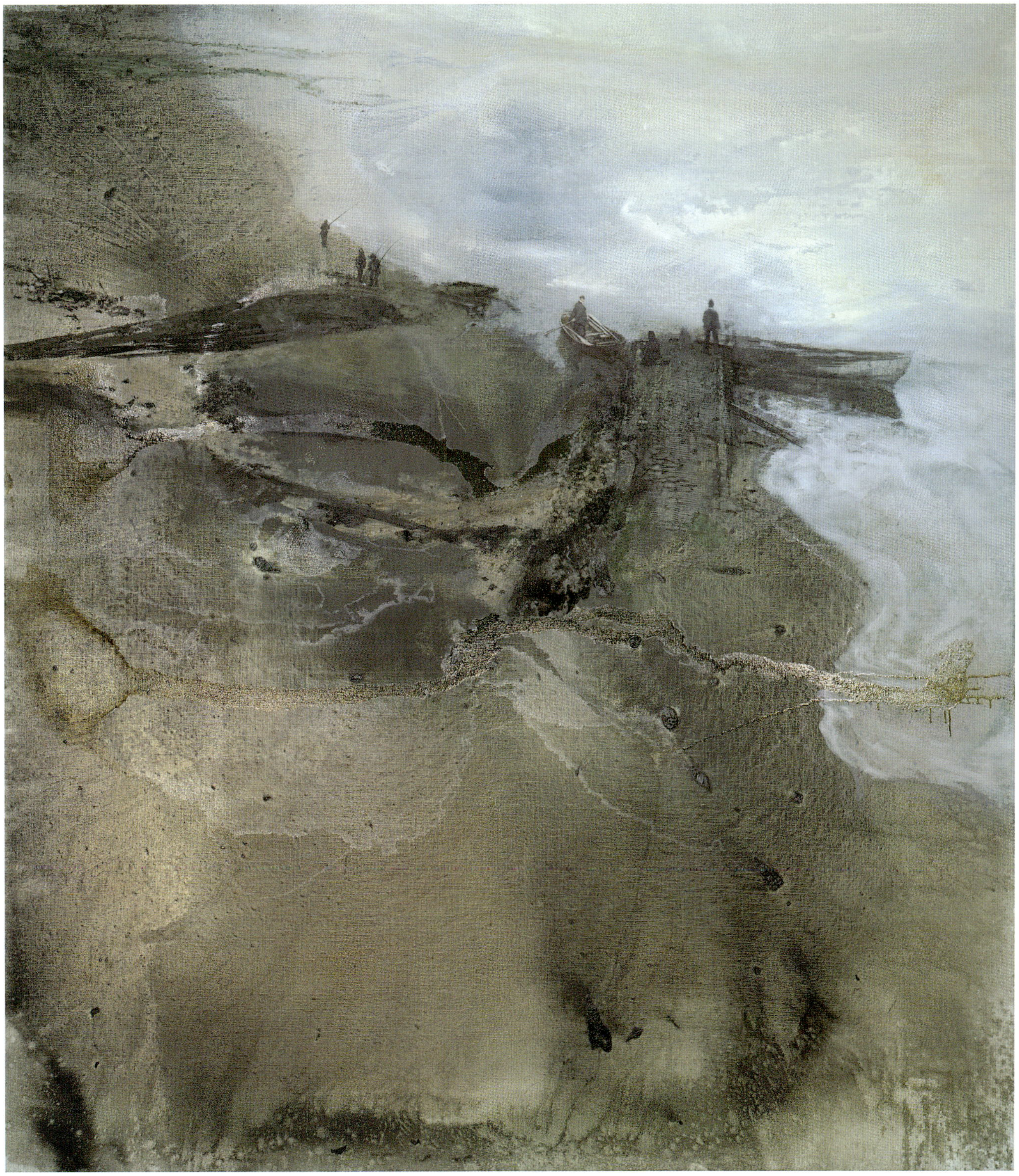

95
Thames Painting: The Estuary
1994–5
Oil and mixed media on canvas
219.8 x 189.1

list of exhibited works

Dimensions are given in centimetres, height before width

early works

1
August for the People
1951
Oil on board
143.5 x 122
College Art Collections, University College London

2
London Jazz Club/100 Oxford Street
1951–2
Oil on canvas
50.8 x 76.2
Peter Stanford

3
The Rocking Horse
1952
Oil on hardboard
122 x 182.9
Private Collection

4
A Man Who Suddenly Fell Over
1952
Oil on hardboard
121 x 173
Tate. Purchased 1958

5
Little Boy Running
1953
Oil on board
51 x 38
Private Collection

6
Lorenza Mazzetti in Italy
1954
Oil on canvas
196.3 x 145.3
Private Collection

7
Four People Sunbathing
1955
Oil on board
122 x 95.5
Arts Council Collection, Hayward Gallery, London

8
Man in a Landscape (Digswell Man II)
1959
Oil on canvas
135.5 x 119.5
Arts Council Collection, Hayward Gallery, London

9
Flats
1959
Oil on board
105.5 x 139.7
Arts Council Collection, Hayward Gallery, London

portraits

10
Late Evening on a Summer Day
1957
Oil on canvas
137 x 344
Private Collection

11
Portrait of John Lessore
1958
Oil on canvas
61 x 56
Private Collection, Northern Ireland

12
Self-Portrait
1959
Oil on hardboard
76 x 66
Sheila and Richard Attenborough

13
The Family in the Garden
1960–2
Oil on canvas
198.2 x 299.8
Centro de Arte Moderna Joeé de Azeredo Perdigao, Fundaçao Calouste Gulbenkian

14
Portrait of Tim Behrens
1962
Oil on board
122 x 122
Museo Thyssen-Bornemisza, Madrid

15
Portrait of John Deakin
1963
Oil on board
92 x 90
Astrup Fearnley Museum of Modern Art, Oslo

parties

16
The Colony Room I
1962
Oil on hardboard
121.9 x 182.8
The St John Wilson Trust

17
The Colony Room II
1962
Oil on hardboard
91.5 x 99
Private Collection

18
The Deer Park
1962
Oil on board
214 x 244.5
Tate. Purchased 1974

19
Study for 'All Night Long'
1963–4
Oil on canvas
100 x 74.5
Arts Council Collection, Hayward Gallery, London

20
All Night Long
1963–4
Oil on composition board (3 panels)
183.5 x 368.3
National Gallery of Victoria, Melbourne. Felton Bequest 1964

21
Good and Bad at Games
1964–8
Oil and silkscreen on canvas (triptych)
152.4 x 203.4 (each canvas)
National Gallery of Australia, Canberra

22
The Lord Mayor's Reception in Norwich Castle Keep on the eve of the installation of the first Chancellor of the University of East Anglia
1966–9
Oil and silkscreen on turaphot linen on canvas
213.3 x 213.3
Norfolk Museums Service, Norwich Castle Museum

23
Head of a Man
*c.*1967
Oil on board
19.5 x 21
Private Collection

24
Study of a Head for a Group of Figures No 4
1967
Oil on board
21 x 19.3
Private Collection

25
Study of a Head for a Group of Figures No 6
1967
Oil on board
22 x 15
Arts Council Collection, Hayward Gallery, London

26
Study of a Head for a Group of Figures No 7 1967
Oil on board
23.7 x 23.7
Private Collection

27
Study of a Head for a Group of Figures No 8 1967
Oil on board
22.2 x 22
Private Collection

28
Study of a Head for a Group of Figures No 9
1967
Oil on board
22.5 x 21
Private Collection

29
Study of a Head for a Group of Figures No 10
1967
Oil on board
31.6 x 16.5
Arts Council Collection, Hayward Gallery, London

30
Study of a Head with Green Turban
1967
Oil on board
21.5 x 16.5
Colin St John Wilson

31
Study of a Head of Arthur Brown (for 'Lights')
1968
Oil on board
20 x 17.7
Private Collection, London

32
Study of a Head for 'Lights' No 1
1968
Oil on board
34.2 x 15.2
Private Collection

33
Study of a Head for 'Lights' No 2
1968
Oil on board
15 x 17.5
Arts Council Collection, Hayward Gallery, London

34
Study of a Head for 'Lights' No 5
1968
Oil on board
21 x 19.4
Private Collection

35
The Blue and Yellow of the Yacht Club
1969
Oil on hardboard
61 x 61
Whitworth Art Gallery, University of Manchester

lights

36
Lights I: Out-of-Doors
1970
Acrylic on canvas
142.3 x 312
Private Collection

37
Liner
1971–2
Acrylic on canvas
152.5 x 183
Private Collection

38
Lights II: The Ship Engulfed
1972
Acrylic on canvas
183 x 153.5
Arts Council Collection, Hayward Gallery, London

39
Lights III: The Black Balloon
1973
Acrylic on canvas
160 x 129.5
Private Collection

40
Lights IV: The Pier and the Road
1973
Acrylic on canvas
152.4 x 213.4
Metropolitan Museum of Art, New York. Purchase, Mr and Mrs Milton Petrie Gift, 1981

41
Lights V: The Pier Pavilion
1973
Acrylic on canvas
152.4 x 213.3
Museo Thyssen-Bornemisza, Madrid

42
Lights VI: The Spa
1974
Acrylic on canvas
152 x 182
Private Collection

43
Lights VII: A Shadow
1974
Acrylic on canvas
182.9 x 182.9
Private Collection

44
Cabin: Sketch I
1975
Acrylic on canvas
24.7 x 29.8
Colin St John Wilson

45
Cabin: Sketch II
1975
Acrylic on canvas
30.4 x 30.4
Private Collection

46
Cabin: Sketch III
1975
Acrylic on canvas
38 x 38
Private Collection

47
Cabin
1975
Acrylic on canvas
152.4 x 213
Private Collection

school

48
School I
1977
Acrylic on canvas
152.5 x 213
Private Collection

49
Pike and Roach: Study for 'School II'
1977
Watercolour
15.8 x 23.5
Arts Council Collection, Hayward Gallery, London

50
Pike and Roach III: Study for 'School II'
1977
Watercolour
15 x 22.5
Private Collection

51
School II: Pike and Roach
1977
Acrylic on canvas
122 x 122
Private Collection

52
The Sun Reflected in the River
1977
Acrylic on paper
32 x 22.9
Private Collection

53
A Pond: Spring
1977
Acrylic and watercolour on paper
22 x 22
Private Collection

54
Early Summer, 7am, 'The Old River'
1977
Watercolour
22.6 x 32.4
Whitworth Art Gallery, University of Manchester

55
Early Summer: 'The Old River'
1977
Watercolour
15.2 x 22.6
Private Collection

56
Early Summer: Stretch of Water: 'The Old River'
1977
Watercolour
10.2 x 32.4
Private Collection

57
School III: Butterfly Fish and Damsel Fish
1978
Acrylic on canvas
152.4 x 213.3
Private Collection

58
School IV: Barracuda under Skipjack Tuna
1978
Acrylic on canvas
175.2 x 175.2
Private Collection

59
Melanie and Me Swimming
1978–9
Oil on canvas
182.9 x 182.9
Tate. Purchased 1979

60
Angler: Geldeston, The Glittering River 2
1981
Watercolour
27.5 x 34
Private Collection

61
First Sketch for Sundance, Escargot, Lady Ottoline and Lynda
1981
Watercolour and acrylic on paper
Private Collection

holiday

62
Glenartney: Sketch from the Harness Room
1975–6
Acrylic and pencil on paper
27.5 x 49
Private Collection

63
A Design: The Garden at Drummond from Higher Ground
1976
Oil and acrylic on canvas
132 x 313.6
Private Collection

64
Glenartney: August 1976, about 6pm, Coire Fearna Beat, Straith a 'Ghlinne
1976
Acrylic on sandpaper
20 x 26
Private Collection

65
Early Morning in Hot Weather: Glenartney
1976–7
Acrylic on sandpaper
22.8 x 27.3
Private Collection

66
Drummond: the Multi-coloured Parterre; Fractions of the Grand Design
1977
Acrylic on canvas
183 x 183
Private Collection

67
Peter's Day: 3rd Stalk
1979
Acrylic on canvas
183 x 183
Private Collection

68
Alistair's Day: 2nd Stalk
1980
Acrylic on canvas
183 x 183
Private Collection

69
Alistair's Day: 2nd Shot 1980
Acrylic on canvas
127 x 127
Private Collection

70
Running with the Deer
1980
Acrylic on canvas
127 x 127
Private Collection

71
Glenartney, 19 October '89. The Imperial
1989
Oil on canvas
30.5 x 40.6
Private Collection

72
October '90, with Jock on Dundurn
1991
Oil on board
30.5 x 25.4
Private Collection

73
Mist Clearing, Glenartney
1991
Oil on board
26.7 x 35.5
Private Collection

74
The Forest Beat through a Telescope
1991
Oil on canvas
35.5 x 40.6
Private Collection

75
'Give me the Rifle…!' 6.30pm, 17th October, Glenartney
1991
Oil on canvas
30.5 x 40.6
Private Collection

76
Recollection of a Moment in October 1989 – The Tobasnich Burn: Glenartney
1992
Oil on board
30.5 x 25.5
The British Council

rock of ages cleft for me

77
Laughter Uluru (Ayers Rock)/ The Cathedral I
1985
Acrylic on canvas
228.6 x 274.3
Tate. Purchased with assistance from the Friends of the Tate Gallery 1993

78
The Cathedral, The North East Face/Uluru (Ayers Rock)
1985
Acrylic on canvas
243.8 x 426.7
Astrup Fearnley Museum of Modern Art, Oslo

79
Permanent Water Mutidjula, by the Kunia massif (Maggie Springs, Ayers Rock)
1985–6
Acrylic on canvas
213.4 x 259.1
Private Collection

80
Valley of the Winds Katatjuta (The Olgas) 1985–6
Acrylic on canvas
213.4 x 289.6
Private Collection

81
In Shade, Foot of Olga Gorge, Katatjuta (The Olgas)
1987
Acrylic on canvas
213.4 x 228.6
Ivor Braka Ltd, London

82
The Cathedral, The Southern Faces/Uluru (Ayers Rock)
1987
Acrylic on canvas
243.8 x 388.6
The Trustees of the Derek Williams Estate on loan to the National Museums and Galleries of Wales

british landscape

83
SAX A.D. 832 – Second Painting
1982
Oil and acrylic on canvas
152.4 x 152.4
Elaine and Melvin Merians

84
Daylesford
1983–4
Oil on canvas
122 x 183
Carmen Thyssen-Bornemisza Collection

85
Oare, the Vale of Pewsey
1989–91
Oil on canvas
182.9 x 212.1
Private Collection

86
A View from Uamh Mhor
1990–1
Oil on canvas
177.8 x 355.6
Private Collection

87
Edinburgh (Old Town)
1990–3
Oil on canvas
183 x 274.3
Scottish National Gallery of Modern Art, Edinburgh, purchased with assistance from the National Art Collections Fund

late works

88
Self-Portrait
1988
Oil on board
25 x 20.3
Private Collection

89
Portrait of June
1992
Oil on board
30.5 x 25.5
Edwin C. Cohen

90
Portrait of Jane Willoughby
1989–91
Oil on canvas
40.7 x 35.6
Elaine and Melvin Merians

91
Portrait of Serena
1989–91
Oil on canvas
40.7 x 35.6
Private Collection

92
Portrait of David Astor
1993
Oil on canvas
52 x 47
F D L Astor

93
Portrait of Colin St John Wilson
1993–5
Oil on canvas
30.5 x 25.5
Colin St John Wilson

94
The Thames at Low Tide
1994–5
Oil on canvas
182.9 x 167.6
Private Collection

95
Thames Painting: The Estuary
1994–5
Oil and mixed media on canvas
219.8 x 189.1
The St John Wilson Trust

96
Source of the Thames
1994–5
Oil on canvas
183 x 213.5
Estate of the Artist courtesy Timothy Taylor Gallery

FIG.26
MA, Pembroke Studios, London, *c.*1974
Photo: Harry Diamond

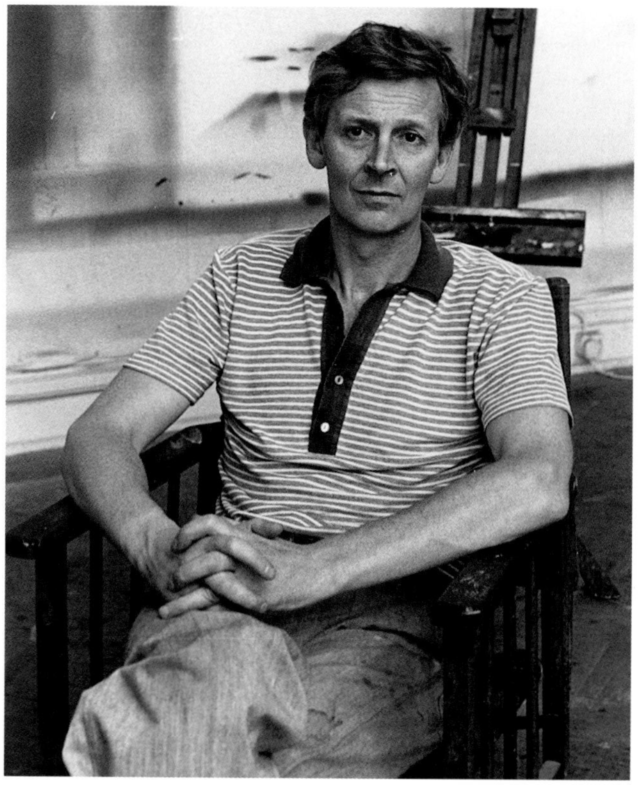

chronology

Compiled by Ben Tufnell

References are to papers held in the Tate Archive (TG 2000/25)

1928
Born 30 October in Norwich. 'My father was an insurance official with the Norwich Union Life Insurance Society until he retired in 1957. His forbears were Norfolk people except for his maternal grandmother who was Dutch. My mother's parents come from Derbyshire. They have spent their married life in Norwich' (Tate Gallery Cataloguing Form, probably 1958–9).

1947
Attends Saturday morning classes at Norwich School of Art for one term, studying oil painting under Lesley Davenport.

1947–9
National service, including nineteen months in Egypt.

1949–53
Studies at the Slade School of Art, London. Taught by William Coldstream, Lucian Freud, William Townsend and Lawrence Gowing, who later writes an introductory essay for MA's 1980 Hayward Gallery retrospective, remarking that as a student MA showed 'not only technical capacity, but uncommon imaginative equipment ... I remember wondering if this lanky, diffident young man could possibly explore the oddness of these perceptions of his' (*Michael Andrews,* Arts Council 1980, p.8).

Contemporaries at the Slade include Craigie Aitchison, Tim Behrens, Raymond Briggs, Bernard Cohen, Harold Cohen, Barry Daniels, Andrew Forge, Elizabeth Frink, Francis Hoyland, Myles Murphy, Paula Rego, Euan Uglow and Victor Willing. During this period MA lives variously at Cartright Gardens, Euston, and with the poet Peter Stanford in Epsom, Surrey.

1952
August for the People 1951 (no.1, p.64) wins second prize in the Slade Summer Competition. Acts in fellow student Lorenza Mazzetti's film of Kafka's *Metamorphosis*. MA's Diploma picture is *A Man Who Suddenly Fell Over* 1952 (no.4, p.66). Exhibits in *Nine Young Painters* at ICA, London, with Richard Hamilton and Victor Willing.

1953
Scholarship in painting at the British School in Rome. Returns to UK after only six months, apparently finding Italy 'too provincial'.

1954
Acts with Eduardo Paolozzi in Lorenza Mazzetti's film *Together* (originally titled 'Glass Marble'). MA and Paolozzi play two deaf-and-dumb labourers in the London docks. The film is screened at the National Film Theatre in February 1956 as part of the original Free Cinema programme, and represents Britain at the Cannes Film Festival.

1955
Samuel Beckett's *Waiting for Godot* first performed in London. Francis Bacon exhibits at ICA. Victor Willing exhibits at Hanover Gallery. Alberto Giacometti exhibits at Hayward Gallery.

1956
Lives with Victor and Hazel Willing in Lancaster Gate, London.

1957
Lives in Norwich, sharing studio with Jeffrey Camp at a friend's house in Chester Place. Paints a mural after Bonnard at Muriel Belcher's Soho drinking club, The Colony Room. Publication of Norman Mailer's *The Deer Park*.

1958
Lives at the Digswell Arts Trust, Hertfordshire. Teaches at the Slade. Students include John Wonnacott. First solo exhibition at Beaux Arts Gallery, London. John Russell describes the show as 'One of the most remarkable English debuts of the last ten years'. Of MA's slow pace of work he comments, 'he has won himself the kind of reputation which can be summed up in the words, "Marvellous, if he'd only get on with it." (*Sunday Times*, 12 Jan.). David Sylvester writes that MA's paintings have 'the substance and presence of a *necessary* utterance... Many a talented painter would produce an exhibition out of the thought Andrews puts into a picture' (*Listener*, 16 Jan.).

Tate Gallery acquires *A Man Who Suddenly Fell Over*. Asked by TG cataloguer to list important events in his life MA writes, 'It was the way one memorable state of affairs was succeeded by the next with hardly any interval that seems important now, rather than events.'

1959
Teaches at Norwich School of Art. Students include Colin Self, who admires MA as a 'hero mentor'. *La Dolce Vita* (dir. Federico Fellini) released.

1960
Teaches at Chelsea School of Art, London, with Lawrence Gowing. 'Notes and Preoccupations' published in *X: A Quarterly Review*. Towards end of the year moves to Cantley, just outside Norwich. Begins working on *The Family in the Garden* (no.13, p.75) in the garden at 13 Park Lane, Norwich. Due to his difficulty in finishing pictures to his satisfaction MA struggles financially. Helen Lessore, Director of the Beaux Arts Gallery, frequently sends him more money than he is owed. 'I

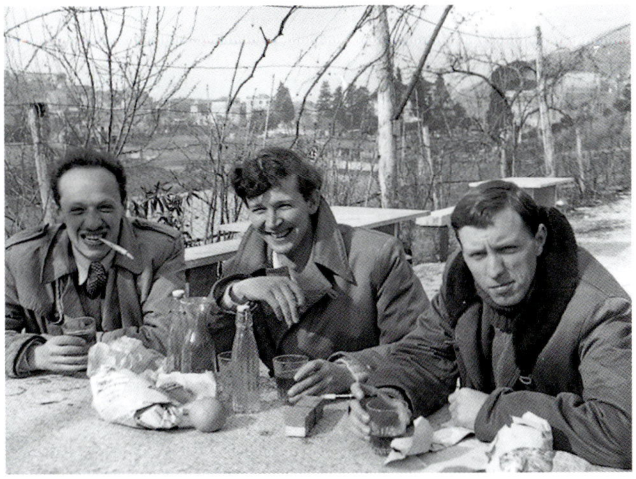

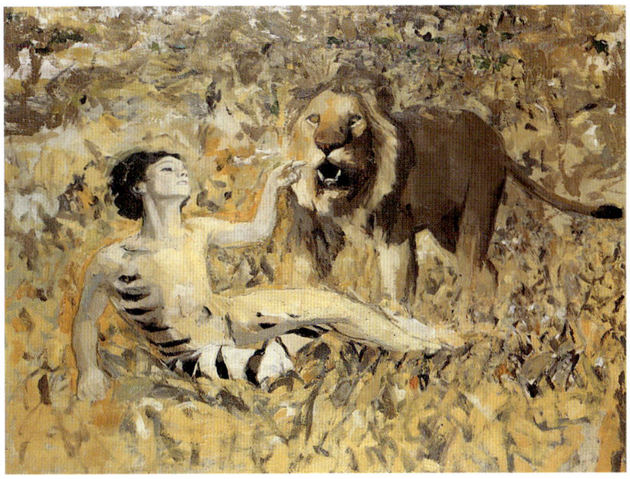

FIG.27
Derek Greaves, MA and Heinz Inlander, Rome, 1953

FIG.28
Liony Piony 1956–7, oil on canvas, 96.5 x 127
Private Collection

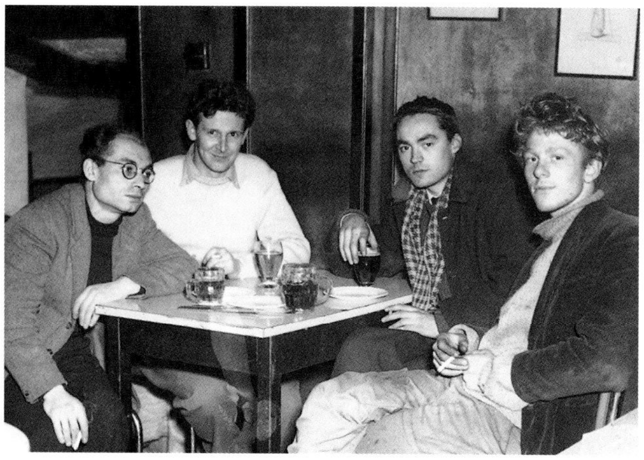

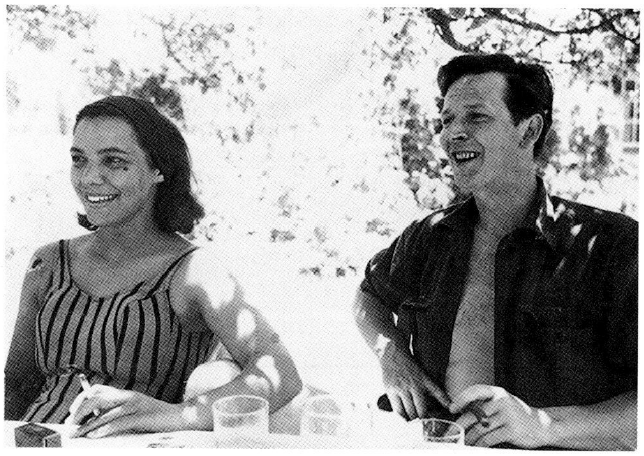

FIG.29
Harry Diamond, MA, Nicholas Garland and Tim Behrens in the Caves de France, Soho, *c.*1958
Photo: John Deakin

FIG.30
MA and June, Portugal, 1964

hate to think of you living on Nescafe and woodbines' (22 Mar.). 'Do you have meals with your family? Otherwise I can't see how you're going to manage with £30 till November. If you want any more ask now, while I've got it. Do you eat enough? You're very thin' (15 Sept.).

1961
Moves to London, living first at Noel Road, with Robin and Susan Campbell, and then at Duncan Terrace, Islington. Social circle includes Francis Bacon, Frank Auerbach, Tim Behrens, Peter Blake, Lucian Freud, John Deakin, Harry Diamond, Bruce Bernard and Philip Oakes.

1962
Completes *The Family in the Garden*. Paints two versions of *The Colony Room* (nos.16, 17, pp.82–3) followed by *The Deer Park* (no.18, p.81). Elected member of The London Group. Publication of the first *Sunday Times* colour supplement, which will prove a rich source of imagery for MA.

Marilyn Monroe commits suicide.

1963
Second solo exhibition at Beaux Arts Gallery, London. Begins *All Night Long* (no.20, p.87). Teaches at the Slade with R.B. Kitaj and Harold Cohen. Starts living with June Keeley.
John Profumo, Secretary of State for War, resigns over affair with Christine Keeler.

1964
Begins *Good and Bad at Games* (no.21, p.88). A 'conversation' with Victor Willing, 'Morality and the Model', published by Rodrigo Moynihan in *Art and Literature*, Paris. Exhibits *The Colony Room I* in the *Pittsburgh International*, Carnegie Institute, Pittsburgh. Included in *54–64 Painting and Sculpture of a Decade* at Tate Gallery, London. Visits Victor Willing and Paula Rego in Portugal, staying with Paula Rego's parents. National Gallery of Victoria, Melbourne acquires *All Night Long*.

1965
Commission from the Museums Committee of the Castle Museum, Norwich. Nigel Henderson helps assemble the silkscreens for *The Lord Mayor's Reception* (no.22, p.90). MA's father dies.

1966
Stops teaching. Begins the studies for *Lights*. Joins Marlborough Gallery (over the next five years exhibitions are variously scheduled for March 1968, March 1969, April 1970 and April 1971, and postponed at MA's behest).

Lucian Freud paints *Michael Andrews and June* 1965–6 (private collection).

Blow Up (dir. Michaelangelo Antonioni) celebrates 'swinging London'.

1967
MA begins to envisage a party painting-as-environment. He plans to project large painted heads onto the walls, like 'Geronimo at the Freak Out', an event he had collected images of (Archive MA19). Begins to accumulate images of light and sound shows by bands such as Pink Floyd, and gatherings of the counter-culture. While not a part of the counter-culture MA is fascinated by it, finding in particular parallels with his interest in Zen philosophy. In April *Studio International* includes an article on Hornsey College of Art's Light/Sound Workshop and 'short-throw projection techniques' (Archive MA19). Festival of Flower Children in London. The Beatles release *Sergeant Pepper's Lonely Hearts Club Band*, with cover by Peter Blake featuring a gathering of 'luminaries' selected by the artist and band members. Cream release *Disraeli Gears* (see *Study of a Head for 'Lights' No.7* 1968 Private Collection) and The Rolling Stones release *Their Satanic Majesties Request* (see *Study of a Head for 'Lights' No 4* 1968 Private Collection and *Study of a Figure for 'Lights' No.1* 1969 Private Collection).

1968
Completes *Good and Bad at Games,* in part inspired by the

private view card for the Giacometti exhibition at the Tate Gallery the previous year. The painting, which includes portraits of Victor Willing, Paula Rego, Craigie Aitchison, June and MA himself, is purchased by the actor Michael Caine. Moves to Pembroke Studios in West London, with June. MA's mother dies.

Fire by The Crazy World of Arthur Brown is No. 1 in UK. *2001: A Space Odyssey* (dir. Stanley Kubrick) released.

1969
Completes *The Lord Mayor's Reception*. Philip Oakes reports in the *Sunday Times* (12 Oct.) that the painting 'instantly became the subject of ferocious wrangling – some objectors claiming it was overpriced because Andrews had merely painted over a collage of party people which had been printed onto photo-linen. [MA responded:] "They felt they weren't getting their money's worth ... They put it to the vote, and finally it just sneaked in by one vote. I rather approved of the shindig because I think there's something wrong if *everyone* likes your painting." Continues work on the series of heads for *Lights*. At this point the series is to include not only rock stars but other 'Receptors of Light' such as 'Myles [Murphy], June, [and] Craigie [Aitchison]' (Archive MA24).

Apollo 11 astronaut Neil Armstrong is first man on the moon. MA begins to collect imagery of moon landings and space walks as part of his research for *Lights*. The Rolling Stones play a free concert in Hyde Park, London.

1970
Daughter Melanie is born. Holiday cruise to Madeira. Urged to consider making prints by Marlborough Gallery, MA experiments with making photo-lithographs of collages with printmaker Chris Prater. Makes notes for pictures consisting of sheets of printed transparencies mounted between plexiglass. Completes the first of the *Lights* series, *Lights I: Out-of-Doors* (no.36, p.97).

1971
Holiday in Portugal, staying with Paula Rego's parents.

1972
MA leaves Marlborough Gallery and joins Anthony d'Offay Gallery.

1973
Uses Visitor's Studio at Royal College of Art for six months.

1974
Uses Eduardo Paolozzi's studio in Glebe Place, Chelsea. *Michael Andrews: Lights series* at Anthony d'Offay Gallery, London. The show consists of just four paintings: *Lights IV: The Pier and the Road* 1973 (no.40, p.100), *Lights V: The Pier Pavilion* 1973 (no.41, p.101), *Lights VI: The Spa* 1974 (no.42, p.102), and *Lights VII: A Shadow* 1974 (no.43, p.103). William Packer writes, 'Michael Andrews has secured for himself a position in English painting as the éminence grise of the middle generation: on every side we hear nothing but admiration and respect for his work, with, in the same breath, resigned regret that so little of it is ever seen ... so long and painstaking is the process of painting it. [These] are strange and disturbing paintings, calm images that are fraught either with the possibility of some dire violation, or with the poignancy of irrecoverable happiness ... [it is] a small but extraordinary show, confirming Andrews' authority as an artist' (*Financial Times,* 3 Dec.). Tate Gallery acquires *The Deer Park* 1962.

1975
First visit to Scotland, to Glenartney in Perthshire. From this point on MA takes annual holidays in Scotland.

1976
First experience of deer stalking. R.B. Kitaj articulates the idea of a 'School of London' in the introduction to his exhibition of artists' drawings of the figure, *The Human Clay*, at Hayward Gallery.

1977
Moves to Geldeston, near Beccles on the Norfolk/Suffolk border. Holds a small exhibition (28 Feb.–5 Mar.) at James Kirkman's house in London. The exhibition consists of *Liner* 1971–2 (no.37, p.104), *Lights II: The Ship Engulfed* 1972 (no.38, p.98), the two Drummond Castle paintings (nos.63, 66, p.124–5), and a group of studies. Commissions photographer Jean-Loup Cornet to take images to be used as source material for *School* and *Holiday* series.

1978
Michael Andrews: paintings 1977–78 at Anthony d'Offay Gallery, London. The exhibition includes the four *School* paintings and a group of watercolours. Begins stalking pictures.

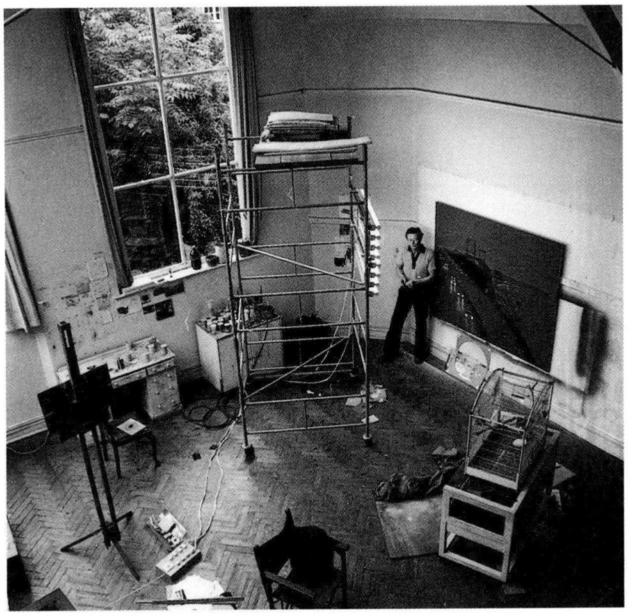

FIG.31
MA at Pembroke Studios, with birdcage and *Lights VI: The Spa*, *c.*1974
Photo: Jorge Lewinski

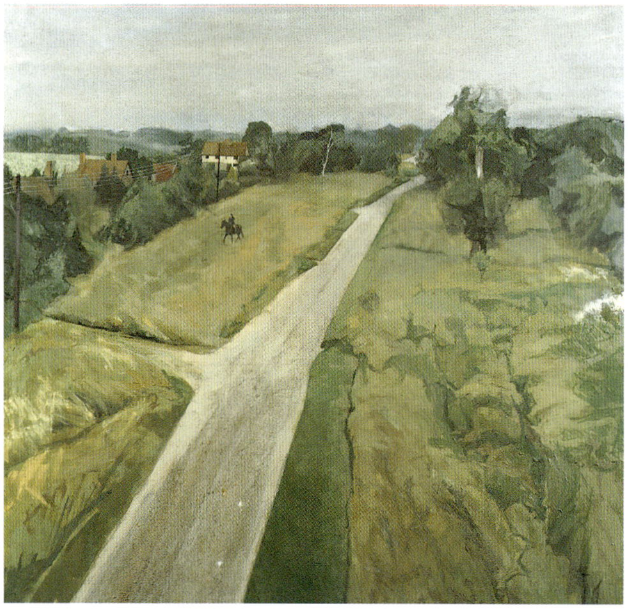

FIG.32
SAX A.D. 832 – First Painting 1982, acrylic on canvas, 152.5 x 152.5
Private Collection

1979
Completes *Melanie and Me Swimming* (no.59, p.121), which is subsequently acquired by the Tate Gallery. Included in the first *British Art Show*, organised by the Arts Council.

1980
Retrospective exhibition, *Michael Andrews*, organised by the Arts Council, is shown at Hayward Gallery, London, and then tours to Fruitmarket Gallery, Edinburgh, and Whitworth Art Gallery, Manchester. John McEwen writes that MA is 'private to an exquisitely English degree. [He] has an almost mythical reputation among his ... art-world contemporaries. He is what most English artists dream of being: the acceptable outsider' (*Spectator* 15 Nov.). William Packer writes, 'He reveals himself as an artist full of talent and singularly ambitious, consistently prepared to take on the largest technical and formal problems, and, to his great credit, to risk and frequently to achieve the most dreadful croppers' (*Financial Times* 18 Nov.).

1981
Moves to Saxlingham Nethergate, near Norwich, and uses a studio in a former chapel at Tasburgh. Included in *Eight Figurative Painters* at Yale Center for British Art, New Haven. Undertakes commission to paint Chateau Lafite for Baron Eric de Rothschild. *Lights IV: The Pier and the Road* 1973 acquired by Metropolitan Museum of Art, New York.

1982
Completes first version of *SAX A.D. 832* (no.83, p.145), depicting the village green at Saxlingham Nethergate. Accepts commission from Baron Thyssen-Bornemisza to paint Daylesford in Gloucestershire (no.84, p.146).

1983
Completes second version of *SAX A.D. 832*. Travels to Australia and visits Ayers Rock. Investigates possibilities of making a series of etchings with printmaker Danny Levy of the Scarlet Press. He envisages five suites of prints: Chateau Lafite (and the people working there), Stalking/Glenartney, Ayers Rock, Saxlingham, and Melanie. Begins portrait of Sir David Wills fishing at Knockando.

1984
Included in *The Hard-Won Image: Traditional Method and Subject in Recent British Art* at the Tate Gallery, London, and *Modern Masters from the Thyssen-Bornemisza Collection* at the Royal Academy, London.

1986
Rock of ages cleft for me: recent paintings by Michael Andrews at Anthony d'Offay Gallery, London. The show includes first five large Ayers Rock paintings, and a group of small studies.

1987
Included in *A School of London: six figurative painters*, British Council touring exhibition, at Kunstnernes Hus, Oslo; Louisiana Museum of Modern Art, Humlebaek; Ca' Pesaro, Venice; and Kunstmuseum Düsseldorf.

1988
Appointed Trustee of the National Gallery, London. Made a Fellow of University College, London.

1989
Resigns as Trustee of the National Gallery.

1990
Included in *The Pursuit of the Real: British Figurative Painting from Sickert to Bacon* at Manchester City Art Gallery and Barbican Art Gallery, London. Begins *A View from Uamh Mhor* (no.86, p.150) and *Edinburgh (Old Town)* (no.87, p.148). Film about his work by Anna Benson Gyles for BBC TV, *As it appears so it is* (broadcast 29 Jan. 1991).

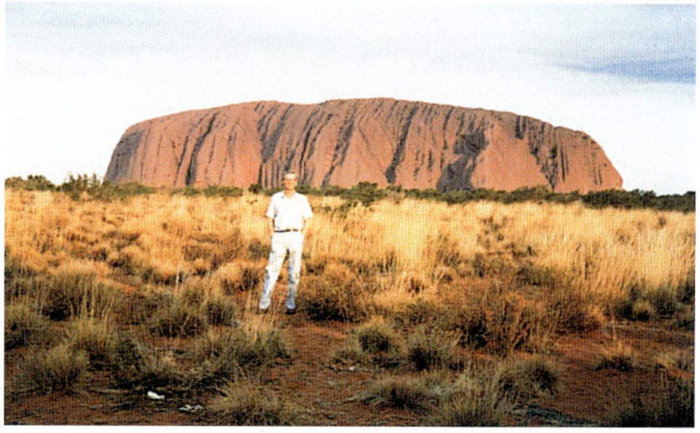

FIG.33
MA at Ayers Rock, 1983

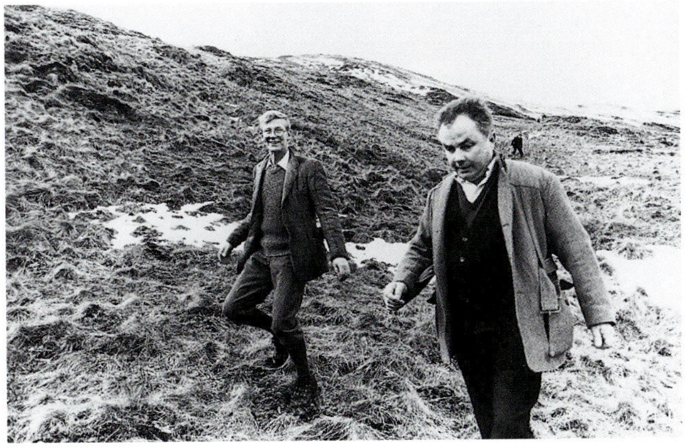

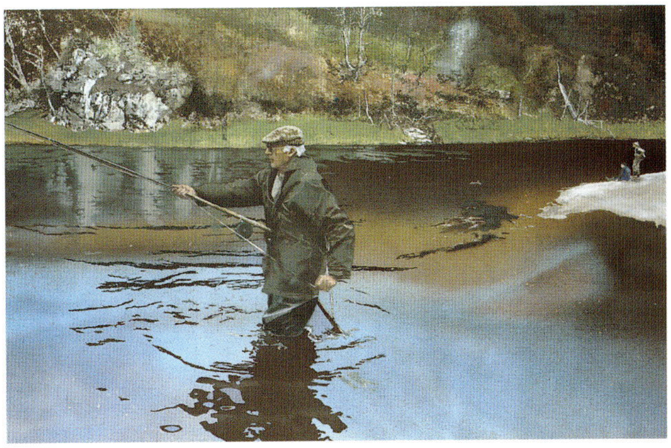

FIG.34
MA and Bruce Bernard at Glenartney, *c.*1987

FIG.35
Knockando, 1983–4, acrylic on canvas, 122 x 183
Private Collection

1991
Michael Andrews: 'The Delectable Mountain' at Whitechapel Art Gallery, London. Tours to Fondation National des Arts Graphiques et Plastiques, Paris, Scottish National Gallery of Modern Art, Edinburgh (which adds *Michael Andrews: The Scottish Paintings*) and Grey Art Gallery and Study Centre, New York University. Press response in UK is mixed. John Russell Taylor writes, 'The pictures are striking in their size, but that does not quite justify the reverence with which they are usually greeted. They seem spread thin not only in physical paint, but also in their inspiration: decorative, but lacking in intensity of response' (*Times* 8 Feb.). Marina Vaizey writes, 'a stupendous suite of paintings ... form an exhibition ... of sensational impact which almost seems to wrap around the spectator. He makes us think not only about the way things look, but how we take that appearance and irradiate it with our very human feelings, animating the landscape with our search for a meaning beyond what we can – simply – see' (*Sunday Times* 10 Feb.).

1992
Visits New York and considers making a painting of Central Park. Moves to London. Lives on Albert Bridge Road in Battersea and has a studio in Sydney Close, Chelsea. *A View from Uamh Mhor* is Picture of the Year at the Royal Academy Summer Exhibition. *Edinburgh (Old Town)* acquired by Scottish National Gallery of Modern Art.

1993
Elected to Royal Academy in May. In December he resigns.

1994
Undergoes operation for cancer.

1995
Leaves Anthony d'Offay Gallery. Completes *The Thames at Low Tide* and *Thames Painting: The Estuary* (nos.94–5, pp.157–9), having delayed treatment for cancer. Included in *From London: Bacon, Freud, Kossoff, Andrews, Auerbach, Kitaj* at Scottish National Gallery of Modern Art, Edinburgh; Musée National d'Histoire et d'Art, Luxembourg; Musée Cantonal des Beaux-Arts, Lausanne; and Fundació Caixa de Catalunya, La Pedrera, Barcelona. *The Colony Room I* opens the exhibition *Identity and Alterity: figures of the body 1895/1995* at the Venice Biennale.

Dies 19 July 1995, aged 66. The funeral is at St Mary's, Battersea, and MA is buried at Glenartney in Perthshire.

1998
Michael Andrews: The Thames Paintings at Timothy Taylor Gallery, London.

2000
Michael Andrews: Luces at Museo Thyssen-Bornemisza, Madrid.

2001
Michael Andrews at Tate Britain, London.

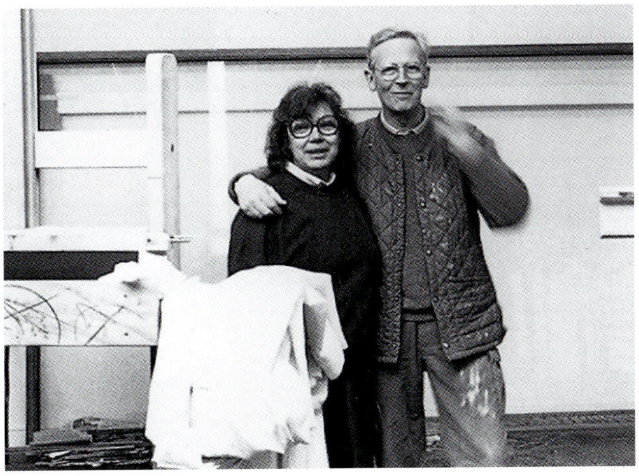

FIG.36
MA and June in the studio, Saxlingham Nethergate (detail)
Photo: Bruce Bernard

bibliography

This selective bibliography has been compiled by Krzysztof Cieszkowski of the Tate Library.

The items within each section are listed chronologically. Square brackets indicate information supplied from sources other than the item itself.

A more extensive version of this bibliography is available from the Tate Library.

Texts by the artist

'Notes and preoccupations', in *X: a quarterly review*, Mar. 1960, vol.1 no.2, pp.137–141, with 3p. of illus. between pp.136–7; French trans. publ. in *L'école de Londres: de Bacon à Bevan*, exh. cat., Fondation Dina Vierny – Musée Maillol, Paris, 1998–9, pp.112–15.

'Morality and the model' [dialogue between MA and Victor Willing], in *Art and Literature,* Paris and Lausanne, Summer 1964, no.2, pp.49–64, incl. 8p. of illus., with 1 work by MA.

[statements], *Survey 66: figurative painters,* exh. cat., Hampstead Arts Centre, London 1966, p.18; acc. by Peter Carey, 'He [MA] made the following remarks to me during a conversation that we had about his use of photography'.

[statement], in *Rock of ages cleft for me: recent paintings by Michael Andrews,* exh. cat., Anthony d'Offay Gallery, London 1986, p.[5].

[interview], in BBC TV 'Omnibus' programme, recorded 1990, broadcast 29 Jan. 1991; excerpts in *Michael Andrews: the Scottish paintings*, exh. cat., Scottish National Gallery of Modern Art, Edinburgh 1991, and *British figurative painting of the 20th century,* exh. cat., Israel Museum, Jerusalem, with British Council, 1992–3; French trans. of excerpt in *L'école de Londres: de Bacon à Bevan,* exh. cat., Fondation Dina Vierny – Musée Maillol, Paris, 1998–9), p.116.

Solo exhibition catalogues

Michael Andrews (15 works). Beaux Arts Gallery, London, 2–29 Jan. 1958; biog.; [4]p.

Michael Andrews (29 works). Beaux Arts Gallery, London, 10 Jan.–13 Feb. 1963; biog.; [8]p., 3 illus.

Michael Andrews (4 works). Anthony d'Offay Gallery, London, 19 Nov.–13 Dec. 1974; biography; [12]p., 6 illus (1 col.).

Michael Andrews: paintings 1977–78 [17 works]. Anthony d'Offay, London, 24 May–24 June 1978; 4p.

Michael Andrews (132 works). Hayward Gallery, London, 31 Oct. 1980–11 Jan. 1981; Fruit Market Gallery, Edinburgh, 24 Jan.–21 Feb. 1981; Whitworth Art Gallery, University of Manchester, 6 Mar.–20 Apr. 1981; organised by Arts Council of Great Britain; pref. by Joanna Drew, Catherine Lampert; text by Lawrence Gowing; text by David Sylvester (1st publ. in *The Listener,* 16 Jan. 1958); cat. entries by James Kirkman; biog., bibliog.; 93p., 103 illus. (24 col.).

Rock of ages cleft for me: recent paintings by Michael Andrews [15 works]. Anthony d'Offay Gallery, London, 28 May–4 July 1986; statement by MA; text by William Feaver; [21]p., 21 illus. (4 col).

Michael Andrews: 'The delectable mountain': the Ayers Rock series and other landscape paintings. Whitechapel Art Gallery, London, 1 Feb.–24 Mar. 1991; Fondation National des Arts Graphiques et Plastiques, Paris, June–July 1991; Scottish National Gallery of Modern Art, 10 Aug.–29 Sept. 1991; Grey Art Gallery & Study Center, New York University, Jan.–Feb. 1992; pref. by Catherine Lampert; texts by Bruce Bernard, Jonathan Raban; biog., bibliog.; [64]p., 30 illus. (27 col.).

Michael Andrews: the Scottish paintings (18 works). Scottish National Gallery of Modern Art, Edinburgh, 10 Aug.–29 Sept. 1991; statement by the artist (from BBC TV 'Omnibus' interview, 29 Jan. 1991), text by Richard Calvocoressi; [32]p., 24 illus. (16 col.).

Michael Andrews: the Thames paintings. Timothy Taylor Gallery,

London, 20 May–20 June 1998; text by William Feaver; biog., list of exhibitions, bibliog.; 28p., 14 illus. (13 col.).

Michael Andrews: Luces / Lights (7 works). Museo Thyssen-Bornemisza, Madrid, 20 June–1 Oct. 2000; 'In Focus' series number 9; pref. by H.R.H. The Prince of Wales, &c; texts by William Feaver, Belén Gopegui; chrono., bibliog.; 70p., 43 illus. (21 col.).

Group exhibition catalogues

Four young artists: Michael Andrews, Susannah Butt, Barbara Braithwaite, Anne Rees-Mogg [20 works]. Beaux Arts Gallery, London, 6–29 Mar. 1952.

Drawings for pictures [3 works]. Arts Council of Great Britain, 1953; introd. by David Sylvester.

The Arts Council Collection of Paintings & Drawings, part four: since the war [1 work]. Arts Council of Great Britain, touring 25 Jan.–6 Dec. 1958 (Edinburgh, Bristol, Southampton, Bolton, Leeds, Birmingham, Newcastle, Eastbourne, Nottingham, Plymouth); introd. by Andrew Forge.

British self-portraits from Sickert to the present day [1 work]. Arts Council of Great Britain touring exhibition, 10 Feb.–8 Sept. 1962 (Newcastle, Leeds, Birmingham, Aberystwyth, Leicester, Salford, Guildford, Bournemouth); text by Lawrence Gowing.

British painting in the Sixties [2 works, in Whitechapel AG section]. Tate Gallery. London, and Whitechapel Art Gallery, London, 1–30 June 1963; organised by the Contemporary Art Society.

54–64: painting & sculpture of a decade [1 work]. Tate Gallery, London, 22 Apr.–28 June 1964; organised by Calouste Gulbenkian Foundation.

Exhibitions of sculpture by Bernard Meadows [...] and paintings by Michael Andrews [12 works]. Norfolk Contemporary Arts Society at Assembly House, Norwich, 29 May–5 June 1964.

Last anthology [1 work]. Beaux Arts Gallery, London, 8 Oct.–6 Nov. 1964.

The 1964 Pittsburgh International: exhibition of contemporary painting and sculpture [1 work]. Museum of Art, Carnegie Institute, Pittsburgh, 30 Oct. 1964–10 Jan. 1965.

English painting 1951–1967: Norfolk & Norwich Triennial Festival [4 works]. Norwich Castle Museum, 31 May–2 July 1967.

Helen Lessore and the Beaux Arts Gallery [2 works]. Marlborough Fine Art, London, Feb. 1968; introd. by Andrew Forge.

The Slade 1871–1971: a centenary exhibition [1 work]. Royal Academy of Arts, London, 20 Nov.–12 Dec. 1971; introd. by William Coldstream, Bruce Laughton.

The human clay: an exhibition selected by R.B. Kitaj [6 works]. Hayward Gallery, London, [5–30 Aug.] 1976, and touring; organised by Arts Council of Great Britain; text by R.B. Kitaj.

Peter Moores Liverpool Project 4: Real life [3 works]. Walker Arts Gallery, Liverpool, 2 June–6 Sept. 1977; introd. by Edward Lucie-Smith [*et al.*].

British painting 1952–1977 [3 works]. Royal Academy of Arts, London, 24 Sept.–20 Nov. 1977; introd. by Frederick Gore.

Narrative paintings: figurative art of two generations [1 work]. Arnolfini, Bristol, 1 Sept.–20 Oct. 1979; Institute of Contemporary Arts, London, 25 Oct.–25 Nov. 1979, and touring until 1980 (Stoke-on-Trent, Edinburgh); text by Timothy Hyman (ref. pp.[8], [25]).

The British art show: recent paintings and sculpture by 112 artists [1 work]. Arts Council of Great Britain, at Mappin Art Gallery, Sheffield, 1 Dec. 1979–27 Jan. 1980, and touring until May 1980 (Newcastle, Bristol); introd. by William Packer.

Eight figurative painters [7 works]. Yale Center for British Art, New Haven (CT), 14 Oct. 1981–3 Jan. 1982; Museum of Art, Santa Barbara, 29 Jan.–28 Mar. 1982; texts by Andrew Forge, Lawrence Gowing.

The hard-won image: traditional method and subject in recent British art [3 works]. Tate Gallery, London, 4 July–9 Sept. 1984; text by Richard Morphet.

Modern masters from the Thyssen-Bornemisza Collection [1 work]. Royal Academy of Arts, London, 12 Oct.–19 Dec. 1984.

The proper study: contemporary figurative paintings from Britain [6 works]. British Council, at Lalit Kala Akademi, Delhi, 1–31 Dec. 1984; Jehangir Nicholson Museum of Modern Art, Bombay, 1–28 Feb. 1985; introd. by Norbert Lynton; text on MA by William Feaver.

A singular vision: paintings of the figure by contemporary British artists [1 work]. Royal Albert Memorial Museum, Exeter, 19 Jan.–23 Feb. 1985, and touring until 13 Oct. 1985 (Milton Keynes, Southport, Newcastle, Barnsley, South London Art Gallery); introd. by Naomi Fabian, Patrick George.

British art of the 20th century: the modern movement [2 works]. Royal Academy of Arts, London, 15 Jan.–5 Apr. 1987; cat. ed. by Susan Compton; texts by Dawn Ades: 'Figure and place: a context for fine post-war artists', pp.73–80 (ref. pp.78–80), and 'The School of London', pp.308–311 (ref. p.311); biog. by Monica Bohm-Duchen, p.418.

A School of London: six figurative painters [9 works]. British Council, at Kunstnernes Hus, Oslo, 9 May–14 June 1987; Louisiana Museum of Modern Art, Humlebaek, 27 June–16 Aug. 1987; Museo d'Arte Moderna, Ca' Pesaro, Venice, 5 Sept.–18 Oct. 1987; Kunstmuseum Düsseldorf, 6 Nov. 1987–10 Jan. 1988; introd. by Michael Peppiatt.

The pursuit of the real: British figurative painting from Sickert to Bacon [5 works]. Manchester City Gallery, 10 Mar.–11 Apr. 1990; Barbican Art Gallery, London, 10 May–8 July 1990; Glasgow City Art Gallery, 28 July–16 Sept. 1990; publ. by Lund Humphries, London; texts by Tim Wilcox, Andrew Causey, Lynda Checketts, Michael Peppiatt.

The British imagination: twentieth-century paintings, sculpture, and drawings [4 works]. Hirschl & Adler Galleries, New York, 10 Nov. 1990–12 Jan. 1991; introd. by Edward Lucie-Smith.

The transformation of appearance: Andrews, Auerbach, Bacon, Freud, Kossoff [4 works]. Sainsbury Centre for Visual Arts, University of East Anglia, Norwich, 24 Sept.–8 Dec. 1991; organised by Tate Gallery, London; text by Paul Moorhouse.

Ready steady go: painting of the Sixties from the Arts Council Collection [1 work]. South Bank Centre, at the Royal Festival Hall, London, 21 Jan.–23 Feb. 1992; and touring until Oct. 1993 (Stockport, Wakefield, Burnley, Ipswich, Coventry, Nottingham, Wrexham, Swansea, Dudley, Bath); introd. by Hilary Lane, Alan Sinfield.

Royal Academy of Arts summer exhibition [1 work], 7 June–16 Aug. 1992 (MA's painting *A View from Uamh Mhor* won the Korn/Ferry International Picture of the Year Award).

Norfolk portraits [1 work]. Norwich Castle Museum, 5 Sept.–29 Nov. 1992; cat. incl., Andrew Moore with Charlotte Crawley, *Family & friends: a regional survey of British portraiture,* London: HMSO, 1992.

British figurative painting of the 20th century [4 works]. Israel Museum, Jerusalem, Nov. 1992–Feb. 1993; organised with British Council, London; text ed. by Yigal Zalmona; introd. by James Hyman; statements by MA from BBC TV 'Omnibus' interview (29 Jan. 1991) repr. on p.27.

Dobbel virkelighet / Double reality: "The School of London" [7 works]. Astrup Fearnley Museet for Moderne Kunst, Oslo, 16 Apr.–9 Oct. 1994; introd. by Hans-Jakob Brun; text on MA by Hilde Morch, pp.12–16 & 89–92.

Identity and alterity: figures of the body 1895/1995 [1 work]. La Biennale di Venezia, 46. esposizione internazionale d'arte, in Palazzo Grassi & Museo Correr, Venice, 11 June–15 Oct. 1995; introd. by Jean Clair; text on MA by Rosana Alberti.

From London: Bacon, Freud, Kossoff, Andrews, Auerbach, Kitaj [14 works]. British Council exhibition, at Scottish National Gallery of Modern Art, Edinburgh, 1 July–5 Sept. 1995; Musée National d'Histoire et d'Art, Luxembourg, 22 Sept.–5 Nov. 1995; Musée Cantonal des Beaux-Arts, Lausanne, 17 Nov. 1995–4 Feb. 1996; Fundació Caixa de Catalunya, La Pedrera, Barcelona, 16 Feb.–16 Apr. 1996; texts by Richard Calvocoressi, David Cohen, Bruce Bernard (ref. pp.10, 12, 33–35, 50, 53–4).

L'école de Londres: de Bacon à Bevan [7 works]. Paris, Fondation Dina Vierny – Musée Maillol, 10 Oct. 1998–20 Jan. 1999; introd. by Michael Peppiatt, Jill Lloyd; incl. trans. texts by MA: *Notes et préoccupations* (1st publ. in *X: a quarterly review,* 1960), and *Une texte* (from BBC TV 'Omnibus' interview, 29 Jan. 1991), pp.112–16.

La Mirada Fuerte: Pintura Figurativa de Londres [10 works]. Museo de Arte Moderno, Mexico City, 4 Apr.–11 June 2000; texts by Andrew Dempsey, Teresa del Conde, William Feaver.

The School of London and their friends: the collection of Elaine and Melvin Merians [5 works]. Yale Center for British Art, New Haven, 11 Oct. 2000–14 Jan. 2001, and travelling to Neuberger Museum of Art, Purchase (NY) until May 2001; texts by Richard Cork, Patrick McCaughey, pp.10–11, 36–9.

Michael Andrews, William Coldstream: 'Mysterious conventionality'. Timothy Taylor Gallery, London, 5 May–5 June 1999; introd. by William Feaver.

Painting the century: 101 portrait masterpieces 1900–2000 [1 work]. National Portrait Gallery, London, 26 Oct. 2000–4 Feb. 2001; introd. by Norbert Lynton, text by Robin Gibson.

Books & parts of books

Mary Chamot, Dennis Farr and Martin Butlin: *Tate Gallery catalogues: the modern British paintings, drawings and sculpture.* London: Oldbourne Press, 1964; vol.1, p.9 (entry for '*A Man Who Suddenly Fell Over*').

Bryan Robertson, John Russell, Lord Snowdon: *Private view.* London, Edinburgh: Thomas Nelson & Sons, 1965; pp.260–263 (incl. text by John Russell, p.262).

John Rothenstein: 'Michael Andrews', in *Modern English painters, 3, Wood to Hockney.* London: Macdonald and Jane's, 1974; pp.201–10, pl.27–8.

'Michael Andrews, b.1928: T.1897: *The Deer Park, 1962*', in *The Tate Gallery 1974–6: illustrated catalogue of acquisitions.* London: Tate Gallery, 1978; pp.47–8.

'Michael Andrews, b.1928: T.2334: *Melanie and me swimming, 1978–9*', in *The Tate Gallery 1978–80: illustrated catalogue of acquisitions.* London: Tate Gallery, 1981; p.58.

Helen Lessore: *A partial testament: essays on some moderns in the great tradition.* London: Tate Gallery, 1986; pp.35–53.

Alastair Hicks: *The School of London: the resurgence of contemporary painting.* Oxford: Phaidon, 1989; pp.50–3.

Alastair Hicks: *New British art in the Saatchi Collection.* London: Thames and Hudson, 1989; pp.22–5, 165.

Simon Wilson: 'Michael Andrews, b.1928: *The Deer Park, 1962*', in *The Tate Gallery: an illustrated companion,* 2nd ed. London: Tate Gallery, 1991; p.252.

Colin St. John Wilson: *The artist at work: on the working methods of William Coldstream and Michael Andrews.* London: Lund Humphries, 1999; pp.8–9, 35–71, 74–5, 79–80.

Articles

David Sylvester: 'Round the London art galleries' [incl. review of Beaux Arts Gallery group exhib.], in *Listener,* 13 Mar. 1952, vol.47 no.1202, p.432.

Albert Garrett: 'The new realism in English art', in *Studio,* June 1954, vol.147 no.735, pp.161–9 (ref. p.168, illus. on p.169).

'Mr. Michael Andrews' [on occasion of Beaux Arts Gallery exhib.], in *The Times,* 8 Jan. 1958.

John Russell: 'A name to watch' [review of Beaux Arts Gallery exhib.], in *Sunday Times,* 12 Jan. 1958.

David Sylvester: 'Michael Andrews' [review of Beaux Arts Gallery exhib.], in *Listener,* 16 Jan. 1958, vol.59 no.1503, p.105; repr. in *Michael Andrews,* exh. cat., Arts Council, 1980–1, pp.49–50; and (in a slightly altered form) in David Sylvester, *About modern art: critical essays 1948–96,* London: Chatto & Windus, 1996, pp.163–6.

Keith Sutton: 'Portrait of the artist–Michael Andrews' [with portrait-drawing of MA by Keith Sutton], in *Art News and Review,* 18 Jan. 1958, vol.9 no.26, p.3.

Robert Melville: 'Exhibitions: painting' [incl. review of Beaux Arts Gallery exhib.], in *Architectural Review,* Feb. 1958, vol.123 no.133, pp.204–5.

David Sylvester: 'Michael Andrews: 'mysterious conventionality'', in *Sunday Times (colour supplement),* 13 Jan. 1963, pp.12–14.

'Pictures that tell one what it is like to be a painter: from our art critic' [review of Beaux Arts Gallery exhib.], in *The Times,* 16 Jan. 1963, p.11.

Andrew Forge: 'Local attachments' [incl. review of Beaux Art Gallery exhib.], in *New Statesman,* 25 Jan. 1963, pp.130–2.

Keith Roberts: 'Current and forthcoming exhibitions' [incl. review of Beaux Arts Gallery exhib.], in *Burlington Magazine,* Feb. 1963, vol.105 no.719, pp.82–84 (ref. p.83).

Michael Levey: 'Around the galleries' [incl. review of Beaux Arts Gallery exhib.], in *The London Magazine,* Apr. 1963, vol.3 no.1, pp.75–8 (ref. p.77).

Philip Oakes: 'One-man party', in *Sunday Times,* 12 Nov. 1969.

William Feaver: 'Stranded dinosaurs', in *London Magazine,*

July–Aug. 1970, vol.10 no.4, pp.95–105 (ref. pp.99, 101, illus. on pp.98–9).
William Packer: 'Michael Andrews' [review of d'Offay exhib.], in *Financial Times,* 3 Dec. 1974.
Catherine Lampert: 'Michael Andrews' [review of d'Offay exhib.], in *Studio International,* Jan.–Feb. 1975, vol.189 no.973, pp.13–14.
Geraldine Norman: 'Signature tune' [interview with Francis Bacon & MA], in *The Times,* 9 July 1977, p.11.
William Feaver: 'The artist as elusive onlooker' [on the occasion of d'Offay exhib.], in *Observer Magazine,* 28 May 1978, pp.26–7.
Edward Lucie-Smith: 'Michael Andrews – Anthony d'Offay' [review of exhib.], in *Art and Artists,* June 1978, vol.13 no.2 (no.147), p.43.
Lawrence Gowing: 'Painter of fact and feeling' [on occasion of Arts Council exhib.], in *The Sunday Times* (colour magazine), 26 Oct. 1980, p.112.
John Russell Taylor: 'The haunting quality of Michael Andrews' [incl. review of Arts Council exhib.], in *The Times,* 11 Nov. 1980, p.11.
Frances Spalding: 'The air balloon goes pop' [review of Arts Council exhib.], in *Times Literary Supplement,* 14 Nov. 1980, p.1291.
William Packer: 'Michael Andrews' [review of Arts Council exhib.], in *The Financial Times,* 18 Nov. 1980, p.21.
Lynda Morris: 'Images of London' [incl. review of Arts Council exhib.], in *The Listener,* 20 Nov. 1980, vol.104 no.2686, pp.706–7.
Edward Lucie-Smith: 'London: winter' [incl. review of Arts Council exhib.], in *Art International,* Jan.–Feb. 1981, vol.24 nos.5–6, pp.70–113 (ref. pp.98–102)
William Feaver: 'Pointillism, plein air and piggybacks' [incl. review of Arts Council exhib.], in *Artnews,* Feb. 1981, vol.80 no.2, pp.201–2 (ref. p.201).
Richard Shone: 'Glasgow and Edinburgh: William Strang and Michael Andrews' [incl. review of Arts Council exh.], in *Burlington Magazine,* Feb. 1981, vol.123 no.935, pp.116, 119, illus. on p.121.
Simon Passmore: 'Fractions of the grand design: Michael Andrews at the Hayward Gallery', in *Contemporary Review,* Apr. 1981, no.238, pp.209–12.
Jeffrey Weiss: 'Eight figurative painters' [review of Yale exhib.], in *Arts Magazine,* Feb. 1982, vol.56 no.6, p.9.
William Feaver: [review of Tate Gallery exhib.], in *Observer Review,* 8 July 1984, p.17.
William Feaver: 'Out of Australia' [on occasion of d'Offay exhib.], in *The Observer Magazine,* 1 June 1986, pp.36–37.
William Packer: 'Parallel paths to manifest excellence' [review of d'Offay exhib.], in *Financial Times,* 24 June 1986, p.23.
Peter Fuller: 'Michael Andrews: recent paintings' [review of d'Offay exhib,], in *Burlington Magazine,* July 1986, vol.128 no.1000, pp.330–2.
Michael Peppiatt: 'Could there be a School of London?', in *Art International,* Autumn 1987, [new series] no.1, pp.6–24.
Michael Peppiatt: 'Six new masters: why stodgy old London is now the art capital of the world', in *Connoisseur,* Sept. 1987, pp.79–85.
Mary Sara: 'The pursuit of the real: British figurative painting from Sickert to Bacon' [review of Manchester exhib.], in *Green Book,* 1990, vol.3 no.5, pp.40–42, 54–55 (ref. pp.42, 54).
Tom Lubbock: 'Smooth assault on a spray-gunned summit' [incl. review of Whitechapel exhib.], in *Independent on Sunday,* 3 Feb. 1991, p.18.
William Feaver: 'Time, the sublime and gold in them thar hills' [incl. review of Whitechapel exhib.], in *Observer,* 3 Feb. 1991, p.52.
William Packer: 'Symbolism in the landscape' [incl. review of Whitechapel exhib.], in *Financial Times,* 5 Feb. 1991, p.17.
John McEwen: 'Losing himself in a lifeless picnic on Hanging Rock' [incl. review of Whitechapel exhib.], in *Sunday Telegraph,* 10 Feb. 1991, p.xiv.
Marina Vaizey: 'At the peak of achievement' [incl. review of Whitechapel exhib.], in *Sunday Times,* 10 Feb. 1991, p.5.8.
Sue Hubbard: 'Rock of ages' [review of Whitechapel exhib.], in *New Statesman and Society,* 15 Feb. 1991, p.40.
Brian Sewell: 'Beaten about the bush' [review of Whitechapel exhib.], in *Evening Standard,* 28 Feb. 1991, p.19.
James Burr: 'The lure of the sea: Albert Pinkham Ryder / Michael Andrews / Alan Reynolds' [incl. review of Whitechapel exhibition], in *Apollo,* Apr. 1991, vol.133 no.350, p.279.
Howard Jacobson: 'No head for heights' [on occasion of Whitechapel & touring exhib.], in *Modern Painters,* Summer 1991, vol.4 no.2, pp.66–8.
William Feaver: 'Verbals up the garden path' [incl. review of Edinburgh exhib.], in *Observer,* 18 Aug. 1991, p.48.
Richard Calvocoressi: 'Flight in the heather' [review of Edinburgh exhib.], in *Spectator,* 24 Aug. 1991, pp.33–4.
William Feaver: 'Ruminative eyes' [incl. review of Whitechapel exhib.], in *Observer,* 29 Dec. 1991, p.40.
Michael Peppiatt: 'A school or not a school' [review of Edinburgh group exhib.], in *Modern Painters,* Summer 1995, vol.8 no.2, pp.64–66.
William Feaver: 'Michael Andrews: As it seems, so it clearly is' [obituary], in *Guardian,* 21 July 1995, p.15.
'Michael Andrews' [obituary], in *Daily Telegraph,* 22 July 1995, p.17.
'Michael Andrews' [obituary], in *Times,* 22 July 1995, p.14.
Catherine Lampert: 'Michael Andrews' [obituary], in *Independent,* 24 July 1995, p.14.
Martin Gayford: 'The river that ran within him' [review of Timothy Taylor Gallery exhib.], in *Sunday Telegraph,* 24 May 1998.
Martin Gayford: 'Farewell to the river' [review of Timothy Taylor Gallery exhib.], in *Daily Telegraph,* 10 June 1998.
William Packer: 'Elegies by the riverside' [review of Timothy Taylor Gallery exhib.], in *Financial Times Weekend,* 13–14 June 1998, p.vii.
William Feaver: 'Yard birds' [incl. review of Timothy Taylor Gallery exhib.], in *Observer,* 14 June 1998.
Ben Tufnell: 'Illuminations: Michael Andrews, Norman Mailer and Rimbaud', in *British Art Journal,* Spring 2001, vol.II, no.3.

Lenders to the Exhibition

Estate of the Artist 96
F D L Astor 92
Sheila and Richard Attenborough 12
Ivor Braka Ltd, London 81
The British Council 76
Canberra, National Gallery of Australia 21
Cardiff, The Trustees of the Derek Williams Estate and the National Museums and Galleries of Wales 82
Edwin C Cohen 89
Edinburgh, Scottish National Gallery of Modern Art 87
Lisbon, Centro de Arte Moderna José de Azeredo Perdigao, Fundaçao Calouste Gulbenkian 13
London, Arts Council Collection, Hayward Gallery 7, 9, 19, 25, 29, 33, 38, 49
London, College Art Collections, University College London 1
London, Tate 4, 18, 59, 77
Mr and Mrs Herbert L Lucas 88
Madrid, Museo Thyssen-Bornemisza 14, 41
Manchester, Whitworth Art Gallery, University of Manchester 35, 54
Melbourne, National Gallery of Victoria 20
Elaine and Melvin Merians 83, 90
New York, Metropolitan Museum of Art 40
Norwich, Norfolk Museums Service, Norwich Castle Museum 22
Oslo, Astrup Fearnley Museum of Modern Art 15, 78
Private Collections 3, 5, 6, 8, 10, 11, 17, 23, 24, 26, 27, 28, 31, 32, 34, 36, 37, 39, 42, 43, 45, 46, 47, 48, 50, 51, 52, 53, 55, 56, 57, 58, 60, 61, 62, 63, 64, 65, 66, 67, 68, 69, 70, 71, 72, 73, 74, 75, 79, 80, 85, 86, 91, 94
The St John Wilson Trust 16, 95
Peter Stanford 2
Colin St John Wilson 30, 44, 93
Carmen Thyssen-Bornemisza 84

Acknowledgements

Copyright credits:
All works by Michael Andrews © Estate of the Artist

Photographs by Bruce Bernard © Estate of Bruce Bernard; John Deakin © The James Moores Collection; Harry Diamond © The Artist; William Feaver © The Artist; Jorge Lewinski © The Artist

Photographic credits:

Figure illustrations
Courtesy of June Andrews 3, 6, 14, 17, 24, 27, 29–31, 33, 34, 36
Courtesy of the British Film Institute 4
National Gallery of Australia, Canberra 1
Courtesy Harry Diamond 26
Courtesy Anthony d'Offay Gallery 13, 32, 35
William Feaver 19–22, 25
The James Moores Collection *frontispiece*
Jorge Lewinski 8,9
Colin St John Wilson 5, 7, 18
Tate Archive / Tate Photography / Rodney Tidnam 10–12, 15, 16
Tate Photography / Andrew Dunkley, Marcus Leith 23, 28

Catalogue illustrations
Arts Council Collection, Hayward Gallery, London / Mike Fear / John Webb
National Gallery of Australia, Canberra
National Museums and Galleries of Wales, Cardiff
François Couget
Prudence Cuming Associates Ltd
Anthony d'Offay Gallery / Prudence Cuming Associates Ltd
Scottish National Gallery of Modern Art, Edinburgh
Centro de Arte Moderna José de Azeredo Perdigao, Fundação Caloutse Gulbenkian / Mario de Oliviera
Larkfield Colour Group
National Gallery of Victoria, Melbourne, Australia
The Metropolitan Museum of Art
Norfolk Museums Service (Norwich Castle Museum)
Astrup Fearnley Collection, Oslo
Antonia Reeve
Bryan F. Rutledge
Colin St John Wilson
The St John Wilson Trust
Tate Photography / Andrew Dunkley, David Lambert, Marcella Leith, Marcus Leith, Rodney Tidnam,
Tate Picture Library
Timothy Taylor Gallery
Carmen Thyssen-Bornemisza Collection
Museo Thyssen-Bornemisza. Madrid
College Art Collections, University College London / Prudence Cuming Associates Ltd
The Whitworth Art Gallery, The University of Manchester

SUPPORTING TATE

Tate relies on a large number of supporters – individuals, foundations, companies and public sector sources – to enable it to deliver its programme of activities, both on and off its gallery sites. This support is essential in order to acquire works of art for the Collection, run education, outreach and exhibition programmes, care for the Collection in storage and enable art to be displayed, both digitally and physically, inside and outside Tate. Your donation will make a real difference and enable others to enjoy Tate and its Collections both now and in the future. There are a variety of ways in which you can help support the Tate and also benefit as a UK or US taxpayer. Please contact us at:

The Development Office
Tate
Millbank
London SWIP 4RG
Tel: 020 7887 8942
Fax: 020 7887 8738

Tate American Fund
1285 Avenue of the Americas (35th fl)
New York NY 10019
Tel: 001 212 713 8497
Fax: 001 212 713 8655

Donations
Donations, of whatever size, from individuals, companies and trusts are welcome, either to support particular areas of interest, or to contribute to general running costs.

Gifts of Shares
Since April 2000, we can accept gifts of quoted share and securities. These are not subject to capital gains tax. For higher rate taxpayers, a gift of shares saves income tax as well as capital gains tax. For further information please contact the Campaigns Section of the Development Office.

Tate Annual Fund
A donation to the Annual Fund at Tate benefits a variety of projects throughout the organisation, from the development of new conservation techniques to education programmes for people of all ages.

Gift Aid
Through Gift Aid, you can provide significant additional revenue to Tate. Gift Aid applies to gifts of any size, whether regular or one-off, since we can claim back the tax on your charitable donation. Higher rate taxpayers are also able to claim additional personal tax relief. Contact us for further information and a Gift-Aid Declaration.

Legacies and Bequests
Bequests to Tate may take the form of either a residual share of your estate, a specific cash sum or item of property such as a work of art. Tax advantages may be obtained by making a legacy in favour of Tate; in addition, if you own a work of art of national importance you may wish to leave it to us as a direct bequest or to the Government in lieu of tax. Please check with Tate when you draw up your will that we are able to accept your bequest.

Tate American Fund and Tate American Patrons
The American Fund for the Tate Gallery was formed in 1986 to facilitate gifts of works of art, donations and bequests to Tate from United States residents. United States taxpayers who wish to support Tate on an annual basis can join the American Patrons of the Tate Gallery and enjoy membership benefits and events in the United States and United Kingdom (single membership $1000 and double $1500). Both organisations receive full tax exempt status from the IRS. Please contact the Tate American Fund for further details.

Membership Programmes
Tate Members enjoy unlimited free admission throughout the year to all exhibitions at Tate Britain, Tate Liverpool, Tate Modern and Tate St Ives, as well as a number of other benefits such as exclusive use of our Members' Rooms and a free annual subscription to *Tate: The Art Magazine*.

Whilst enjoying the exclusive privileges of membership, you are also helping secure Tate's position at the very heart of British and modern art. Your support actively contributes to new purchases of important art, ensuring that the Tate's Collection continues to be relevant and comprehensive, as well as funding projects in London, Liverpool and St Ives that increase access and understanding for everyone.

Patrons
Tate Patrons are people who share a keen interest in art and are committed to giving significant financial support to the Tate on an annual basis, specifically to support acquisitions. There are four levels of Patron, including Associate Patron (£250) Patrons of New Art (£500), Patrons of New Art (£500), Patrons of British Art (£500) and Patrons Circle (£1000). Benefits include opportunities to sit on acquisition committees, special access to the Collection and entry with a family member to all Tate exhibitions.

Corporate Membership
Corporate Membership at Tate Liverpool and Tate Britain, and support for the Business Circle at Tate St Ives, offer companies opportunities for corporate entertaining and the chance for a wide variety of employee benefits. These include special private views, free admission to paying exhibitions, out-of-hours visits and tours, invitations to VIP events and talks at members' offices. Tate Britain is currently only available for entertaining by companies who are either corporate members or current sponsors.

Founding Corporate Partners
Companies are also able to join the special Founding Corporate Partners scheme which offers unique access to corporate entertaining and benefits at Tate Modern and Tate Britain in London, until the end of March 2003. Further details are available on request.

Corporate Investment
The Tate Gallery has developed a range of imaginative partnerships with the corporate sector, ranging from international interpretation and exhibition programmes to local outreach and staff development programmes. We are particularly known for high-profile business to business marketing initiatives and employee benefit packages. Please contact the Corporate Fundraising team for further details.

Charity Details
The Tate Gallery is an exempt charity; the Museums & Galleries Act 1992 added the Tate Gallery to the list of exempt charities defined in the 1960 Charities Act. The Friends of the Tate Gallery is a registered charity (number 313021). Tate Foundation is a registered charity (number 1085314).

Tate Britain Donors to the Centenary Development Campaign

Founder
The Heritage Lottery Fund

Founding Benefactors
Sir Harry and Lady Djanogly
The Kresge Foundation
Sir Edwin and Lady Manton
Lord and Lady Sainsbury of Preston Candover
The Wolfson Foundation

Major Donors
The Annenberg Foundation
Ron Beller and Jennifer Moses
Alex and Angela Bernstein
Ivor Braka
The Clore Duffield Foundation
Maurice and Janet Dwek
Bob and Kate Gavron
Sir Paul Getty KBE
Mr and Mrs Karpidas
Peter and Maria Kellner
Catherine and Pierre Lagrange
Ruth and Stuart Lipton
William A Palmer
John and Jill Ritblat
Barrie and Emmanuel Roman
Charlotte Stevenson
Tate Gallery Centenary Gala
The Trusthouse Charitable Foundation
David and Emma Verey
Clodagh and Leslie Waddington
Sam Whitbread

Donors
The Asprey Family Charitable Foundation
The Charlotte Bonham Carter Charitable Trust
Giles and Sonia Coode-Adams
Thomas Dane
The D'Oyly Carte Charitable Trust
The Dulverton Trust
Friends of the Tate Gallery
Alan Gibbs
Mr and Mrs Edward Gihuly
Helyn and Ralph Goldenberg
Pehr and Christina Gyllenhammar
Jay Jopling
Howard and Linda Karshan
Anders and Ulla Ljungh
Lloyds TSB Foundation for England and Wales
David and Pauline Mann-Vogelpoel
Sir Peter and Lady Osborne
Mr Frederick Paulsen
The Pet Shop Boys
The P F Charitable Trust
The Polizzi Charitable Trust
Mrs Coral Samuel CBE
David and Sophie Shalit
Mr and Mrs Sven Skarendahl

Pauline Denyer-Smith and Paul Smith
Mr and Mrs Nicholas Stanley
The Jack Steinberg Charitable Trust
Carter and Mary Thatcher
Dinah Verey
Gordon D Watson
The Duke of Westminster OBE TD DL
Mr and Mrs Stephen Wilberding
Michael S Wilson
And those donors who wish to remain anonymous

Tate Collection

Founders

Sir Henry Tate
Sir Joseph Duveen
Lord Duveen
The Clore Duffield Foundation

Founding Benefactors

The Kreitman Foundation

Benefactors

American Fund for the Tate Gallery
Gilbert and Janet de Botton
The Friends of the Tate Gallery
The Heritage Lottery Fund
National Art Collections Fund
National Heritage Memorial Fund
The Patrons of British Art
The Patrons of New Art

Major Donors

Robert Lehman Foundation Inc

Donors

Howard and Roberta Ahmanson
Lord and Lady Attenborough
Mr Tom Bendhem
Robert Borgerhoff Mulder
The British Council
Neville and Marlene Burston
Mrs John Chandris
The Clothworkers Foundation
Edwin C Cohen
The Daiwa Anglo-Japanese Foundation
Judith and Kenneth Dayton
Foundation for Sport and the Arts
Mr Christopher Foley
The Gapper Charitable Trust
The Gertz Foundation
Great Britain Sasakawa Foundation
HSBC Artscard
Sir Joseph Hotung
Mr and Mrs Michael Hue-Williams
The Idlewild Trust
The Japan Foundation
The Kessler Family Re-Union
Mr Patrick Koerfer
Samual H Kress Foundation
The Henry Moore Foundation
The Leverhulme Trust
Friends of the Newfoundland Dog and Members of the Newfoundland Club of America
Peter and Eileen Norton, The Peter Norton Foundation
Mr David Posnett
The Radcliffe Trust
The Rayne Foundation
Mr Simon Robertson
Lord and Lady Rothschild
Mrs Jean Sainsbury
Scouloudi Foundation
Stanley Foundation Limited
Mr and Mrs A Alfred Taubman
The Vandervell Foundation
Mr and Mrs Leslie Waddington
And those donors who wish to remain anonymous

Collection Sponsor

Carillion plc, Paintings Conservation (1995-2000)

Tate Founding Corporate Partners

AMP
Avaya UK
BNP Paribas
CGNU plc
Clifford Chance
Dresdner Kleinwort Wasserstein
Energis Communications
Freshfields Bruckhaus Deringer
GLG Partners
Goldman Sachs International
Lazard
Lehman Brothers
London & Cambridge Properties Limited
London Electricity plc, EDF Group
Pearson plc
Prudential plc
Railtrack PLC
Reuters
Rolls-Royce plc
Schroders
UBS PaineWebber, Inc.
UBS Warburg
Whitehead Mann GKR

Tate Britain Corporate Members

Partner Level
Merrill Lynch
Associate Level
Cantor Fitzgerald
Drivers Jonas
Global Asset Management
Honda (UK)
Hugo Boss
Lazard
Linklaters
Morgan Stanley
Nomura International plc
Oracle
Robert Fleming Holdings Limited
Simmons & Simmons
The EMI Group
Tishman Speyer Properties
UBS AG

Tate Britain Donors

Major Donors

The Bowland Charitable Trust
Mr and Mrs James Brice
Robert Lehman Foundation, Inc
The Henry Luce Foundation
The Henry Moore Foundation

Donors

Howard and Roberta Ahmanson
David and Janice Blackburn
Blackwall Green
Cadogan Charity
Ricki and Robert Conway
The Elephant Trust
Garban Intercapital
The Hedley Foundation
Robert Holden Ltd
ICI
The Stanley Thomas Johnson Foundation
John Lyons Charity
Kiers Foundation
The Kirby Laing Foundation
Leche Trust
London Arts
The Paul Mellon Centre
The Mercers' Company
Sally and Anthony Salz
Judith Rothschild Foundation
The Wates Foundation
And those donors who wish to remain anonymous

Tate Britain Sponsors

Founding Sponsors

BP
– Campaign for the Creation of Tate Britain (1998–2000)
– Displays from the Collection (1990–2002)
Tate Britain Launch (2000)

BT
– Tate Online (2001–2003)

Ernst & Young
– Cézanne (1996)
– Bonnard (1998)

Benefactor Sponsors

Channel 4
– The Turner Prize (1991–2001)

Prudential plc
– Grand Tour (1996)
– The Age of Rossetti, Burne Jones and Watts: Symbolism in Britain 1860-1910 (1997)
– The Art of Bloomsbury (1999)
– Stanley Spencer (2001)

Major Sponsors

Aon Risk Services Ltd in association with ITT London & Edinburgh
– In Celebration: The Art of the Country House (1998)

Glaxo Wellcome plc
– Turner on the Seine (1999)
– William Blake (2000)

The Independent Newspapers
– Media Sponsor for William Blake (2000)
– Media Sponsor for Stanley Spencer (2001)

Magnox Electric
– Turner's Watercolour Explorations (1997)
– Turner & the Scientists (1998)

Morgan Stanley
– Constructing Identities (1998)
– John Singer Sargent (1998)
– Visual Paths: Teaching Literacy in the Gallery (1999–2002)

Sun Life and Provincial Holdings plc
– Ruskin, Turner & the Pre-Raphaelites (2000)

Tate & Lyle PLC
– Tate Friends (1991–2000)

Sponsors

AT&T
– Piet Mondrian (1997)

B&Q
– Michael Andrews (2001)

BT
– Tate Britain Launch (2000)

The Economist
– James Gillray: The Art of Caricature (2001)

The Guardian / The Observer
– Jackson Pollock (1999)
– Media Sponsor for the Tate 2000 launch (2000)

Hiscox plc
– Tate Britain Members Room (1995–2001)

Reuters
– Art Now: Art and Money Online (2001)

Rowe & Maw
– Turner's Gallery, House and Library (2001)